T0383187

THE
"SUCCESS or DIE"
ULTIMATUM

Steven Borris • Daniel Borris

THE
"SUCCESS or DIE"
ULTIMATUM

SAVING COMPANIES WITH BLENDED, LONG-TERM IMPROVEMENT FORMULAS

CRC Press
Taylor & Francis Group
Boca Raton   London   New York

CRC Press is an imprint of the
Taylor & Francis Group, an **informa** business

A PRODUCTIVITY PRESS BOOK

CRC Press
Taylor & Francis Group
6000 Broken Sound Parkway NW, Suite 300
Boca Raton, FL 33487-2742

© 2015 by Taylor & Francis Group, LLC
CRC Press is an imprint of Taylor & Francis Group, an Informa business

No claim to original U.S. Government works

Printed on acid-free paper
Version Date: 20150219

International Standard Book Number-13: 978-1-4822-9903-8 (Hardback)

Visit the Taylor & Francis Web site at
http://www.taylorandfrancis.com

and the CRC Press Web site at
http://www.crcpress.com

Contents

Preface

I was working on a different book when Danny called. I remember, I was wearing my Garfield padded slippers because the colder air flowing beneath the house made my feet cold as the air relentlessly crept up through the wooden floorboards when I was sitting typing. Danny's call was a welcome excuse for a break and a chance to warm my feet a bit.

Danny and I have spent most of our lives hundreds of miles apart and, for the last few decades, thousands of miles apart, me in Scotland and Danny in Canada, but spending long periods anywhere (or everywhere) in the world. The interesting thing is that we have followed a remarkably similar career path, with a large part of it being dedicated to making real company improvements.

While chatting about work, we shared so many similarities and stories that we thought it would be worthwhile to put our heads together and see what we could create that would help folks improve their businesses. It was obvious that there is a trend toward exclusive processes, like Six Sigma (which I have used when needed), but many use it before considering the application of simpler techniques. We believed that many of the most useful techniques were being overlooked by not using the simple ways first (remember KISS—Keep It Simple, Stupid?). We wanted to resurrect some of the older techniques—the ones we knew to work and to work well.

Mostly, the book is about finding and fixing issues. But we also saw complexity in newly formed working relationships, so we included how companies work with consultants. Are there misunderstandings on why they are needed or used? How do managers handle the decision made by their bosses to use them? How do they interact with managers to get things done positively? How can you handle the folks who are actively against improvements? How hard is it to build a culture of improvement in some organizations, and how do we involve folks and get things done on the front line?

We discussed the usual format of how-to books and felt that it might not be the best vehicle to pass on knowledge.

When I think of the books that most influenced me, I remember *The Goal* more than most. I could see myself in the factory manager/engineer's position and relate to all the issues—especially how my wife was affected every time I needed to work late. We liked that it had simple characters and used the story as a framework for illustrating issues.

So, despite not being fiction writers, we decided to have a go and use real experiences to illustrate issues and, more importantly, solutions. It was a long, hard road. It is hardly *Harry Potter*! Our characters exhibit a conglomeration of traits we have encountered in real life but are not related to any specific people. The same holds true for the problems we cover.

We tap into some complex diagnostic techniques, such as Four-Field Mapping and process mapping, and some simple techniques, like face-to-face discussions to gather data. We explain some simple statistics and introduce how Minitab® can be used to speed up and simplify data analysis. We also explain one way to use Statistical Process Control (SPC) to anticipate problems from data and what the results mean. We introduce the benefits of the "morning meeting" and allocating tasks and responsibilities to eliminate issues. We cover project planning, strategy, and even the use of Lean manufacturing and several other very useful techniques.

We also wanted to show that every company suffers the same issues, so we selected four different companies and used them as illustrations: a call center, a pharmaceutical company, a tier one automotive parts supplier, and a metals distributor and processor. This allowed us to cover a range of problems—different in nature but also sharing similarities.

I can't see any way the content of this book will not help you to improve the profit margin of your company or give you insight into what you could choose to learn and apply next.

Danny and I are pleased with what we have created. We hope you will be, too.

Acknowledgments

We thank Austin Davey for his help and permission to use Minitab® and the diagrams, and Judy Bass from McGraw-Hill for permission to use any diagrams from my previous works. For their help and support on the publication of this book, we thank Michael Sinocchi, Marsha Pronin, and Iris Fahrer from Taylor & Francis.

About the Authors

Steven Borris

I began working as a junior lab tech at Paisley University, which I attended as a day-release student at the Glasgow College of Technology (now The Caledonian University) while studying applied physics. Working in a university had many advantages. For one, I had 15 private tutors. In addition to learning about equipment maintenance, I was also using my physics training daily in the labs and was taught how to train students in laboratory experimentation and how to develop new ways of doing things.

From there, I moved on to Strathclyde University, the UK Health Service, and the semiconductor industry, where I installed and maintained complex equipment across Europe with Eaton, a global power-management company based in the United Kingdom. Customer training was a high priority both with Eaton and later with their largest competitor, Varian, as their Northern Europe in-plant training manager. Training included operations, maintenance, and production processes and root cause fault-finding. I learned very quickly that most equipment issues were caused by poor training—not poor technicians or poor equipment—so I began writing procedures and training the people involved.

National Semiconductor provided my introduction to Total Productive Maintenance (TPM), where I managed the Education and Training Pillar and was an active member of the pilot team. I was so impressed at the success of the implementation of TPM and the benefits of a formalized improvement process that I changed the direction of my career. I was also trained in Reliability Centered Maintenance (RCM) and developed the course that we used to train others.

After forming my own company, I worked with companies such as Premier Foods and Interbrew. During this period, I wrote my first book, *Total Productive Maintenance* (McGraw-Hill Scientific, New York, 2005). The book also focused on RCM, Lean manufacturing, quick changeovers (SMED), 5S, and problem-solving techniques.

I had the opportunity to help build an organization designed to improve the productivity of Scottish manufacturing, which was something that I had wanted to do since learning the benefits of TPM. So I took a position with SMAS, the Scottish Manufacturing Advisory Service. During my time at SMAS, I worked with directors, CEOs, owners, and employees at all levels while diagnosing, training, and fixing company issues across Scotland. As a bonus, I was one of the few who were also trained in Six Sigma and in the formal business advisor course, a required course for Scottish government account executives.

I felt that there was inadequate material available for proper diagnosis of company practices, so I wrote my second book, *Strategic Lean Mapping* (McGraw-Hill Scientific, New York, 2012), covering a range of mapping techniques I had used as well as a capacity map I had developed to solve a specific issue.

I started Productivity Jigsaw Limited in 2012, where I consult and train in TPM, RCM, Lean techniques, and process improvement. I cover most sectors, including semiconductors, life sciences, medical products, manufacturing, recycling, printers, electronics, and others. I can be contacted at steven.borris@productivity-jigsaw.com.

Daniel Borris

My working career began as a tool-and-die maker and as a marine engineer in Scotland. No university for me—I maxed out with a college degree in engineering. I had no choice but to succeed!

I progressed through supervisory roles with Chrysler Corporation and then management roles with American Can International in the UK and North America. My first consulting role was with Kepner Tregoe Associates, a company with a reputation as a gold standard in rational thinking processes.

Ever the reader, I was triggered into fashioning myself as half executive and half consultant. As an executive, I rose over the years to become the chief operating officer with Minacs Worldwide and a managing director with Teletech Australia and NZ. I have managed profit and loss responsibility on five continents.

My grassroots beginnings and the length of my career have given me experience and expertise in business-process outsourcing, call centers, automotive parts manufacturing, metals distribution and processing, plastics, and high-speed packaging.

I am the founder and principal of Daniel Borris & Associates, a Canadian-based management consulting firm, and can be reached at danielborris@yahoo.ca.

Introduction

Imagine you are running a group of companies, the Bow Corporation, and suddenly find out your backers want to shut you down. It turns out that even banks have bosses, and their driver, just like the one you have, is profit. The recession hit us all hard, particularly banks, and they need to bring in new money fast.

Then you discover the profit you have been happy with is no longer good enough. In fact, it's not even close. You have been given an ultimatum: Fix it or be sold. Even if you had the time to fix the problems, you have no idea if it is possible or how you would go about it. What do you do? Maybe consultants are the only way to go.

There is the instant fear of unemployment: having to tell your spouse, find a new job, move home. Jeff Lincoln, the CEO of Bow Corporation, is stunned, "I have let down all my employees. I have failed them all. My confidence is shattered. In one fell swoop, my life has changed again."

The CEO has no time to look around. He has no desire to call in help, but he knows he needs it. So he asks around for a recommendation and, following an interview with two consultants, takes a leap of faith based on his instincts and experience.

During the meeting, one of the consultants lists five options available for finding the issues that they must fix. He knows it can be only a high-level pass, but it will cover as much of the organization as possible and highlight—and quantify—the main issues. Do they use one technique or use them all?

The consultant interview is a two-way discourse. Pretty soon, Jeff has listed many of the problems—at least the ones he knows about. He is a bit embarrassed that there are more issues than he would care to admit. It is a big, big list, ranging from the timescale allowed to save the business to possible management resistance. But the biggest fear is the key ultimatum: Increase profit from 3% to 12% in nine months.

He believes the task is simply impossible.

Hamish McIntyre is the COO and has been assigned as the interface with the consultants. He has the same fears as Jeff, but also has a wife and teenage daughter and only recently relocated his family after accepting the job at Bow.

Then there are the four division presidents: Elizabeth Golden runs Phonethics, a call center that is running at a loss; Hugh Greenlees runs Ronson & Ronson, the metals processing and distribution business that can't make their deliveries; Chuck Nothis runs Next Automotive, saddled with low profits and huge costs for premium transport to get deliveries to clients on time and in the right quantities; and Lucie Bell runs Independent Pharmaceuticals, the jewel in the crown, which makes good profits but has serious downtime issues that make production unreliable and limit manufacturing capacity.

Hugh does not want to have anything to do with the consultants and actively resists the improvement plans, even to the extent of instructing others to do the same.

The consultants do some training in Big Picture mapping to get a general view of the issues and then move on to the individual companies to develop their issues more deeply, find the root causes, and work to fix the issues.

The book provides a guide through a business analysis and highlights solutions to bridge the gap between current performance and the new expanded expectations.

The project plan is used to sequence and prioritize all of the required actions to ensure success within the nine-month time frame.

Each of the four divisions requires the use of a different approach to achieve success in eliminating its specific problems. These range through SPC, identifying constraints, working in small teams, short-interval reporting, management control systems, and problem-solving techniques. The ongoing need is getting everyone on board to support the change initiative that will then allow for a new performance system to be developed.

Finally, if and when you have achieved the short-term results, you have to take a strategic look at the future of the Bow Corporation.

All of the techniques introduced in this book are usable in any company, whatever their sector.

1

The Uninvited Visitors

Dark, black, angry clouds; it feels like it has been raining forever.

Jeff Lincoln looks away from the window and toward his visitors. Two members of the board of directors have dropped by unannounced and are now seated opposite him at his desk. Both are wearing gray, immaculately cut, pinstriped suits, striped shirts, and red power ties. Indeed, if it wasn't for the age difference, one could imagine them as twins dressed by their mother.

The guests are Elijah Tobias, who represents Boston–Edinburgh Ventures, one of Bow's four private equity owners. The other is Patrick Edwards, from Paris Investment Corp, a more aggressive growth fund.

Elijah has been in this game for years and is normally a moderate man, pleasant to deal with. Patrick is not so agreeable: young, dynamic, overbearing, and pushy. He likes to be in control. It seems like he reflects the image of his company.

Jeff wonders why they are here. One thing he is sure of: It can't be good! He composes himself as he asks the burning question. "Well, gentlemen, to what do I owe this unexpected pleasure this morning?"

"It's like this, Jeff," says Elijah, wasting no time. "The board has been uncomfortable for some time now about the level of profits the Bow Corporation is generating. A 3% profit just doesn't cut it in this day and age, and the fact that there has been no top-line growth for years also had us on the ropes. We are here to discuss our options on how we can improve profitability."

"I know the figures are not stellar, but we had our board meeting just last month and no one raised any of these concerns, so why the sudden urgency? What has changed to bring you both here today, Elijah?" Jeff is genuine in his recollection.

"It was most definitely mentioned at the board meeting," interrupts Patrick, leaning forward in his chair. "If you would take the time to read the minutes, you would see that!"

Jeff is surprised at the forcefulness of Patrick's response. "Why the aggression, Patrick?" Jeff asks softly. "You are talking to me as if I am the enemy and not the CEO and chairman of the board."

Patrick changes to a more gentle tone. "Jeff, it's time we had a serious talk." He now realizes attack was not the best approach. He sinks back into his seat and continues. "Although the discussion at our last board meeting on profitability was brief, it was definitely tabled. You seemed to let it slide past at the time, which is why Elijah and I thought we should raise it again, a bit more informally—as a courtesy."

Elijah picks up the discussion. "We will be calling an emergency board meeting next week to make this official, but the equity members are in agreement. We must make significant improvements in our profitability immediately, and I mean *now*. The investors have reached their tipping point. If you do not—or cannot—improve, then each of the investors will forward a motion to put the company on the block. Either we improve quickly or we sell and recover as much of our investment as possible. We realize that due to the current financial climate and your poor performance, the companies will likely need to be broken up and the assets sold independently."

This is a bombshell to Jeff. He can feel his heart pounding, but he keeps calm. "I am sorry guys, where are my manners? Can I get you coffee?" He smiles as he picks up his mug and walks toward the coffeepot. He pauses before he fills his mug, looks back at the table, and asks, "What extent of profitability improvement are we talking about?" Before they answer, he adds, "… and what does 'now' mean?"

Patrick's frustration is obvious in his response. He has already written off the company in his mind and is expecting to sell. His boss has given him financial targets to achieve too, and, for Patrick, a sell-off immediately meets them. He thinks the board's option is an unrealistic gamble and a waste of time. But a decision is a decision. So he answers, "We need the profit to increase from $9 million to $36 million EBIT.* And 'now' means now!"

Elijah adds some clarity. "It's the beginning of a new fiscal year for us. We feel the gains have to be in place nine months from now. By then, the

---

* EBIT is an acronym for "earnings before interest and taxes."

Bow Corporation must be showing a run rate that will sustain $36 million in earnings, before interest and taxes, for the entire fourth quarter of this year. If you feel you cannot lead the company through this change, we will, regretfully, need to ask for your resignation."

Jeff places a tray with coffee, milk, and sugar on the table and smiles. He is stunned into silence but conceals it well. The tray gives him thinking time.

Patrick looks at Elijah and then at Jeff. "If you don't mind, Jeff, we will pass on the coffee. We have another appointment."

As his fellow board members leave his office, Jeff remembers a point on low profitability being raised at the last board meeting. He thought it was just a throwaway comment and not a call to action. Now its intention is clear. His first thought is simply to resign, to get up from his desk and leave the building. He feels insulted and unappreciated. After 25 years of service, this is how it ends?

He sits on his chair and spins to look out the window. Sipping his coffee, his mind goes into freefall. It has been two years since the death of Martha, his wife. It followed a long and painful battle with cancer. This had proved to be the most difficult time in his life. He knows his performance at work suffered—even his performance at life—but he thought he was doing OK.

He remembers before her diagnosis, how little time he'd been able to spend at home, having no idea that this time could never be recovered. Even when she was ill, there were so many occasions he had to travel or work late. At first his colleagues were fully supportive and covered for him. Some true friends still do but, over time, most just stopped. They had their own lives to live and jobs to do. After all, surely enough was enough. They just needed to get on with it.

Now he recognizes that he has been running on autopilot for the past two years, concerned at some level with the company's stagnating performance, yet unable or unwilling to do anything about it. He knew it was happening. He even hired Hamish McIntyre as chief operating officer less than a year ago to fill the gap. This was a new position in the company.

At 63 years of age, Jeff is far from dead. He remembers when he was aggressive, dominating, and maybe even a bit unpleasant—like Patrick. Indeed, he was proud to know he would fearlessly stand toe to toe with anyone and argue his point. He could make decisions in seconds, *knowing* he would be right.

Now, he thinks differently about decisions, preferring to make the real "right" ones the first time. He involves his employees whenever possible and rarely loses his temper. He has managed the conglomerate's four company presidents personally, even though his hope was that Hamish would take the reins and improve things, allowing him to gently slip into retirement.

In retrospect, it was obvious that Hamish would need time to get settled, to get his feet under the table. Maybe not a year, though. Jeff was still grieving and had simply been coasting along. He had effectively relinquished control without realizing it, but no one had taken over. This meeting with Patrick and Elijah has been like a slap in the face. In that instant, he knew things couldn't continue as is. Now he is awake and determined not to walk away in the shame of failure.

His decision is made: It is time to do something different.

How on earth can he find out what is wrong with four companies and fix their problems? He considers hiring consultants to help. With the timescales given, help will be essential. By hook or by crook, he will get the results.

Jeff speaks softly, talking to himself "… I promise to do everything in my power to get Hamish ready for the role of CEO. Then, as soon as the results are assured, I will retire!"

As he sips his coffee, he notices the rain is no longer bouncing off the windowpanes. He crosses over and leans on the windowsill and looks out. The clouds have broken and the sun is finally forcing its way through.

2

The Consultant

"Richard, can you pick up the phone? It's Eddie."

Richard twists the corner of the page of his book and lays it down beside the Kindle. He prefers the feel of real books. Mind you, the Kindle does have some advantages: It remembers the last page read. The book, on the other hand, has so many dog-eared pages already that a new fold just adds to the choices.

He reaches out his arm to pick up the phone and lets out a low groan. There is a base with a flashing light, but no phone. He thinks, "Wouldn't it be a good idea to tie the handset to the base with a cable? It would make it so much easier to find." He scans the room while simultaneously lifting the cushions off the chair. The phone is sitting next to the coffeemaker—again. "Maybe I should move the base there," he thinks.

"Eddie, great to hear from you, how have you been? How are Julie and the kids?" Richard chats as he makes himself another cup of coffee.

"The family is great, thanks, Richard. You know that I'm the problem in our house, it's sad to say," Eddie hesitates and chuckles. "I'm *really* busy at work," he says, stretching out the word *really*. "In fact, that is why I am calling. I was talking to Jeff Lincoln yesterday. He's the CEO of a group of companies. He has big problems with his call centers and manufacturing plants. The more he told me of the situation, the more I thought that you were the guy to help. I don't have the same skill sets as you and your team. In fact, being a lawyer, most folk would say I have no skills at all!" Both Richard and Eddie laugh.

Richard moves toward his desk as he listens. Sitting down, he picks a red, hardback book from a rack, opens it to a new page, grabs a pen, and writes the date on the top of the page. "What did you say the CEO's name was?"

"Jeff Lincoln. The company is the Bow Corporation."

"I think I have heard of them. They're a privately held conglomerate, right? Owned by a group of private equity firms?"

"Correct, smart-ass," Eddie quips. "You have far too much time on your hands!"

"Eddie, you know me, I spend so much time traveling I have a chair with my name on it at the airport. Traveling sounds glamorous, but it is just an opportunity to sit on uncomfortable chairs, read books and newspapers, and watch in-flight movies." Richard draws a bullet point on the page and starts to color it in. "What is it that's keeping Jeff awake?"

"It's the usual, buddy: profitability, growth, and all the other stuff that clutters things up. The real issue, though, is that the private equity guys backing them are not at all happy with current performance. Since the financial crisis, the owners are looking for ways to maximize their investments. They have asked Jeff to increase his profits—by a huge amount. With four divisions and a tight time limit, it's more than Jeff can handle, and he's looking for some help."

"What are the group's total sales and earnings before taxes, any idea?" asks Richard, pen hovering above the page.

"About $300 million annually, but the real issue is that they only run about 3% earnings, not much better than inflation. The performance used to be better—that's why I am calling you. I will send you an e-mail with contact info and some details."

"Excellent, I'll have a look and give you a call back. Would you prefer if I spoke to Jeff first?"

Eddie pauses to consider. "Good idea. I'll give him a call and tell him you will be in touch later today. Keep me informed of any progress."

"Cheers, Eddie. Take care. Learn how to delegate and get a life!"

Richard picks up his iPad and taps the Google icon with his index finger. When the keyboard appears, he types "Bow Corporation." As the search data appear, he grabs his coffee and moves toward his chair.

3

The CEO

Michael and Richard, the consultants, arrive at Bow's corporate office for a meeting with Jeff Lincoln. Annie, his executive assistant, shows them to his office. After introducing himself and shaking hands, Jeff asks if they would like tea or coffee. They both opt for the coffee, and Annie is kind enough to fetch some.

Glancing down at his watch, Jeff starts to speak, "I hope you don't mind, but I've asked our chief operating officer to join us. He should get here in around 15 minutes. Eddie tells me you'll be able to help us. Would you mind telling me a bit about your backgrounds while we wait?"

Michael takes a business card from his wallet and hands it to Jeff while explaining that his original background is engineering and maintenance, with much of his time spent on problem solving and training. He has worked on staff of a number of companies but changed direction when he started seeing how the benefits of continuous improvement could change the way a company works—specifically in the areas of quality and profitability. Mike gives a brief overview of the companies and industry sectors he has worked with and quotes a few results from each sector. He suggests that Jeff take a look at the consultants' company website and promises to send him a full CV.

Jeff listens with interest and then asks, "So, what made you change? What started your interest in productivity?"

Mike has answered this question many times before. "I was working in one of the divisions of a major multinational company. It was told by its parent company that it needed to increase its performance across the board or be sold off. A small team of specialists was selected to lead the initiative, and I was chosen as one of the members. I have always enjoyed training and, if I'm honest, trying to fix everyone's problems. I found that the job suited me perfectly. I loved how the simple formality of a process could make what I did even more effective. Striking out on my own just seemed to be a natural progression, as many of the skills overlap, and production is important to engineers too."

Mike's background resonates with Jeff's current situation.

"Richard, as you will appreciate, I'm about to trust you both with key information regarding my company and so, even with Eddie's glowing references, I will still need to check your details." Jeff smiles at Richard and goes on, "So please, since Hamish has not arrived yet, would you tell me your background?"

Richard explains that although he also started his career in engineering, his path oscillated between consultant and manager. It was not a deliberate plan, as such, but more the way the dice landed. When a new opportunity appeared, if the challenge suited, he would take it. He gives Jeff a brief rundown on the sectors and countries in which he has worked. His experience covers five continents. Jeff listens intently, makes no comment, and gives no sign other than the occasional nod of his head.

The coffee arrives and creates a natural break. As everyone sips on it, the door opens and in walks the COO. Hamish McIntyre is a giant of a man, clearly athletic—probably played rugby or football at some time in his life. If he didn't, it would have been a real waste! He crushes each of their hands in turn as he introduces himself in a strong Scottish accent. Both Michael and Richard like him immediately.

"We understand that you are faced with a complex set of issues that need to be resolved and you think we may be able to help?" asks Michael, after allowing Hamish time to get organized.

"We could probably do it ourselves," replies Jeff, "but not quickly enough! However, if we use external support, it will give us additional brainpower and manpower, and it should take the pressure off enough to allow us to continue with our normal responsibilities and avoid any mistakes or backward steps. We simply don't have the time for those!"

"How do you feel about that, Hamish?" asks Michael.

"I'm completely on board," he says. "I'll happily work with you two as partners, but I have to make it clear to you that my authority always must be recognized or my credibility will vanish—and with it will go my ability to lead the operations of this business."

Michael and Richard agree to work together, recognizing that Hamish is the senior partner. They also express their support and gratitude for the confidence he is displaying in accepting outside help.

"In our current situation, we definitely could use the help. The task seems virtually impossible." Hamish looks at Jeff for agreement. "Where do you think we should start?"

Michael replies, "The first step is normally to clarify the current situation. There are some standard techniques we can use."

Michael moves to the flipchart and lists five options.

1. *Big Picture mapping*: This is the most effective when used to cover as much of the organization as possible at a high level. It will identify and quantify the main issues and, often, the source of the problems.
2. *Selection of projects*: We can zoom in on specific issues highlighted in the big picture map by using process or other mapping techniques. Mapping can take time, which is the main drawback. But the benefits normally outweigh the time taken.
3. *SWOT analysis*: This is a faster option, but provides less detail than mapping. It covers the Strengths, Weaknesses, Opportunities, and any Threats (SWOT) to the organization or company.
4. *Brainstorming*: Although a function of the other two techniques, brainstorming will produce a list of symptoms that can be analyzed.
5. *Talking to people*: Simple and yet effective, this can highlight many issues that managers are unaware of.

Mike concludes, "The main objective is finding the issues that, when fixed, will eliminate the biggest—or easiest—problems. Some of them, we will already know about. By careful selection, every issue we eliminate will create savings that can be used to increase production time or, equally important, will create a window of time that will make it easier to free up the staff to work on new problems."

BACKGROUND TO THE PROBLEM

Jeff considers the reply and then begins to explain the high-level issues that he believes they are facing. Mike confirms that it is OK for him to take notes as Jeff speaks. "In a nutshell, our business is financed by four private equity firms, and the return on investment doesn't meet their expectations. They have been patient for the last couple of years. Unfortunately, during this time, with the financial crash and the recession, things have gotten worse. There always comes a point in time when poor performance creates a crisis, and our time has come."

Jeff continues, "The board of directors, which comprises representatives of the four private equity firms and me, have decided that they want to take the company public to drive a liquidity event. It seems obvious that we must improve the overall profitability of the business—and quickly—to ensure acceptance from the market for any public offering. If we are unable to do this, the company will be broken up and sold. Although the targets are aggressive, they are also our lifeline. If we can achieve the targets, there will be no sale, and the group will survive. The downside is that we only have nine months to do it."

"Not an easy task, but it depends on the expected increase," says Michael. "Would you mind if we capture some of the high-level points now? It will give us a good starting point for further analysis and the basis of a charter listing what we need to achieve."

"Good idea," says Jeff. "Before you leave the room, though, I'll need you to sign these nondisclosures." He holds up some papers that he has already prepared. The overall urgency becomes clearer.

Richard moves toward the flip chart. "Let's appraise the situation together. I'll capture the main points." Both Jeff and Hamish begin to offer issues. As Richard duly captures them on the flip chart, clarifying the details as he goes, Mike refers to his own notes to ensure that no points are missed.

Hamish keeps jumping to solution mode, but Richard steers him to concentrate on only the key points at this time. There is no conscious effort made to prioritize or sequence the issues. Often the most important ones tumble out first, as they are on the top of one's mind. But the most recent ones can sneak out, too.

The list grows quickly:

- Turnaround viability must be proven in nine months.
- Company sales are currently at $300 million.
- Each business has differing degrees of sales ($) and profit (%).
- There is a 3% average profit on EBIT (earnings before interest and taxes).
- Four diversified companies make up the business, each led by a divisional president.
- The businesses include automotive parts, pharmaceuticals, a call center, and a metal processing and distribution company.

- The key issues include quality (scrap), rework, on-time delivery, process bottlenecks, and customer-satisfaction levels.
- There may be resistance from the divisional presidents to outside help.
- A project plan is required.
- If viable, a strategy is required for presentation to the board covering the next three years.
- The private equity investors require a 12% return on sales (EBIT) as a run rate by nine months from now.

The list had started quickly but slows as Hamish and Jeff run out of issues. When all of the points have been captured, the four review them once more. "How do you both feel about the list? Does it represent your current view of reality?" asks Richard.

Jeff and Hamish exchange a look of agreement and nod their heads pensively. "I think so," says Jeff.

"It looks OK as a high-level start," Hamish agrees. "What's next?"

"Well," says Michael, "the list is pretty comprehensive but lacks detail. At division level, we need to confirm the issues, prioritize them for resolution, form teams to work on the issues, train as required and, of course, find root causes. And, we need to do it quickly."

Richard adds, "By doing this, we can baseline the current performance using key performance indicators (KPIs). If we have no data or KPIs, we can begin collection, but we can also make simple estimates to avoid delays. The main advantage of KPIs is that they give us an established baseline and we can see, at a glance, if we have made any improvements. Our reality is the main KPI we need to ensure, and that is the EBIT. The analysis will also introduce us to the players across the business and help determine who would be best to participate in the improvement teams. The makeup of the teams is very important, as they will drive the results."

Hamish calls his personal assistant. "Janice, would you set a date for the first meeting with the division managers? We will need at least a half day, but a full day would be better. If you can, please try and minimize disruption to any critical appointments already made, but if necessary, you might have to do a bit of shuffling around. Can you also please clear my calendar for tomorrow? I have a meeting with Richard and Michael for 8 a.m. I will draw up the agenda myself."

Janice confirms. They had already discussed the importance of the meeting.

Mike jots down some notes for analyzing any situation:

- The correct people have to be present.
- The issues have to be made visible, with data where possible.
- The team has to agree that the list is complete for the current level of the analysis.
- Responsibility assignment has to be agreed upon.
- The next steps have to be established with timescales.

4

The COO

The two consultants arrive 20 minutes early; both Michael and Richard are sticklers for being on time. Janice shows them straight in and they find Hamish already seated behind his desk.

They say a person's office can tell a lot about them, and Hamish's office suggests a very interesting person. There's a battered rugby ball in prominent view and, yes, there are the framed rugby shirts on the wall. His desk and oval meeting table are cluttered in a very organized way, as is the top of his credenza. There is a picture of an attractive woman and another of a teenage girl on his desk. Hamish motions them to the seats opposite him.

"Morning, Hamish." Richard and Michael shake Hamish's gigantic paw.

"Good morning, gentlemen. Would you like coffee?" And there is Janice; she hasn't even waited to be asked. As she pours the coffee Hamish asks, "How would you like to plan this project?"

Richard answers, "Well, we were hoping that you might be able to flesh out some of the details from our meeting yesterday, and then we could discuss your expectations of the outcome of our working together. We are also glad of the chance to get to know you a little better. Maybe you could tell us a little about yourself?" Richard looks at the photographs on the desk and checks Hamish's hand for a ring. "Is this your wife and daughter?"

Hamish chuckles, "Yes, happily married with one beautiful teenage daughter who, like me, dotes on her mother." He touches his wife's picture. "I guess we all suffer from executive marriages and wish we could spend more time with our families." He laughs and adds, "Mind you, if we can't solve our problems, it looks like I will get my wish."

"What about the rugby?" Richard asks.

"Rugby is a lifelong passion. The ball was given to me by the team captain after a cup final, and the shirts are from my university days. These days, business is my game, but I still thrive on competition and like to keep myself fit." As he clears a space on his desk for Mike's notepad, he apologizes. "Sorry about the mess in here. I seem to function best with everything in my reach and, believe it or not, I can find exactly what I'm looking for in these piles very quickly. I've found that in my world, out of sight means out of mind, and I can't afford that."

"I'm relatively new here. I started about 12 months ago after a few years as COO of an engineering shop. I was headhunted. My background fit the profile they were looking for. In general, I've been well accepted here although, as you would expect, there has been the occasional personality clash. There were a couple of internal candidates who thought they should have been given the job—you will meet them later ... but it's always a little tough for some when a new guy is brought in from outside."

"I think what I want from you guys is a fresh pair of eyes and extra manpower to get this done. We need a fresh injection of talent and different ideas to help achieve the degree of change that's required—particularly within the expected timelines. Even with your help, I think the timeline is really tight."

"I also need you to be tactful and respectful to the people who are here—including me. We all have egos, and some of us could easily bruise when you start asking us to change. We need to establish a clear method of approach, a detailed plan as to how you and I will approach this."

Hamish points into the air. "Oh yes, it almost slipped my mind. I will be leading this initiative—not you two. You will be reporting to me, and I will be heavily engaged!"

They nod their agreement. Richard adds, "That's exactly the way we like it, Hamish. We believe your total commitment and buy-in is essential in creating an improvement culture. Your leadership and support will help ensure everyone else's, too."

"All right, I have one more question for you two guys. How much is this going to cost me, and when will it hit my budget?"

"We can work for a standard rate or agree on a reduced rate plus a percentage of the savings we achieve. Naturally, our out-of-pocket expenses would be on top. We support what Jeff and you plan to do, Hamish, and we want to be a part of it. This is why we have included the second option. We can share any risk with you, although we have no doubt we can achieve this turnaround if we all work together."

Hamish seems satisfied and nods his head in agreement. "I think that sounds pretty fair. I'm also beginning to trust you, which isn't bad for me in such a short period of time. So, what do we do next?"

Michael takes the lead. "Let's look at the details behind the situation you and Jeff described yesterday. With a little more clarification, we can easily move to the next step, which, with your approval, will be a meeting with the four division presidents, chaired by you and facilitated by us. This will be the first major analysis into the specific businesses, and from this we will identify if there are any crossover issues between divisions. It'll also afford an opportunity for us all to get to know each other—to see how each other thinks and hopefully build a little rapport and the beginnings of trust with the division presidents. We also need their buy-in if we are to succeed."

Michael and Richard begin to work on the issues following standard procedures. The best way to find the right answers is to ask the right questions. Clarification is best achieved through asking lots of open questions, like:

- What exactly do you mean by that?
- Is there anything else that bothers you around this issue?
- What makes you believe this to be true?
- Is there anything else you think will clarify this issue a little further?

Using these questioning and discussion techniques, the consultants work through yesterday's issues list and refine it. Once complete, they review the situation and agree that it is a good representation of the current state (Table 4.1).

"It looks like we have a winner in Independent Pharmaceuticals," says Richard.

"I agree, Richard. It is a great little company. They do have a few problems they just don't seem able to get their heads around, but there is a lot of potential there. As a pharmaceutical business, it should run with much better margins," says Hamish.

"Has Janice been able to arrange the half-day meeting with the regional presidents?" asks Richard.

"Tomorrow morning at 8 a.m. I've already given them a heads-up. Be bright-eyed and bushy-tailed, boys. I'll see you tomorrow in the boardroom."

Mike prepares a few notes on clarifying issues.

- Ask questions that look for details.
- Use open-ended questions, like "What exactly do you mean by that?" or "What else?" or "How could we best do that?".
- Identify potential issues and improvements.
- Explore questions like "What threats do you see?" or "What opportunities might there be?" or "Have you ever thought of how you might solve this?".
- Determine what the next steps should be.

TABLE 4.1

The Meeting Summary

Turnaround viability proven in nine months. The private equity investors require a 12% return on sales (EBIT) as a run rate by nine months from now.	• The run rate for the last quarter should be 12% EBIT. • The 12% profit has a bit of leeway. The board is more interested in earning the $36 million than it all being due to increased margins. • This is good news, as it means we can increase sales, and they will accept a slightly lower EBIT. • Before making increased sales, we need to increase manufacturing capacity to cope. • However, productivity improvements do not all make money, as such. They enable more products to be made in the same time. To turn this into profit, any new product must be able to be sold. • Michael and Richard are to assist in monitoring and control plus any necessary adjustments for 12 months. • Improvements that will meet the company's financial targets must be identified and installed. • Control systems that will ensure the sustainability of solutions and the ongoing use of improvement techniques must be installed. • Management and selected hourly representatives must be trained in continuous improvement techniques as required, eventually involving all employees.
Total company sales are currently at $300 million with an average of 3% profit overall (EBIT).	• Every effort will be made to increase sales/markets to assist in achieving the target profits. • Current profit performance of 3% EBIT = $9 million. • Expected performance of 12% EBIT or $36 million as a run rate in nine months.
Each business has differing sales ($) and profit (%).	• Sales for Ronson & Ronson: $110 Million @ 2% EBIT or $2.2 million. • Sales for Next Automotive: $70 million at 3% EBIT or $2.1 million. • Sales for Phonethics: $80 million @ 2% EBIT or $1.6 million. • Sales for Independent Pharmaceutical: $40 million @ 7.5% EBIT or $3.0 million.
Four diversified companies make up the business. Each company is led by a divisional president.	1. Ronson & Ronson: Metals distribution led by Hugh Greenlees. 2. Next Automotive: Automotive parts manufacturer led by Chuck Nothis. 3. Phonethics: Inbound call-center business led by Elizabeth Golden. 4. Independent Pharmaceuticals Limited: Pharmaceutical company led by Lucie Bell.

TABLE 4.1 (*Continued*)

The Meeting Summary

The key issues include quality (scrap), on-time delivery, process bottlenecks, and staffing.	• Details gleaned from managers' meetings and refined at individual divisional meetings. • Processes analyzed to find problems and wastes:
There might be resistance from the divisional presidents to outside help.	• Commitment of the CEO and COO plus a formal expectation of full support will help reduce this. • The consultants must gain their trust. • The divisional presidents must accept responsibility for their business, the change process, and achieving the results.
A project plan is required.	• This will be developed two weeks from now following the initial analysis. • The project plan will be developed by Michael and Richard with extensive input from the COO and the division presidents.
If viable, a strategy is required for the board covering the next three years.	• Michael and Richard will facilitate the process. • It should be outlined by the end of the initial three-month change initiative. • Baselines need to be established for each division. • The divisional presidents must be part of the strategy development team.

5

Hamish

The meeting with Mike and Richard is over, and I have asked Janice to get the boardroom set up for tomorrow's meeting. I feel a little upset and am having problems concentrating. This is not normally a problem for me. I guess I am still reeling from the news. I check the time. It is only 3:30 p.m. Staring at my Outlook calendar, I see I have no appointments, so I open the monthly report spreadsheet and look at the data. I check a couple of columns but just can't get interested.

I take another look at my watch, but now I don't see the time. Instead, I do a quick mental calculation. Six p.m. is the earliest I ever leave the office, but not today! I have decided to go home early. So I click on the "Start" icon and then "Shut Down" and close the lid of my laptop. I normally take it with me, but I know I won't look at it, so I just leave it on the desk.

I get into my car and start the drive home. I look in the rearview mirror and see a glazed look on my face. "Surely that's not me?" Thankfully, I only live 45 minutes away. Passing my favorite bar, I consider stopping for a beer but decide against it. Instead, I stop at the river and watch the swans for a while. I feel they must know me by now. I come here often and photograph them. It never occurred to me until now that I have photos of them when they were babies!

I smile at the thought of the birds, calm and elegant on the top but their legs going fast and furious below the water. They have just had seven babies—OK, cygnets, the size of a closed fist and furry, like chicks. They are swimming in a straight line with Dad in front and Mom at the back. Just imagine, seven kids, and I think *I* have problems!

The last couple of weeks have been chaotic, and now I'm also having meetings with consultants! Although they are pleasant enough, I have come to the rude awakening that someone, probably the entire board and senior managers, will all be looking over my shoulder, judging everything I do. Some might even be hoping I fail.

I know the consultants are here to help and that I am in charge, and yet I still have niggling doubts. I think I am worried that folks will think I can't do my job, and having two consultants, not just one, screams that I need help. I know I should have been on top of the situation before now, but I felt I had time.

Why am I feeling so uncomfortable? I can't kid myself. For some time now—truth be told, since I have been here—it has been obvious that the group is not working as well as it should. It's not even close to what I would like. It's sort of broken. It's not that the wheels have fallen off, but they are more than a tad wobbly.

Helen, my wife, is a nurse. She works irregular shifts, and today I need her counsel. That's why I am going home early. I walk into the hall and shuffle out of my coat. As I hang it on the rack, I notice her perfume. I look around and she is standing at my side.

She looks at her watch and taps the face, wondering where the time has gone. It never occurred to her that I would ever come home early. "Hamish! What are you doing home so early? Did something happen?"

My daughter, Zen, who has just arrived home from school, rushes downstairs and hugs me. She plants a big kiss on my cheek.

"Wow!" I exclaim. "Everything is fine, there's nothing wrong. Mind you, if I had known I would get a welcome like this, I would sneak home early more often!"

I look at Helen. She still has her look of disbelief, so I feel the need to explain more. "It's just that there are some things at work that are making me uneasy, and I think we should talk about them as a family."

We all walk into the living room together, and I tell them the whole story of what's going on. "So you can see there will be lots of pressure on me for the next year or so." I need to be more honest. I never knew it would be so difficult. I hesitate and then add, "I might even lose—or need to change—my job, and I'd like to know what you think of that?"

Both Helen and Zen start speaking at once, falling over each other. Then Zen sits back to allow her mother to speak. "Do you really think you might lose your job, Hamish?"

"Anything is possible. The company wants to quadruple the profits in nine months. Can you imagine that? It probably impossible! Mind you, at least they are really low at the moment, so four times could be a lot worse, I suppose."

Helen and I laugh.

"But you didn't cause this," says Zen. "Why would you lose your job, Dad?"

"I've been there a year, darling, and quite honestly I haven't done very much. The profits went up for a short time after I pushed a few buttons, but they slipped right back to where we started pretty quickly. Jeff, my boss, didn't seem too bothered with it, and so neither was I. It's as if I was hypnotized by Kaa, the swaying cobra from *Jungle Book*." Zen looks a bit confused, but I was really speaking to Helen. "I knew I should have been a self-starter and that I should have kept right on pushing, but Jeff's lack of concern was like an anchor; it just dragged me down to exactly the same place."

"We have my job, Hamish; we will survive. And you know we both love and support you."

"And I don't need any money, Dad," says Zen.

I tried to fight back the tears that were filling my eyes. "That means so much to me," I say, hugging my wife and daughter. "Anyway, the worst case is that I'll get a decent package, enough to last us for at least six months, and I'll find something new in the interim. Your job will carry us for a while if necessary, and we have enough savings to keep us going for another year."

We all hug and cry a little. It's been just a year since we moved to Newtown, and we are still settling in. It was difficult initially: a new school for Zen, a new hospital for Helen, new neighbors, new everything. But we have always been a close family, and that is helping us deal with things now. Besides, it has not sunk in yet.

"I thought you were sick, that you were going to die or something!" says Helen. "God knows I see enough of that in the hospital without having it come home to roost. If losing your job is the worst-case scenario, then we have nothing to worry about." Helen gives me a kiss on the cheek and whispers, "It's nothing; don't worry. I love you."

I straighten up on my seat. "I've let a few things slide at work. There are poor relations between me and a couple of my direct reports, and I've simply ignored it. It has to stop. In particular, I need to sort out the situation with Greenlees. I've let him get away with murder!"

"You complain about him all the time," says Helen. "He's been driving you crazy. Why haven't you sorted him out?"

"It's a toughie," I answer. "I've worked for some terrible bosses in the past who have been bullies. If they don't like you, they will make your life hell. They can even affect your health. It's a terrible thing to see or to be at the receiving end of. It's even harder to prove. So, I suppose my stance has been to be the opposite. Now it just seems obvious to me that there is a time and a place for all types of behavior—a time to be understanding and forgiving and a time to be tough."

"You don't need to give up your principles just to sort out a relationship. Just be fair and open." Helen takes my hand.

"I have to be careful, though. These will be sensitive times for everyone in the company, and I can't appear to be changing overnight. In fact, the folks will need a lot more support and encouragement from me. It's funny; I've been chasing this promotion for years, not having a clue what a chief operating officer's job in a large company actually was. I just wanted it for the status, the money and, ironically, the security. Now, after all this chasing, I had finally caught it. I guess we do have to be careful what we wish for!"

We share a chuckle.

"Worst case is really not so bad…I'm staying the course on this one. What better way to learn the craft of being a senior executive than being right in the middle of it? If I quit now, I'm done forever!"

"What will you have to do different?" asks Helen.

"Well.…" I hadn't really thought that far ahead, but I try to answer. "My behavior will go a long way in determining my results, and so there are definitely things I should do differently. I guess I just need to do more … be more visible to my employees, make people more accountable for their performance, involve folks more in identifying production and admin problems, address more people problems—head on, if necessary—and I really need to be seen supporting Jeff Lincoln and these two consultants. If I don't do these things, I'm dead in the water. So I will do this and more. I might be a little late getting home from time to time, and I will probably have to go in on weekends for a couple of hours each day, just to keep on top of things. Are you two OK with this?"

"Hamish, neither Zen nor I took you on as a temporary assignment," Helen smiles. "Go get them, Tiger!"

I let out a little roar, more like a kitten than a tiger.

Helen adds, "Oops, there's no dinner made for you two, and I have to dash to work. Patients arriving at emergency don't understand when the nurse is late. Can you take care of yourselves tonight?"

"Come on, Zen. I'll treat you to McDonald's." I wonder if tigers purr like cats.

6

Division Presidents

Hamish learned the importance of first impressions in his previous job. He worked for an engineering company that had survived 30 years of slow deterioration—just. He remembers how he always felt embarrassed when customers visited, and yet everyone else who worked in the factory no longer noticed. Although the factory was clean *and* made good-quality product *and* ran at a reasonable profit, it was far from being able to impress.

He probably would have just become like everyone else, except for a chance introduction to a new methodology at a conference he attended. There were no seminars of interest, so he decided to sit in on a Lean manufacturing session to kill some time. He was so impressed, he wanted to implement it at his workplace, but his boss would not buy in to the idea.

One of the topics that impressed him—and had stayed with him ever since—was a process called 5S. He had heard of it being applied to factory floor organization, but was surprised to learn that it should also be applied to offices, company reception areas, and even the outside of the buildings. Just like when buying a house, the trainer said, it was very important that any visitors get a positive first impression. House sellers even recommend a sneak attack on the senses, with the smell of fresh coffee and baking, all intended to subconsciously influence the visitor. In fact, this very tactic has led to a huge market for people who redecorate homes that prove hard to sell. Potential customers often had no idea why they didn't like a place: Sometimes the buyers felt it was too dark, or it had a smell of pets or was too cluttered. Some were even put off by too many pictures of the families of the current owners! It seems they just couldn't see themselves living there. They felt displaced by the family in the pictures. He remembered another comment about customers who judge a restaurant by the cleanliness of the toilets.

However, the point was really brought home to him when he picked up a very important, potential customer from the airport. As he looked for a parking space at the factory, he noticed the expression on the face of the visitor as he bumped over the potholes in the parking lot and, again, when they were approaching the building. He had always been aware of the fact that the factory entrance needed painting and the reception area was a bit shabby, but now he felt downright embarrassed. He found himself apologizing and even lied about planned improvements—and Hamish rarely lied. He became acutely aware of another of the 5S trainer's comments: that what a visitor sees outside the factory can create a similar perception about the product. "If people don't care about the state of the place in which they work, why would they bother about the quality of the product?"

However, his lies were only a short-lived deception, as he soon introduced a new visitor's parking lot, a new entrance, and a redesigned reception area. He then moved his attention onto the various divisions and, because his budget was tight, he prioritized the improvements to the areas visiting clients would see first: the stairway leading to the management floor, the conference room, and the corridor leading to a factory-floor inspection window. The condition of the rest of the factory improved as fast as the budget could be made available. It was not long before all of the divisions and their respective factories were at a much higher standard.

Consequently, Hamish had wasted no time in starting to improve Bow's head office. He was particularly proud of his conference room. It had been completely refurbished and had an air of importance. The new conference table, as well as a state-of-the-art communications system with a plasma TV and a high-definition projection system, just screamed professionalism. Every customer commented on the room and the quality of the presentations. Even Bow employees were impressed.

Prior to the introductory meeting with the division presidents, Hamish and Janice check that the boardroom is ready. Hamish is unusually unsettled about today's meeting.

The consultants, Michael and Richard, arrive at 7:30 a.m., and Janice shows them to the boardroom. A busy girl is Janice. She seems to do everything administrative around here. Clearly, there isn't any overspending at corporate on admin support. They are not the first to arrive; an attractive and well-dressed lady is pouring herself a coffee. She turns and smiles as they approach.

"Good morning, I'm Elizabeth Golden," she says, holding out her hand. Both consultants return her smile, shake her hand, and introduce themselves. Her handshake is firm, but as one would expect, not quite as bone crushing as Hamish's. They make idle chatter about the weather as the others begin to drift in. By 7:55 a.m., everyone has arrived and there is some preliminary chatting, pretty much with everyone smiling.

"Right then, let's take a seat," invites Hamish.

Once they are all settled, he opens the meeting. "It may just be coincidence," Richard thinks, "but the four regional presidents are sitting in a row on one side of the table and the three of us are on the other, like two opposing armies before a battle."

"There's no surprise here folks, I'm sorry to say." Hamish shakes his head, "This has been coming for a while. I know all of you have been working hard to improve the financial performance of your companies, and I have to agree there has been some success. This has been noted by the CEO *and* the board of directors."

Hamish looks at the document in front of him before proceeding. "For the past several months, things have leveled off. This is both good and bad. Good because it shows we have sustained our performance improvements, but bad because there has been no further improvement. Unfortunately, we are a l-o-n-g way from the performance level that the board has set for us. That's why Jeff and I have engaged Richard and Michael to help us move forward." Hamish gestures toward the two consultants. "They come highly recommended. Their skill sets complement each other's and ours, Michael being an engineer and efficiency expert and Richard being a blend of consultant and executive, a sort of corporate retread." The group laughs, and even Richard manages a slight chuckle. "Seriously, though, both of these guys have a great track record, and people tell us that they are also decent fellows." Hamish looks at his presidents and nods his head. "Could everyone please introduce yourself and tell Richard and Michael a bit about your business and what you think might be your biggest opportunities for improvement?"

Looking round the table, the consultants see that the group is quite young, mostly late thirties to mid-forties. All look confident and yet, as you would expect, there is an air of defensiveness.

The president of Phonethics is first to speak. "Hi, I'm Elizabeth Golden, and I run the call-center business. We are outsourcers, and so the calls our agents handle are from our clients' customers. When our agents answer the phone, they answer with the clients' name and, for all intents and purposes, behave as would our clients' own employees—except better!" The group laughs and makes some good-humored comments.

"What do you think might be your improvement options, Elizabeth?" asks Richard.

"Well, there's always room for improvement," says Elizabeth, "and that's actually part of the problem. Our performance tends to be benchmarked against our clients' own in-house call centers and the other outsourcers they use. So, even though we are performing in the top quartile of all the locations that handle incoming calls, there is still endless pressure to do even better."

Elizabeth gathers her thoughts and continues, "There is, naturally, a heavy focus on customer satisfaction, and although we have to be staffed to handle the incoming call levels, we sometimes find ourselves overstaffed in the quiet periods due to the shifts in the pattern of the incoming calls during peak intervals. When we plan to cut the numbers, some clients object, as they expect us to staff to the same level as during high call-volume intervals. It's really a question of *where* do we give? Where is the balance to be struck between giving the clients what they want and making a profit?"

"Thanks, Elizabeth. Would you like to go next, Hugh?" says Hamish.

"Sure…" Hugh Greenlees places his pen on top of his pad and takes a sip of water. He is very deliberate, even slow in coming forward. Both Mike and Richard sense the alarm bells: His body language suggests he is likely to be difficult. "I've been in the metals processing and distribution business for more than 20 years and, quite frankly, I can't imagine that either of you two gentlemen can help me at all. No offense!" He grins, leans back, and crosses his arms in the wait-and-see mode.

"No offense taken," responds Richard. There is always at least one "Hugh" somewhere in the group. In fact, if we consider the "Five Men in a Boat" analogy,* there can be as many as 5% to 10% in any organization. There's a long silence. It seems like minutes, but it was probably only 20 seconds.

"All right, Hugh, continue if you would, please," says Hamish.

"Well, I know no one is jumping for joy at our achieving a 2% profit margin. To be fair to my team, it is really a 3% rise, but I'll tell you it was damned hard work getting there from minus 1%. Nobody else in this company could have done it!" Hugh has defended his results.

Richard sees Hamish bristle and bite his tongue, but his answer is calm. "We really appreciate your efforts, Hugh. Please keep going. Perhaps you could tell us where you feel you might have opportunities for improvement?"

---

* The "Five Men in a Boat" analogy compares the willingness of a company culture to participate in a change program to the folks in a boat. It is symmetrical with the person at the front being the most willing (like 10% of workers) and the person at the rear being the least willing (like 10% of workers). The second person represents 15% that are keen to apply it and the man in the middle is Mr. Average and accounts for around 50% who don't object but are not drivers of the process. The fourth person represents the 15% who don't overtly object but have serious reservations about change.

"That is a difficult question. So far we have done everything possible to improve. But, I guess, if you insist on pushing me to decide.…" Hugh goes silent again and stares down at the table, his lips tightly clamped together.

Richard intervenes, "Hugh, with a profit level of only 2%, surely there has to be at least one thing you feel that is limiting your success." Richard smiles and continues, "Is it a lack of orders, not enough employees, unreliable equipment, space problems, late deliveries from suppliers, incomplete shipments requiring repeat work, difficult customers who expect priority treatment, long lead times? Surely you must suffer some of the same problems as almost every other industry—at least to some degree? We are not looking for definite causes at the moment, just symptoms—the problems you see that might give us some clues as to where we might start looking for opportunity."

Hugh hisses his reply, "We were running like clockwork, no problems at all. Then the corporate office had the idea of shutting the plant in Lexington and transferring all the work to us. It was a bad idea!" His lips are still tight and his nostrils flare as he speaks, "No, it was a terrible idea."

His momentum is building, "There was no planning. All of the work was simply diverted to us. Why? Not because we had extra capacity—as if anyone even bothered to find out! It was because we were performing at 95% on-time delivery! Their logic, if there was any, seemed to be that something that is working well can always work better. Before the extra throughput expectation, we were able to have eight trucks loaded and on the road by 8 a.m." Hugh pauses again for effect and takes a deep breath. "Now the expectation is that we can do 14 trucks! Nearly double the work—an actual increase of 75%." A few of his colleagues are nodding in support.

He continues, "Sometimes a man wonders where these types of decisions are made, in which ivory tower? Nobody discussed it with me. Our on-time delivery has dropped to 60%, and there are days when no more than 10 trucks even get out on deliveries. So, where's the opportunity? Increasing capacity! We can't do any more with what we have now." He glances at his colleagues, looking for their approval. "Help us—if you can!"

Michael and Richard are used to fiery, but this is quite aggressive for a first meeting.

Hamish doesn't bat an eye. "Thanks, Hugh, can you go next please, Lucie?"

As you would expect from the president of a high-tech pharmaceutical business, Lucie Bell does not lack confidence as she tells her story. "When you produce something that people pop into their mouths with the intent of it making them feel better or healthier, it's an awesome responsibility. And when you add this to the legislation we need to deal with, I'm sure you can imagine our watchwords are always 'safety' and 'quality.' Independent Pharmaceuticals may seem like a small company, but it touches millions of people every day who use our products: men, women and children. I would not be happy if even one of our customers became ill or, God forbid, died from taking our products."

"There is a consequence to this: The slightest suspicion of a problem often leads to long delays. Product might be required to undergo extra quality testing, sorting, and even rework or be scrapped. Naturally there are cost issues to this."

"As a company, we are a generic pharmaceutical manufacturer. We produce products that are no longer covered by patent. While protected by a patent, only the company that developed the product has the legal right to make and sell it—except under license. When the patent runs out, however, it means that anyone can make a similar product, provided it can match or surpass the quality of the original product."

"We consider what we do to be a true service to the community, as a lot of people have no drug plans or insurance. They have to pay for their own prescriptions. Generic products are cheaper than the original drugs, and so our customers benefit from the lower cost of our products. As we serve pretty much all of the pharmacies in our state, there is most certainly an opportunity for expansion of our product lines. We could even expand to include other states."

"The opportunity, as I see it, is in increasing production capacity and to help clear any bottlenecks we have in our production system. Our people are ready and willing and will work with you; we will absolutely welcome any and all help you can give us." Lucie looks directly at Michael and Richard. Her sincerity is obvious.

"Thanks, Lucie, your openness is an absolute delight," says Hamish, with an overt, ever-so-slight sideways glance at Hugh, which is not lost on him. "Chuck, your turn, my friend—the best saved for last?"

Chuck Nothis grins from ear to ear. He is relatively young for such a senior position, probably in his early thirties. "Gentlemen, welcome." He speaks directly to the consultants with no small degree of flourish. "I started in Next Automotive as an apprentice tool-and-die maker, then production foreman, plant manager, and now president, all in what seems like a few years. I'm very grateful for the opportunity to be in the position I have. We have just one location, and we make pretty much everything in metal that the tier 1 automotive companies use."

"We tend to make relatively small parts, stampings, small subassemblies, and that kind of thing. We have good-quality press lines, have the required state-of-the-art welding machines for assembly, and we have a top-quality paint line. In short, what this means is that our subassemblies arrive at the customer ready for final assembly into the vehicles. We also have our own die-repair and maintenance shops. I guess I feel fortunate that I've worked all over the plant: I know the business as well as anyone, and I tend to get the respect of the people who work in the plant."

"Quality and *just-in-time* delivery are essential entry-level requirements to supply the original equipment manufacturers. All of our budgets and prices are set up with the guarantee that we will deliver on time. We have no budget for premium freight costs to ship late product to the customer. If any parts miss the scheduled delivery, the extra cost of a special truck, courier, or air freight comes straight off our bottom line. We promise a delivery date that our customer uses to schedule production, so getting the goods to the customer 'just-in-time' is our responsibility."

"Unfortunately, we are late to ship quite often. More often than I care to admit. Currently, my business's premium freight cost is running at $300,000 per year. It's a miracle we make any profit at all. I've had project teams on this for a year trying to get to the bottom of it, and although there are plenty of recommendations, the problem still persists. If you can help me eliminate this, I will be forever in your debt. Mind you, I suspect you might need to reengineer the entire business." Chuck ends with another animated flourish, as if he is straight out of *The Three Musketeers*. The entire room smiles, even Hugh.

"And thank you, Chuck," says Hamish. "Now, what are the next steps, gentlemen?"

Richard nudges Michael. "It just so happens that my colleague, Michael, is an expert in organizational mapping, and he has been simply dying to lead you through the process with the intent that, together, we can uncover some of the key problems and maybe even find some root cause issues that will give us quick benefit. Of course, we realize that this is simply the beginning. We will have lots of further analysis and work to do coming out of the exercise. Michael, the floor is yours."

THE "CORPORATE" BIG PICTURE MAP

Mike likes to keep meetings as informal as possible, as it encourages group participation. Even though he did not anticipate anyone holding back today—until he met Hugh, that is—he decides to start from a seated position. "There is a popular misconception that consultants come into a company and just change everything, ignoring all the good work that has already been done. I guess this is partially true. Changes are put in place, but they should *not* be the consultant's changes. Any changes should be those of the employees, made through training sessions, analyses, discussions with the management, interaction with the employees' improvement teams, and working *with* the consultant. All changes should be your changes, how you want to improve."

"Just like hypnotism, it is not possible to make someone do something they don't want to. Indeed, within limits, forcing change pretty much guarantees a failed improvement. This single point applies to company owners, CEOs, presidents, managers, engineers, office and admin staff, warehousemen, and even cleaners. It applies to everyone in the organization."

"Success depends on developing a culture of improvement where employees *want* to make changes and, to use on old clichéd phrase, they will 'go the extra mile' just to make it happen." Mike looks at all the people around the table as he waits for a response. There is none, so he adds, "Any questions so far?"

Still no feedback.

He goes on to discuss management structures: command and control, where managers just tell folks what to do and expect them to do it, and empowerment, where workers are involved in how their jobs are carried out. There is always a degree of debate as to which one works best, particularly among Lean practitioners, who generally prefer willing participation.

"Personally, I prefer empowerment," Mike admits, "but I would like to be clear. I would, if necessary, resort to firmer methods if all attempts to understand and reason with an employee fail. Just like problems with equipment or processes, we need to have some kind of escalation procedure. In the best-run companies, it should be difficult to see the beach—the dividing line where the sand becomes the water."

"That sounds like how I like to work," Lucie comments, with a beaming grin.

Chuck adds, "Me too. I would say, 'What do you guys think?'" Chuck looks at the other team members, who nod in agreement.

Mike has already guessed that Hugh is a pure command-and-control man, but tries not to let it influence what he says. He goes on to explain that although everyone has just discussed their main issues, they are just *symptoms* of the problems each division is having, and that to fix them it will be necessary to find the root causes. Improvement is never about fixing only symptoms.

Mike explains that because of the deadline they all face, he and Richard will use three key approaches to make improvements quickly:

1. Work on the issues we already know about.

    We will estimate how much they cost the company in cash and, equally important, in how it impacts the customer. By quantifying the issues, it is easier to decide what to fix first and, if necessary, what we should spend to fix it. But remember, throwing money at a problem is not a solution. It has to be the right solution, and the best is often low cost or free.

2. Carry out a high-level diagnosis in each company, using mapping techniques—probably starting with the Big Picture map.

    The purpose here is to get as much input as is practical to help prioritize the detailed diagnoses. This will also help us to identify some issues that might not have been previously recognized. There are always a few.

3. Create process maps of the problem areas selected and quantify the issues in detail.

"I have said this before, but it is worth repeating as often as possible." Mike looks a bit more serious. "The success of any improvement program depends on everyone participating. Your support is crucial. As managers, you can make or break this project. It is not practical to map an organization as a single entity." Mike is starting to think out loud—he does that sometimes.

He is concerned that Hugh believes his issues are unique and can't be fixed, and Chuck also thinks he has done everything possible. Lucie has tried, too, but she is open to suggestions. So far, he is not sure about Elizabeth. She has a different situation in many respects, but seems to have resigned herself to failing. The thing is, everyone has the same problems, pretty much. They have been around for years, and there are recognized techniques to fix many of them.

"Do you mind if we try and throw a simple map together? It might help us make a couple of points and will only take half an hour. At the very least, you will learn that the best feature of a map is that we can use it for whatever we need. Worst case, it will help reinforce the main mapping exercise." Mike thinks a corporate map might work in this case. It is worth the investment of half an hour.

Mike explains how a *normal* map is a loop from customers through the administration offices and technical offices to the suppliers. There is also a link from suppliers to company for delivery and from company dispatch to customers. There are also the other departments like warehousing and quality control, as well as any small "stores," often called *supermarkets*, required closer to the work areas. And, of course, there are the production lines.

The map will include high-level information: lead times for services and deliveries, any waiting times or delays and, of course, any major problems. It also includes the lines of communication between departments and any important information—located in cleverly named *data boxes*.

In Mike's map, each division is treated as if it were a production line. As he draws the map, Mike explains that he and Richard will repeat this same process in each division, working with the senior management team. Here they have only the presidents. It is much better to involve all the managers in a company, as it draws from a much greater depth of experience. So the main benefit for now is an initial familiarization and a visual summary of the issues discussed so far. Normally they use sticky notes and create the map on a wall. The difficulty with a corporate map with so many divisions could possibly be the height of the room!

Mike asks the division presidents for details as the map is being sketched and writes each comment on a red sticky note. He just sticks the notes randomly along the relevant "division" row they apply to. After listing the main problems, he marks each note with the division it refers to and then groups them together in an Affinity Diagram.

Breakdowns, maintenance, setups, and changeovers fall under a new header—*throughput*—as they stop production. Waiting for instructions, no materials, and no operators also reduce throughput, but it could be argued that they are performance related. The delays reduce the total amount able to be produced due to the time lost, so the group agrees on the header *capacity*.

Due to space limitations, Mike writes the summaries in data boxes at the end of the division row they refer to. The result is the map shown in Figure 6.1.

Mike apologizes for the crushed detail of the map, as he was only sketching it on a flip chart. "But," he adds, "just imagine the room available for detail on a wall. It is virtually limitless. You will find some folks prefer a computer program, but again imagine how little of the map you would be able to see at once. It would be as condensed as this map, meaning data you would want to show would need to be on a different page or screen. Indeed, we would possibly get even less information on a screen than we do here."

To emphasize the point he intends to make, he sticks the sticky notes on a wall. First, all the notes from one division are laid out in a row. Then all the "breakdowns" are sorted to align in a vertical row. The maintenance work, for example, is then aligned vertically, too, keeping the row order by division. The same is done for all the other notes.

Mike steps back and looks at the map and the sticky notes on the wall. "Not bad for a half an hour's work. Now, what do they tell us?" (See Figures 6.1 and 6.2.)

Hugh snaps, "That it doesn't have enough detail and, as I expected, it only tells us what we already know."

No one else comments. Mike resists the urge to ask why he has not fixed the problems when he knows the causes, but he holds back. "What I see is that, apart from the call center, which we would expect to appear different in this direct comparison with three manufacturing facilities, all the companies have the same problems: mainly capacity and throughput. Besides, even the call center has capacity issues and will probably have many of the same admin-related issues, too." Mike waits for a reaction—again, nothing!

"But, if you don't mind, I would like to repeat, the issues—the symptoms we see—will not all be caused by the same root causes, although many will turn out to be variations of the same causes." Mike waits once more to see if anyone has any comments. When no one speaks, he proceeds. "The problems we have listed are only symptoms: We need to find your root causes. So, unless there are any questions, I don't see much gain in adding more detail at the moment. We should get on with the original training plan."

"Moving on, what I would like to do, if it is OK with you guys, is to give you a more detailed outline of the benefits of mapping—particularly the diagnosis value—and how we will apply it in each of your companies.

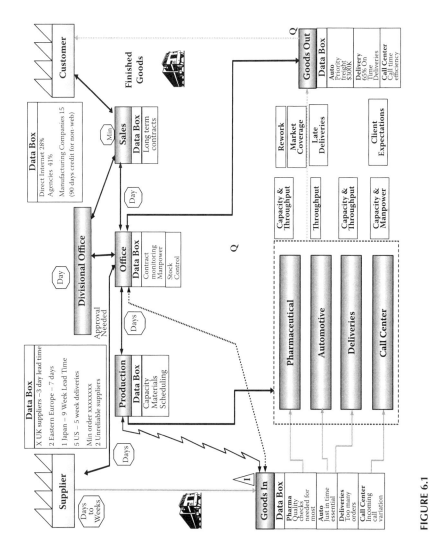

FIGURE 6.1

A simple corporate Big Picture map.

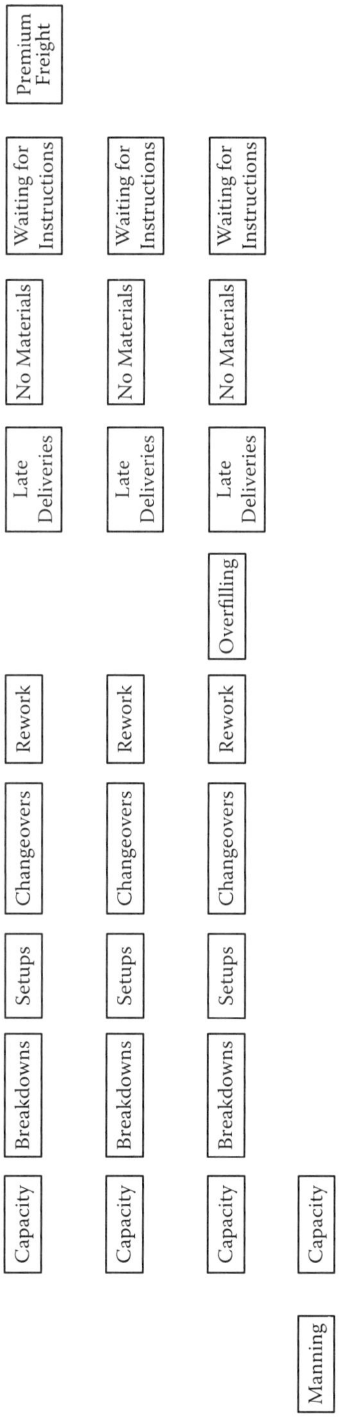

Manning	Capacity	Breakdowns	Setups	Changeovers	Rework	Overfilling	Late Deliveries	No Materials	Waiting for Instructions	Premium Freight
	Capacity	Breakdowns	Setups	Changeovers	Rework		Late Deliveries	No Materials	Waiting for Instructions	
	Capacity	Breakdowns	Setups	Changeovers	Rework	Overfilling	Late Deliveries	No Materials	Waiting for Instructions	
	Capacity									

FIGURE 6.2
Problem comparison.

The corporate map will have given you a taste, but we will add some background and discuss the other tools we will be using so that you can tell the folks in your divisions what to expect. How does that sound?" Mike asks.

Everyone nods in agreement as Mike checks the time. "Why don't we take a break while I set up a short presentation."

The table at the rear of the room has been replenished with fresh tea, coffee, soft drinks, and cookies. Only Hugh has left the room; the others chat as they select something to drink.

7

Big Picture Map

Mike and Richard are now seated at the top of the table on either side of the CEO's usual position. Hamish has moved to the opposite end of the table. He likes to see everyone in the room and to be able to see the presentation without looking back and forth at each slide. Mike has set up his laptop, a notepad, and a printout of a presentation. A flip chart is positioned at each side of the projection screen. As Mike checks the quality of the projection, he comments, "This is a really nice system." Hamish smiles.

Hamish decides it is time to proceed. "While we wait for Hugh to return, I would like to reemphasize how important I believe this intervention is to our company. That's why I invited you all here today—the whole senior management team. I believe full attendance is critical if we are to go forward as a coherent group."

Hamish looks at the empty chair. As he speaks, he notices a mark on the conference table and rubs it with his finger as he speaks. "I wanted you all to meet Mike and Richard as soon as possible. We'll all be spending a lot of time working with them—and each other—over the next several months."

He dips the corner of his napkin into his glass of water and rubs the spot on the table again. "For practical reasons, I decided that it's best to get us all together in one group. Apart from trying to save the company, we need to change. It is crucial that we set a long-term goal to encourage a culture of improvement. I believe the culture shift clearly says that we intend to think long term and that selling the companies is a goal to be avoided."

Moving to a dry part of the napkin, he watches it soak up the water on the table. "We must involve everyone in the company in finding and solving our problems, to tap into their experience. Without group interaction, there will be fewer ideas, and we might tend to get a limited view of the situation. I also want all the divisions to be working to a standard plan. So you will all be trained in the same techniques as your employees."

He pauses again and smiles at the clean table top. Lifting his gaze, he scans around the table, looking at each person in turn. Slowing down the speed of his speech, he confirms his message. "I completely agree with the approach we plan to use," he continues. "With a representative from every division involved at the steering level, we can get immediate input for ideas, any problems we have now, and any concerns you might anticipate."

"Apparently it's common for one department in a company to cause problems for another and yet have no idea that they are doing it. Departments can operate in real isolation—like silos. I'm not sure how that will affect us at a divisional level, but we do have a common administration department, and that might create some issues. The corporate map is interesting. I never really considered the divisions as a linked system before. I also like how the 'different' issues you have mentioned so far may be only variations of the same problems."

"So, to finish, it's important that we see this as an opportunity to make changes that will benefit our organization into the future. It is not a stepping stone to a shutdown—not if I have anything to do with it. To do this, we need to know what our *opportunities* for improvement are. If I was to be a bit less politically correct, but more honest, I would simply say that we need to know what we have to fix or change if we are going to meet the board's targets and survive. We had better get started," Hamish says, looking at the clock on the wall and the empty chair. "We can't wait any longer for Hugh."

Again, Mike remains seated as he speaks to the group. "I would like you all to ask questions, make jokes and, above all, please be honest with your answers. I hope you will find our sessions to be fun or, at the very least, interesting. If you disagree with something I say, challenge me. It's important that you believe in the techniques we will be using." Mike looks at the different faces as he speaks and continues, "Not everyone will agree initially, but even the most difficult critics are usually won over in the end. These techniques have been around for years and have survived for one single reason: They work."

"If you have any questions regarding the meetings, feel free to ask Richard or myself." Richard nods. "We will also give you our contact details. I am not sure if you will find this reassuring or not, but any comments you make to us will be confidential. The entire project is about building an improvement culture, understanding and implementing new ways of thinking and of working. It is *never* about personalities or blame." The managers look at Hamish, who nods in agreement.

Hugh knocks on the door and enters. He apologizes for being delayed but makes no excuse. He wanders over to the refreshments table and pauses, deciding what to have. Then he slowly pours himself a coffee, adds milk and sugar, and leisurely stirs it before throwing the plastic spoon into the wastebasket. He then moves to the table and sits down.

Mike smiles at Hamish, "Everyone in this room will be tasked with promoting the new methodology. There will also be a range of new 'tools' we will use, but most of the success will depend on the work being carried out by the employees. To this end, as Hamish has said, we need to promote and support the desired culture at every opportunity."

All eyes turn to Mike. "We will be involving the employees to help find and fix the problems. Lean promotes a degree of empowerment that must be supported by everyone in this room if we want it to succeed. It will be the task of every one of us to identify training needs, help find the problems, discuss and allocate which problems to work on, and help the teams to analyze, evaluate, and implement the solutions. In fact, the teams will use many of the techniques that you will also use. Any questions so far?"

Still nothing.

"The Big Picture map is one of my favorite diagnostic tools. I like to use it because it gives us the chance to 'see' how your company works and where the key issues appear. Often, we can even see the source of problems."

"What do mean when you say 'see'?" asks Lucie.

Mike replies, "I guess it is like the difference between reading a description of a place and looking at a photograph. In the written version, we are free to imagine what the writer means, filling in any gaps as we think they would be—just not as they are. Plus, we are also inclined to accept anything the author says. In a photograph, however, we can see for ourselves and don't need to imagine anything."

"The completed map will be like a high-level flow diagram, with all the steps laid out in order. The main difference is that it follows the actual path, the flow of materials and information used to create your products. It starts and ends at the customer, who is the most important person in the organization."

"Since the map will be on a wall, you will actually be able to see everything: all the links between the steps, steps that depend on other actions, steps where options are selected, where materials are delivered, where any of the Lean wastes apply, any relevant data—like production rates, manning, and equipment performance levels. It will also show you what and where the issues are and even where they are created. Even better than that, because we color-code problems in red, they stand out clearly. Some say too clearly, as they are impossible to miss. I have a slide that will show you what the maps will look like. We will see it shortly. Does that help?" asks Mike.

Lucie nods, "I like the sound of that."

Mike continues, "What we plan to do is straightforward:"

1. We need to find out where we are now, and that will set the baseline for our improvements.
2. Then we define where we want to be—or need to be. In our case, that is where the board of directors has told us we must be.
3. The difference—the gap—will be filled with the things we need to fix to achieve the goal.

"All we need to do then is prioritize the issues, select the folks to work on the problems, teach them any new skills they will need, and help them to reach successful resolutions of the problems. And please understand this: Setting a financial target is *not* the way anyone should approach improvement. We should be tackling problems that benefit the company, working at a controlled rate, within the resources the company can provide, and the timescale should be forever. Strange as that sounds, it is true."

"We don't avoid the financial benefits, though; we should always know what each problem costs us. It helps us to decide the order in which we implement the solutions. What we are planning to do will be much more difficult due to the deadlines facing us. What we plan to do is called *continuous improvement* for a reason. It is *not* a quick hit, a one-time set of projects."

Mike presses on the mouse and the first slide appears. It is a PowerPoint slide of a simple Big Picture map. He looks at Lucie and says, "Even the simple diagram of a map looks a bit complicated, but the way we put the map together and add the data will become clearer as we proceed. There is a nice, easy process to follow."

Mike moves to the flip chart behind him and starts to draw a skeleton of the map. As he draws it, he mentions some of the key issues.

- The first step is to create the map.
- We do not consider any problems until the map is complete. We do this because it is easy to get sidetracked and lose the flow of the teamwork.

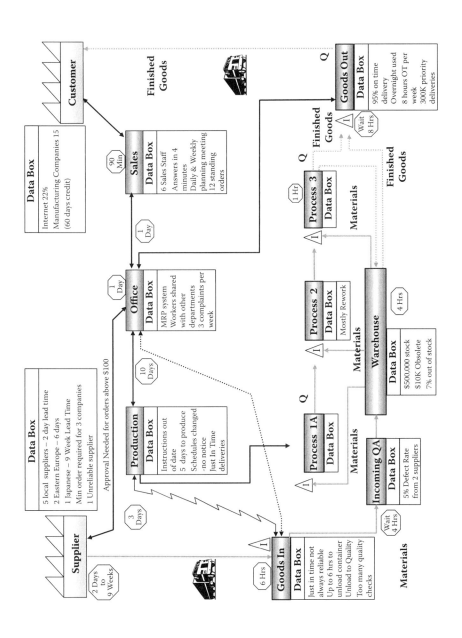

- We can use a "parking lot"—a flip chart—to record any points made, just in case we forget. But no discussion is the goal. You can talk for a minute or so, but end it as quickly as possible.
- The map is organized to show all the functional departments in the company—not the rooms or areas in which they work.
- It also includes the customers and the suppliers.
- They are represented as one "factory" symbol for customers and one for suppliers. The details are listed in a Data Box.
- The map shows the communication lines.
- The map shows who talks to whom, how they communicate, and how often.
- Any issues that are mentioned are recorded in the parking lot.
- The map shows the processes.
- These are not detailed process maps. They are simple representations, often shown as only one box per process or, if the process is complex and the team feels it needs more detail, it can be represented as the main components that make up the line.
- The symbols, arrows for example, can show how the products are made, whether materials are pushed (fed to the work in fixed quantities) or pulled (fed as the amount needed to do the job). The type of arrow can also represent the type of data used—paper or electronic, for example. There are also symbols for quality checks and stores.
- The map shows where the quality is checked.
- The map shows where stock is held.
- The map shows key operational data, which are listed in Data Boxes.
- The map shows the main problems.

"We build the maps in the following order:"

1. Material flow
2. Information and communications flow
3. Production statistics and data
4. Lead times for each stage
5. Inventory storage, stocking points, and quantities held
6. Quality and inspection points
7. Scrap and rework loops

"I plan to talk in terms of manufacturing, but the mapping method applies equally to office tasks. The suppliers would be listed in the same place where the tools needed to do the job come into play; the processes would be the completion of any documents or files; quality would look for data errors; shipping would report results back to customers and clients; and so on. The admin row would carry out the same tasks as a manufacturing company: sales, liaison with clients, controlling throughput, checking quality standards, and designing processes. In a manufacturing process, we start by following the flow of materials used to make the products. The goods come from the supplier, and we track how and where the goods arrive at the company. So we work from left to right, at the bottom third of the page."

"When complete, we follow the path of the information, communications, and paperwork, which defines the administration and technical offices. This starts at the customer and flows from right to left at the top third of the page. When the offices are defined, we add the communication between all offices, customers, suppliers, and production areas."

While drawing the map, as Mike talks of the customers, he draws a simple "factory" with a jagged roof in the top right-hand corner of the map. When he mentions the suppliers, he draws another factory, but this time at the top left-hand side. Unless the company has a security check-in booth or weighs truck loads, *Goods In* is the first place the materials are seen.

The row of boxes at the bottom of the map represents goods in the warehouse, the quality department, the process areas, and the shipping area. The arrow shows the direction of movement.

When he mentions the administration path, Mike draws the row of boxes between the two factories and a direction arrow going from right to left.

Next, he follows the information links. This time the arrows go in all directions and between all the boxes. "The customers deal with the admin folk and sales reps or agents. It is less common, but they might even talk directly to technical support or have a customer manager assigned. Sales talks to the design, production, and warehouse departments to confirm delivery dates. Purchasing also talks to production and sales to find out what needs to be ordered to make the goods. Purchasing then buys the goods from the supplier and agrees on a delivery date."

"The production folks schedule a date to make the goods based on the supplier's delivery details or stock availability in the warehouse. Goods are often quality tested before passing to manufacturing. When ready, the raw materials are delivered and fed to production along with the instructions on what to make. Quality confirms that the products are acceptable, and shipping sends them off to the customer. Admin bills the customer, and the sales folk keep in touch, ready to process the next order and the loop starts again."

Mike continues, "The mapping technique is a formal process and is based on facts. We don't ever discuss people. This avoids, or at least minimizes, the risk of anyone getting upset or defensive when we include an issue that is traced to their department. We also build the map in layers, with no problems being analyzed until the map layout has been completed."

"We will create a similar map for each of your companies in turn. It will surprise you when you see that the maps will all look very similar. What will surprise you even more is that many of the problems you see will also be similar. This is the point I wanted to make with the corporate map."

Mike walks over to the other flip chart. "This chart is to be used as a Parking Lot, where issues raised out of sequence can be recorded for future analysis. Points will be raised as we talk. We don't want to forget anything that might be important."

"The final stage of the map creation will be the identification of the issues. Because it is very important that the map is accurate, participants must feel free to list all issues that they know of or suspect—even if they feel it might make another department look bad. I will say again, departments often have no idea that some of the things they do are having a negative impact on others, especially when they think of the 'cause' as being an efficiency improvement."

"Let me give you a quick example. I did some work for a laboratory that sampled liquids. The booking department had the task of scanning in and labeling all the samples. Because they came from all over the country, the samples tended to arrive quite late in the morning, and the quantities varied throughout the rest of the day. This meant that the lab often did not receive some of the samples until really late the next day, which could result in the analysis running late."

"The manager did some productivity improvements—really nice work. He changed the layout of the booking-in stations, set up self-contained workstations with an input area and an output area, bought a new label printer, and allocated delivery teams to specific workstations. The improvement was a 30% increase in throughput. Every sample that arrived was now prepared and loaded onto trolleys and delivered to the lab before the day shift went home. The booking guys were proud of their achievement."

"The lab employees, however, were not so pleased. By 5 p.m., their labs were jammed full of trolleys; every space and walkway was obstructed.

Every bit of desktop was covered with crates full of samples. It was a disaster: No one could move, and night shifts had to search through the trolleys to find the samples that needed to be analyzed first."

"Another simple example was one where a production layout was arbitrarily changed to make room for extra materials. The change won them space but reduced the productivity of the area by almost 50%. It was interesting that productivity was not a consideration when the change was made. It was simply a reaction to a current issue."

"You will find it is quite common for folks to make isolated improvements that speed up or improve their own section, but often create problems for the folks downstream. There is a natural tendency for departments to work in silos. And yet, with a bit of teamwork and proper process mapping, these problems can be avoided. Just as equipment can create bottlenecks, so can departments, when viewed as part of a complete linear process."

Elizabeth Golden looks at her notes and then at Mike. "Mike, I have a question." All eyes in the room are now looking at her. "Why have we never done this type of exercise before? I mean, if it works that well, why is it not used all the time?"

Mike looks at his notepad. He had a sketch of the table layout and who was sitting where. "Elizabeth, isn't it?" She nods. "That is a really good question." Mike looks down and to the left as he thinks of an answer. "There are several reasons, the main one being that not everyone knows the technique exists, even though it has been around for more than half a century. Plus, many folks feel that formal techniques only happen in training courses like this and are not used in real life where *we don't have time for them*.… After all, 'We all have *real* work to do.' So, many companies seem to spend as little time as possible in formal planning sessions. Some companies make a plan just because *the book* tells them to and then never refer to it again."

"Sitting around this table, we have the top management of four divisions, but this is not enough knowledge to fix all the issues. Contrary to popular belief, it is not so common for all managers to work together or *with* their employees, mostly because they are always too busy working on their own issues. I have also found that a lot of managers feel that *they* are paid to fix the problems—that they must be seen to be the expert that provides the solution and so do not involve anyone else. Personally, I disagree. I think the manager's job is to find the *best* people to work on the problem, give them the tools and support they need, and decide on the best solution.

She can only do that if she explores the options, gets a range of inputs, and then decides."

"But surely that takes a lot longer?" asks Elizabeth.

"It can," Mike replies, "but how many times have you seen the same problems coming back again and again? A problem is not resolved until it no longer returns and actions have been taken to ensure this. Which one is faster: planning a journey in advance or just heading off and following road signs? The extra planning time is more than recovered by knowing where you are going."

Lucie comments, "I agree, I have a problem with a filler unit in a process. Once the bottle is filled, a second machine screws a cap on the bottles. Those screw caps drive me mad because they never fit. It's just as well we've got Bob North to set the machine up—or it would never be running."

Mike glances at his map again. "Lucie…" Mike's eyebrows rise as he waits for confirmation that this is the right name. When Lucie nods, Mike continues, "That is a really good example. I suspect that you could be fixing a symptom and not a root cause. A root cause solution would mean the fault would be gone forever. As I have said, the fix does not end with the machine running again. Action has to be taken to prevent the fault from coming back: a maintenance step or an inspection by quality control being introduced, for example."

Lucie responds, "No, the problems are always different. Sometimes we need to adjust the speed of the feed, or the synchronizing pulse needs to come sooner or later … sometimes, nothing works and we need to send the caps back to the supplier."

"Exactly my point," Mike grins. "But what if the problem is due to variation in the quality of the caps and all the adjustments were needed to compensate? I once knew of a company that had two different cap suppliers: One supplier had a permanent engineer on site to fix any issues; the other only had an occasional issue to address because their caps were simply made more accurately."

"I never thought about it that way," says Lucie. "So how do we know if.…" She pauses, not sure how to end the question.

Mike takes the lead. "What we need to do is analyze the situation in detail. We need to find out how much time is lost in total. That means counting how often the fault occurs and for how long each time. Then we need to look at what the 'symptoms' were, what was done, and when the fault returned. It also helps to know how much the issue costs in lost production. Now that you have highlighted it as an issue, we will find out if the cause is the machine, the setup, the quality of the caps, an issue with the bottle size, or whatever."

Mike walks over to the Parking Lot and writes: "1. Cap-fitting issue."

"But we are getting ahead of ourselves. We are not ready to discuss specific issues. We need to identify all the problems we are experiencing first. This is the main benefit of the process. As I said before, we will apply this same process at every plant and find their problems in as much detail as we need."

Elizabeth looks as if she has another question. Mike invites her to ask. "So, how often do we need to do this?"

"That's another really good question Elizabeth. I would recommend that the output of the plan be turned into a series of monitored projects and the whole plan be reviewed annually, along with the company strategy."

Mike pauses again, "We all know that strategy is a living plan: a vision of where we want to be and what we need to do to get there. It has to adapt when the circumstances change. And, since we always need to improve the way we work, we will always need to know what our main problems are. And, more to the point, we need to know if we actually did fix what we needed to fix and whether we are still working on the correct projects. Does that make sense, Elizabeth?" asks Mike. Elizabeth nods again.

"But…" Elizabeth is still thinking, "if this is a strategy, should we not be thinking about what we want and not what we are doing now?"

Mike answers, "Elizabeth, you are on fire today. You are asking all the right questions! There are two parts to this analysis. The first map is known as the 'Current State' and a second is known as the 'Future State' map. Consider a visit to the supermarket: Do you just buy what you think you might need, or do you do a check—create a *current state* of what you have and then know what to buy?"

"We could just brainstorm for the issues and jump straight to the future state map, but we would not be any wiser about the processes we use now. We don't just want to change the bad stuff but also to find out what we do that is good and see if we can do the same anywhere else. In addition, there will be problems we have not discovered yet—problems that you do not yet see. And, we would not have a baseline for our improvements."

"I know it sounds a bit unlikely, but Lean has identified eight fundamental wastes, symptoms of problems that all companies suffer from—a lot. In the current state map, we work at a high level and look for big issues, but it is probably more valuable when we focus and look at process steps in detail. The Lean wastes are: Transportation, Inventory, Movement,

Waiting, Overprocessing, Overproduction, Defects, and Unused Human Potential. I will introduce you to the principles of Lean and the eight wastes at the analysis part of the map, and you will get a chance to use them. However, if you don't mind, I would prefer to hold back on the explanation until we are ready. Is that OK?"

Elizabeth agrees and Mike continues, "Are you happy with the logic for starting with the current state map?"

Again, Elizabeth agrees.

Mike clicks the mouse and the next slide appears. This time it is a photo of what looks like hundreds of sticky notes on a wall. "This is what our map will look like. It will not be a pretty, computer-designed presentation, but a functional map that is easy to make, easy to change, and will involve everyone in the room to create it. Let's begin."

Mike moves to the wall, which has been "tiled" in flip-chart sheets. The plan is just to have a go at applying what the group has learned. There will not be enough detail, but this will give them a chance to see how the process works. A small table has a stock of sticky notes, pens, and other stationery. "I had to convince Hamish that these sticky note flip charts would not damage the walls before he would agree to me using them." Mike tugs gently at the stuck corner of one of the sheets, as if to remove it, and hurriedly sticks it back on the wall. He grins at Hamish and says, "Did I say that this map should never be taken off the wall?"

They start to assemble a map based on Chuck's company, Next Automotive, and assemble it as described. The Parking Lot begins to fill up as issues are raised at different points during the exercise. Mike and Richard keep the team focused by allowing a tiny bit of discussion before parking the issues.

The team lays out the sequence of the departments, sometimes shuffling them around as they remember a function they had forgotten, which is one of the main reasons for using sticky notes.

Mike mentions the *Gemba*, the Japanese term for the place where the work is done. It is always beneficial to visit the production lines (and the offices) to chat with the employees about any issues they are having. It is a great way to improve the working relationships and generate a feeling of real involvement. It also gives the manager the opportunity to get a feel for the physical distance between the process workstations, any day-to-day delays, equipment performance, or any issues that affect stores, goods in, and shipping.

The technical data is almost a summary of all the plants. "Data boxes" are added—or, to be more accurate, more sticky notes or even sheets of paper, each stuck next to the department or process step they refer to. Since the group is only drawing a generic map, accurate quantities are not required (they would be different for every company), but the measures or KPIs (key performance indicators) would likely be common:

- Order frequencies are next to the customers and the suppliers.
- Customer-complaint data and supplier quality/reliability information are next to sales.
- Deliveries and load/unload times are next to "goods in."
- The production data is a bit more complex. It needs to state how much time was available to produce, general efficiencies, changeover times, reliability data on equipment, overall equipment efficiency (OEE) where known, defect and rework rates, accident data, quality check data, numbers of machines and operators, number of shifts, etc.
- Shipping data: frequencies and transport modes, including late or incorrect delivery data.

In short: as much information as needed should be added. The good bit is, the team can ask for any data they need and find out how easy—or hard—it is to find. If data was missed, it can be added later.

Once the map is complete, the team can add any issues they know about—on red notes, so they stand out. Then the team quantifies their cost to the company over a year (on a spreadsheet) to standardize their impact. The time lost can be converted to man-hours; reduced overtime costs can be included, as can saved facilities costs, material costs, and, if the goods can be sold, they could even consider lost production.

The meeting winds up after a question-and-answer session.

8

Hugh Greenlees

The meeting has just ended. My team has just approved my new ideas. I smile at the folks around the table and say, "I will mail you all a copy of the action plan as we discussed." As I stood up I had another thought and added, "It is probably best you all keep quiet about the information I gave you about our new bosses coming." They nodded in agreement.

I walked back to my office, chatting with a group of the guys. On arrival I looked over my notes from the meeting. It's unusual for me to have more than one purpose for a meeting. Normally I just want the team to approve my ideas. But this time, I wanted to leak the details about the consultants coming and let the guys know my fears. I read over my notes twice, just to make sure there was nothing on paper about the consultants and to add any points about my ideas that I might have forgotten to note.

I find having team approval for an idea gives it more credibility at board meetings and shares any blame if something should go wrong. I called my friends, John and Brian, to thank them for their support. I find their help makes suggestions for changes less likely. So my ideas generally get approved as I want them. I suspect the team might have an idea that I don't want changes but they still offer a few on occasions.

I was planning to ask John and Brian for coffee but we had coffee and cookies at the meeting. I like to keep my guys happy—and free sweets never go wrong.

I am happy about the discussion around the consultants. I thought it was best to make it an informal "leak" providing some inside information. A gentle warning about the incoming management agents, who "are probably looking for staff cuts" to boost profits never goes wrong. I scanned my notes again just to be sure there was nothing about their coming. I like to keep a tight grip on what information is documented for public access.

It is still early, so I make my way to the break room, just to check if there is anyone I should be warning of the visit. Looking through the window I see that there is no one, so I return to my office.

It's 3:00 p.m. on a dull Friday afternoon and I am becoming impatient. I don't feel like coffee, but want to have a private chat with my buddy, Ken Hughes. Ken is the VP of sales, an old mate: we've worked together for years. I employed Ken within a few months of starting with Ronson. I like to have my friends working with me. Picking up my mobile, I poke a photo of a partially bald man, with a bushy brown beard. I stand and move to my awards wall, as the phone dials the number. The wall contains every certificate and training course I have ever attended—all framed.

The phone rings and is immediately answered. "Hello, Ken Hughes…"

"You still here at 3:00 p.m. on a Friday, Hughes?" I ask with a half laugh and half growl. "Get your coat on," I command, "we're going for a beer and a chat."

Ken makes no resistance and jokes, "You must be calling from your car! I didn't know you worked Friday afternoons! Where do you have in mind?"

Ten minutes later we pull in to the parking lot of the local pub. It's real close to the steel warehouse and some of the off-shift guys are there already. Some nod and some say hello. I order a drink for Ken and me and buy a round for the guys who said "Hi." I look around for a secluded table at the rear of the bar.

"What have you got on for the weekend?" Ken asks.

"Pretty much the usual, dinner tonight around 6:30 p.m. and then watch a bit of TV with Betty. It's hockey practice with my two sons tomorrow morning, and the rest of the day it's you and me: a beer or two at lunch and then on to the city to see the hockey final in the evening."

"It's great to get these free tickets from the suppliers isn't it?" We chuckle: we just love our perks.

After a few minutes of silence and the first beer, I make sure no one is near enough to overhear. When confirmed, I finally open up to Ken. "I don't like the fact that McIntyre and those two consultants are snooping around. They think they can just walk into our business as if they own the place!"

"Technically they do," says Ken with a slight laugh.

His humor is short lived. "Ken, I don't want you to tell them any more than you have to and I don't want anyone else to either."

"OK buddy," says Ken. "I'll have a short, informal word with the boys."

"It's an outrage," I growl. "These guys come into our business and think it's OK to tell US how to run it. These consultants will just look around and tell us what's wrong. We already know what's wrong and we are fixing everything we can! If it has not been fixed, it's because there is no fix. Consultants are just a bunch of overpaid know nothing, do nothings!"

"Yes, they are that, Hugh, you're completely right!"

"McIntyre is just as bad. He's been here for a year now and what's he done for us? I'll tell you: he's done… nothing, not one single improvement or bit of support for us. I think he's scared of me!"

"He is that, Hugh!"

"I don't know what the other three division presidents are going to do about this situation, but I know what I'm going to do. I plan to batten down the hatches and keep out of their way—with minimum contact—until it blows over. Yeah, that's what we'll do, these things always blow over."

"All right Hugh, you know me and the boys are with you."

It's 6:30 p.m., time to call my wife and tell her I will be working a bit later and ask if it is OK if I pop into the bar on my way home to give Ken his ticket for tomorrow's game. I notice the second shift start coming into the bar. After a few beers Ken and I finish and head for home, our plan of resistance set in motion.

9

The Confrontation: Ronson & Ronson Metals Distribution

Richard is not looking forward to visiting Ronson & Ronson. Hugh Greenlees's behavior triggered all of his internal alarms at the mapping training session. Consultants know there is often going to be someone like Hugh, but just for once he wished to avoid the usual hassle. There is an element in most people that wants to avoid conflict and unpleasantness. It seems to manifest itself in a kind of apprehension, whether liked or not.

Hamish McIntyre is also very aware of Hugh's behavior and attitude. Indeed, Richard's observation of Hamish during the first meeting with the division heads suggested that he was in no hurry to take Hugh on. Richard was surprised at this: Hamish is perfectly capable of taking command when he wants. Richard assumes Hamish must have his own reasons. This is a meeting Richard would normally attend on his own or with Mike, but this time Hamish specifically asked to come along.

Richard and Hamish arrive at 8 a.m. and are shown into a long Ronson boardroom. It is full to capacity—standing room only. The general hum of conversation in the room completely disappears at their entrance, although the occasional person mutters a subdued "Hello" to Hamish. All the seats are taken except for three: one at the head of the table and two, together, halfway down one side. There are people lined up all the way along the length of both walls. It's obvious that the two empty seats are for Richard and Hamish. The one at the head of the table is no doubt reserved for the man in charge: Hugh.

They sit down and wait. It is unclear whether they can expect a hostile audience, but they are not too sociable at the moment. The meeting was planned for only three people: Hamish, Richard, and Hugh, but Hugh appears to have invited most of the factory. The silence in the room is deafening. It seems that if any message has been sent out through the grapevine or even formally, it must have had negative overtones. Richard suspects that any written messages would be worded so as to be ambiguous and would not be seen as deliberately provocative.

Richard notices the refreshment table and says loudly, "Hamish, do you fancy a coffee?" Richard stands and makes his way through the crowd to the table, pours two coffees, grabs some milk, sugar, and cookies, and makes his way back to his seat.

Before sitting down, he gestures at the refreshment table and says, "If any of you guys would like something to drink, please help yourselves. Hugh will be along in a few minutes, so you should be quick, as we will start the meeting promptly." His offer works, and he is pleased to see several of the group accept it. Every positive action helps!

Hugh finally arrives through a door at the opposite end of the table to his reserved seat. He's a bull of a man, overweight, bulky; he gives the impression of strength and power. As he walks the length of the room to his seat, he touches the shoulder of the occasional person, smiles wryly, and says "good morning" to selected folk. He is rewarded with a steady recognition from the faithful. Taking his seat at the head of the table, he nods and waves to the others in the room. Richard and Hamish feel as if they are supposed to be in the presence of a feudal baron.

When Richard and Hamish entered, the room had gone silent, but when Hugh entered, there was a buzz of anticipation that lasted for a few moments. The chatter dies away quickly when Hugh takes his seat. It feels as if the air has been sucked from the room—the silence seems drawn out, exaggerated, and filled with tension. Hamish and Richard give Hugh his place and say nothing.

Finally Hugh speaks up. "You all know Mr. McIntyre, our COO. He has brought the consultant I told you about. He thinks he can help us with our performance and fix all the stuff we have failed to do."

Richard realizes that Hugh hasn't recognized him by name. By taking this attitude, his behavior is a bit demeaning and might lead his employees in a negative direction. And yet, he's smiling; perhaps he has simply forgotten Richard's name. The business is underperforming; he's sitting at the table with his boss; and he is smiling—not in a friendly way, but smugly! Richard can feel himself beginning to get angry, so he takes a sip of coffee and bites into a chocolate chip cookie.

Hugh looks directly at Richard, almost challenging him. "I know he will want to talk to all of you, so that you can tell him how he can help us."

He emphasizes key words as he speaks; he wants to imply that Richard will do just what they tell him to do. "He will want you to tell him how to solve our problems. So, to save a bit of time and to make that easier for him, I've asked you all along today. Let's go around the room so that you can all introduce yourselves."

Richard takes another bite of his cookie and sips his coffee. One by one, folks say their name and their job: name, rank, and serial number. Those in attendance range from Ken, the vice president of sales, to the plant manager to the trucking supervisors to the shift supervisors. Richard thinks he heard someone say he was a scheduler. Hell, even the janitor might be here! Richard considers looking under the table to see if anyone had brought their dog. Nearly 40 people introduce themselves—a complete waste of 30 minutes from the perspective of Richard and Hamish. Hugh sees it as a win.

Richard is concerned by the number of people in the room, but he hopes to win some time to circle the wagons and state the real objectives. Opposition is not unusual, but it is very rare for someone to openly obstruct the wishes of the board of directors. The best way forward, as far as Richard can see, is to simply state what they need to do and why they need to do it. Explain the support they will need from the employees and then work on picking off any opposition using standard techniques: leading by example, reason, making meaningful positive improvements, and chipping away at any fears one piece at a time.

The silence still dominates the room as Hamish takes the lead. Richard had been expecting that role to fall to him. "Hi guys, first I want to thank you all for taking the time to be here this morning. I know how busy you are. We'll be as brief as possible, but please feel free to ask any questions at the end." Hugh leans back in his seat as Hamish talks to the room, treating them as a group of friends.

Hamish continues, "I want you all to know that both the board of directors and I appreciate the efforts that all of you have made to improve our overall performance. We have definitely seen some positive improvements." Hamish looks around the room and stops when he reaches Hugh. "However, circumstances have changed. As Hugh will have told you, we—you and I—have been told we need to improve our performance. You have successfully managed to take a bad situation, one that you never created, and take a company from a loss of 1% to a profit of 2%. What we have done this far has not been easy and, again, I thank you all for your efforts. But we can't rest on our laurels. We have been given a target and a deadline, and we must move forward."

"This is not something that I take lightly, and it's not something that is driven by a whim on my part. The truth is, like any other business, we have shareholders. They are the people who actually own this company—I don't. They are my bosses as well as yours. The shareholders are the ones who have invested the money that we use to run our business. We often don't think of it this way, but it's the shareholders' money that pays our wages, buys our inventory, pays our leases and our electricity, and keeps the business alive. They invest in us to make them a profit. The sad fact is that the investors could make as much money—and with less risk—if they put the cash they are spending on us into a savings account in the bank."

You could hear a pin drop in the room. Hugh is leaning forward, and he is not smiling.

Hamish explains, "Major world events, particularly in the stock market or the housing market, often seem to impact only the rich and somehow seem divorced from our lives. Sadly, this is definitely not the case. There is a trickle-down effect. You may have heard of the subprime mortgage crisis and loans collapse across the country. Well, this is also having an impact across the world and on our stock markets. It does impact our lives in lots of ways, but here's how it affects us right now."

"As you all know, our business is part of a conglomerate. It simply means we have four different companies in four distinctly different industries. In addition to what we do here, metals processing and distribution, we are in pharmaceuticals, call centers, and automotive parts manufacture." Everyone seems interested. For now, at least, Hugh is not in control of this meeting, and the length and content of Hamish's explanation is clearly causing him discomfort. Everyone in the room now knows why Hamish is the COO.

Hamish continues, looking around the room and making eye contact with each individual. "Our investors expect a certain return on the money they have invested in our company, and right now our performance is falling way below what they expect. So much so, that they have given us a new game plan with much higher goals. I want to emphasize that I do not see this as a threat, but as an opportunity. To this end, we have asked Michael and his partner Richard, here, to work with us to help us meet the required profitability levels." Hamish acknowledges Richard as he speaks.

"I want you to notice that I say *required* and not *desired* levels. We must achieve our goal. As they say in the movies, 'Failure is not an option.' Our task extends right across all four companies: It is not only you who are affected. And, we must start work on improving right now, before we hit any kind of crisis mode."

Hamish extends his arms as though to encompass everyone in the room. "We can't do this without your help. You are our experts. Richard and his team are here to work with us and help us identify what we need to fix, just as Hugh has said. But, they will teach us how to use some different diagnostic techniques. Your knowledge is absolutely essential. We simply cannot do this without each and every one of you."

"These new skills, by the way, will not only benefit our company, they will add to your current skills, making you even more valuable as employees. Richard and Mike will work with you all, helping you. You will be empowered to find and fix the issues. You will be the ones who achieve the targets. Any and all success will be down to all of you here and to your friends and colleagues who were unable to attend this meeting. I recognize that our success depends mostly on you, and you alone."

Hamish looks directly at Hugh and smiles, "Do you have anything you would like to add, Hugh?" The ball has very clearly been handed back to Hugh, and he knows it. Hamish has made it clear he expects visible support. Richard is wondering how Hugh will react.

"Well, it's hard for me to know how consultants can help us improve our business. As you have said, we are the experts, and we are running things as well as we can. We all know we have been pulling out all of the stops. But, to quote an old saying, 'the proof of the pudding is always in the eating,' so let these boys try to help. If there is a victory coming out of it, we lose nothing, and if there's no improvement, it shows we were already doing all that can be done. So, Richard, fire away!"

Hugh has finally acknowledged Richard's name, and they are already 45 minutes into the meeting! Richard is not happy, but he knows he has to get past it.

He smiles and waves at eveyone gathered around the table as he begins to speak. "Hello everyone. Hugh and Hamish are both right: You are the experts, and although we have some experience of the metals processing and distribution business, we can't possibly know what you do. But, we are definitely not here to tell you how to do your job. We have different skills to share with you that have been developed over the past 60 years, and their purpose is principally to help you find and apply new ways that will work better for you."

"The target set for us is not going to be easy to achieve. Indeed, we rarely go into a company with an expected improvement target. After all, we don't know how you work or what your issues are. But, what we do know is that you will be suffering from the same eight basic problems as every other company and, probably, a few specific ones."

"It is just possible that with your help and your know-how, combined with our experience in improving businesses overall, we can do something good together here. I guarantee you this, though; without your help we will fail. Hugh is absolutely right about that. I can only ask that you allow us the opportunity to help and work alongside you. And by 'us' I mean Jeff Lincoln, your company CEO, and Hamish, your COO and, of course, your company president, Hugh. They will help to remove roadblocks and make your improvement path smoother. We will be working across all four businesses, so we will not be on site all the time. You will be working in your own improvement teams, asking for help as required. We do not have a lot of time, nine months maybe. I know it sounds like a line, but we simply will not succeed without you."

Ken Hughes, the vice president of sales, speaks up. His demeanor is odd. It's kind of a combination of passive-aggressive, currying favor from his boss Hugh, and yet recognizing the seniority of the COO. "Well, I'm sure all of us really appreciate your offer of help. We fully understand the urgency to improve, but between us, I believe we are doing everything that can be done. I personally can't see how we can do anything different. We meet every week and discuss progress on plant improvements, our inventory situation, and our sales. And, trust me, when I say that we are hard on ourselves, even though we are supportive of each other." Ken has managed to show compliance with Hugh and yet still give the impression of being a team player. He is asking for help that he believes will not be of any benefit—a neutral comment overall.

While facing toward Richard, Ken's eyes glance at Hugh and then sweep back. "Our inventories are high, but that's no fault of ours. Our senior executives at corporate decided to close our plant in Lexington. Then, with no discussion, they shipped their entire product range through this location, almost doubling our expected throughput. This plant simply can't handle the load. So, naturally our inventory is bulging at the seams. We can't get the stuff out the door fast enough."

"Also, our customers are fed up with us. On-time delivery has dropped from 95% to less than 60%. Sometimes our customers don't get their orders for days, and some have started to go elsewhere for their steel, so our sales are down. What am I to do? What are any of us to do? Low throughput in shipping, poor throughput and utilization of the plant folks, lots of waiting time, late shipping, high inventory, poor customer satisfaction, decreasing sales! Now tell me, please, how you expect to fix that!" One wouldn't think a room could become even more silent, but it does.

Richard responds sensitively, "Ken, this is not the first time we have come across this type of problem. You are right. We don't know your situation—yet—or have any ideas of the opportunities to make improvements. You have been very unfortunate to be put into this situation. It is a pure and simple case of one group of people making a decision without enough (or any) consideration of the impact it will have on the folks that it affects. But, here's the thing: We are where we are."

"I can tell you this from experience: From listening to the points you have just listed, I know there are tools that we can bring to bear. You have identified several of the '8 Lean Wastes' I alluded to earlier—symptoms that we recognize and can help you resolve. It probably won't be easy, but only with your help will we be able to make definite improvements. I can only ask that you give us a chance."

"Here is a fact: If your total achievement has been limited to 3% improvement over the past couple of years, you will never be able to get an extra 10% in nine months. To quote Albert Einstein, 'Insanity is doing the same thing over and over again and expecting different results.' If you keep doing the same things, how can you reasonably expect anything to change?"

Richard now looks around the table, "Talk to us one on one. Tell us your problems. Let us take a look at things, and together we will develop some new ideas and formulate a plan that will take us where we need to go. The key word is *together*. We're committed—and I hate to say this again, but we need your help."

Hugh can't restrain himself any longer. Hamish's talk was very persuasive and avoided a bad situation. But Hugh needs to regain control, so he makes a last dramatic stand—a final curtain call. "Talk to you? Work with you? Give you a chance? Are you deaf? Didn't you hear anything our vice president of sales just said? We didn't create this situation! It was dropped on our heads from a great height. It was done to us, but don't you worry, we will work ourselves out of it! Don't call us, we'll call you!" And with that final comment, Hugh stands up and leaves.

Everyone else in the room is stock still and stunned. This has to be the quietest group of people that has ever attended a meeting. From being a potentially aggressive group of primed, angry employees at the start of the meeting, Hamish turned them around. The gunfight at the OK Corral was avoided. It was not even a duel between the main characters, as Richard and Hamish defused the situation. Now that it's all over, no one knows what to do. Should they just leave? The most senior person they have ever met in the company is still sitting at the table, and their boss has gone! So they wait.

Hamish breaks the silence, "Thanks very much guys. I really appreciate you taking the time to listen to us, and I look forward to us working together. We will be in touch soon." Having been given permission to leave, everyone begins to file out of the room.

Ken Hughes hangs around and makes idle conversation with Hamish, thanking him for coming along and for the offer of help. Ken's a real politician. Hamish and Richard head for the door and out into the parking lot.

"We can use our executive coaching techniques and one-to-one support, but Hugh will be very hard to talk around," Richard comments.

"Wait them out," says Hamish. "One more month of bad results and I will turn up the pressure on Greenlees. Don't you worry, he *will* ask for help."

"A month's wait will put us behind the eight ball," Richard says.

"Don't worry, Richard, you'll make the time up. Besides, there's plenty of other work for you to do in the meantime. A little pressure never hurt anyone." Hamish is actually smiling. This little incident doesn't seem to have fazed him at all. If anything, he seems to have found it quite exhilarating.

10

Next Automotive

With Ronson on the back burner, Richard moves on to Next Automotive. Today is day one.

He arrives at the reception area and is met by the plant manager, Ralph Fines. He seems like a nice guy, perfectly pleasant. Richard likes the fact that he is dressed for work—a blue foreman's coat, no shirt and tie here.

"The boss is running a little late; he often gets caught in traffic on the freeway. He asked me to apologize for him and to ensure that you're comfortable in the meantime. Chuck will be here in about 20 minutes, if that is OK?" asks Ralph.

Richard looks around the small meeting room. Minimalist would be an overstatement. There are four upholstered metal chairs surrounding a Formica-covered metal table. That's pretty much it. The only decoration is a set of light gray squares on the darker gray wall. Tiny pinholes at the top center of each square suggest that pictures used to hang there.

After a brief look out the window at an equally Spartan but well-laid-out yard, Richard wanders out the door and looks around. He sees the sign "Safety Glasses Must Be Worn Beyond This Point." Treating this as an invitation, Richard takes his glasses from his inside pocket, puts them on, and pushes the door open. Initially sticking his head in, he confirms that it is a production area. To get a better view, he steps inside.

The workshop contains the usual stuff: two lines of heavy presses, of which one line is running. There are also groupings of smaller presses around the factory floor. Richard sees some welding machines through gaps in the fireproof curtains. A paint line sits next to one of the heavy presses, with a couple of separate spray booths and a furnace at the far end. On the other side of the wall from the paint line there is a final assembly area. There are no floor markings for walkways or forklifts and no attempt at defining areas for materials, but the floor is clean apart from the occasional tire track, some of which come dangerously close to equipment. There are no obvious signs of bottlenecks, either.

There are a number of people about, some coming in for the start of their shift, Richard supposes, and some getting ready to go home. He likes the fact that they are finishing off what they are working on before leaving. The workers seem happy, no rush to get out, laughing and chatting. But the only real sound is the regular *whump* of the heavy press line, followed by a quieter tinkling as the products drop, one by one, into a box at the end of the conveyor.

Richard smells coffee and follows the scent, wandering into a small office. This is a working office, with lots of papers, files, books, and catalogs. Two desks are sitting back to back, like one large unit. A row of filing cabinets sits against the rear wall. Richard is impressed by the size of the new flat-screen monitors, and the quality looks pretty good, too. There is also a large-screen tube monitor. He recognizes the make as one he used for his digital photography—high-resolution and very accurate color reproduction. He couldn't bring himself to upgrade either.

Richard tracks the scent to the far corner of the room, next to a small metal sink. The drip coffee machine is feeding a glass carafe. He looks around for a mug but needs to settle for a Styrofoam cup. Ignoring the little packets of powdered creamer and sugar, he wanders back to where Ralph had left him. Lo and behold, Chuck Nothis is waiting.

"Good morning," welcomes Chuck, extending his hand. "I see you found Starbucks."

Richard shakes his hand, smiling, "Starbucks never tasted this good!"

"Sorry I was late. Let's go up to my office; it's a little less noisy and more conducive to conversation."

They climb up the creaky, narrow, old wooden staircase and arrive at a mezzanine above the factory. There is a window that runs along the right-hand wall, the full length of the floor. It overlooks the main production area. From here, you can see virtually everything. Along the opposite wall are a few offices, all with their doors wide open. They get a few nervous glances as they pass. At the end, there is another small office. The sign on the door, "Conference Room," is bigger than the office! Richard suspects it might be an old sign, as the room seems to have multiple purposes, including being a temporary storeroom.

They arrive in Chuck's office at the far corner; it's nice, kind of homey. Richard comments on a picture hanging on the wall. It's an old limited edition Lumbers print called "Shopping." Richard tells him that he has a copy of the same print—that he loves the ghostly image of the Old World shop with the modern mall in the background—but he gets no reaction. After a few niceties about the weather, Chuck asks, "How do we do this?"

"It's almost a formula," Richard says. "Although there is no one-size-fits-all solution, there are a few studies to do to help us find the main issues. Then, probing deeper for detail becomes a natural part of the process. Each type of study has its value, but it's the fact that they all come together in the end that's important. There are also some standard tools we use in addition to building a culture of improvement. The order in which the tools are applied will be such that we work on your biggest issues first."

Chuck looks interested, but he really doesn't know what's coming next. "We conduct interviews with your key people and ask them some basic questions. I imagine this is the basis for the abuse we get that all consultants do is ask what is wrong and then regurgitate what they have been told. Strangely enough, most of the company managers that consultants deal with could do the same—they just don't. Here are some of the questions:"

- Tell me about what you do.
- What do you like about your job?
- What makes your job difficult?
- What keeps you awake at night?
- What stops you from doing your job on a daily basis?
- How do you know if you're doing a good job?
- What's the difference between a good day and a bad day for you and then for the factory?
- If you could change one thing to make the factory more efficient, what would it be?
- Do you really feel that anything has to change around here?
- If I came back in one year and looked around the factory, what would be different?

"In fact, Chuck, these are pretty much the questions I will ask you. We want to get a feel for what prevents folks from doing their job. The objective is to find the niggling causes of everyday interruptions. In Lean, we call them wastes. But, even better than that, there are only eight basic Lean wastes. There are also some other 'losses' that are equipment related, like performance, capacity, speed issues, and availability that help us make improvements."

"Interesting," Chuck says, nodding his head in agreement.

Richard continues, "The interview studies have their benefits. They introduce us to the employees, and we can gather a lot of information quickly. The information we get is often very different from the perception of the management. The downside is that the information is subjective, not always accurate, and can be colored by the point of view of the person who is answering the questions."

Because Chuck is an engineer, Richard wants to stick with engineering tools initially. "Another form of study is more objective, it's an observation study where we actually watch what is going on. Have you ever used SMED—the single minute exchange of die? It is used to reduce production changeover times, setup times, and die changes."

Chuck thinks for a minute and answers, "I don't think so. We have done some time and motion studies, but mostly we have done the same changeovers for years. Are you saying we can we speed them up?"

"Yes, we can, but before discussing SMED, Chuck, you have just made a really good point. Time studies often try to reduce the time it takes to carry out specific tasks. Tasks are normally regarded as adding *value* to a process—like drilling a hole. Time study measures the time taken to drill the hole and then tries to drill it faster."

"Lean manufacturing comes at the problem from a different angle. It starts by finding and reducing the wasted time and resources between tasks. For example, consider the time spent looking for the drill, checking the size, sharpening it or checking for damage before using it, or picking up a new one from stores. All these components of the job are seen as *non-value-adding*, as are scrap and reworks. Lean would try and ensure that the right tool is ready to be used at the right machine, when it is needed, so the skilled engineer does what he is skilled at and the laborer does the unskilled, possibly time-wasting tasks—until we eliminate them completely, that is."

"Lean quantifies the savings where possible. So, unless there are seriously obvious, badly organized tasks, Lean removes wastes before concentrating on improving the time taken to drill the hole. The savings are normally bigger."

"I think I am going to like Lean," says Chuck. "I find I want to learn more already. What were you saying about SMED?"

"SMED is an in-depth analysis that maps everything being done from the end of the first production run to reliably running new product that is of 'sellable' quality. There is a reason for the start and stop points being defined that way. The basic function of SMED is to get more production time out of the machine. Making tasks shorter is a benefit, but not the only goal. We look for time-wasting steps like waiting for tools, parts, and materials. We look for jobs that can be prepared *before* the change starts. We can even use multiple employees for parts of the work, if the cost is justified in extra production capability. SMED is a well-established process that can reduce changeover times by 50% or more on a first-time analysis."

Chuck is really interested. "Does it take long to do?"

"No, we usually need a day for initial team training. Then, depending on complexity, it takes roughly a day to do a real changeover and the analysis, and a day to create a new written procedure. If we need to modify any parts, we need to design and make them before fitting, which naturally extends the time. But we estimate what the expected time saving will be. Normally, we work with a team of around six people—operators, technicians, and engineers—who all work together to make the improvements. SMED is one of my favorite tools."

"How do they do the analysis?" asks Chuck.

"The team does a real changeover as normal. This does not mean we have a machine sitting and waiting. It must be running product and make a scheduled stop, just as it would in production. It has to be a normal changeover as it is always done, with no improvements based on what we have learned. It helps if we have data on previous changeover times but, for some reason, that is often not a KPI (key performance indicator) that companies monitor. We have one team member time each step with a stopwatch, one or two to record the steps, one to record a video for later playback, and experienced people to do the changeover."

"The notes are recorded on sticky notes: one per step. We use them on special analysis sheets that split tasks into *internal* (those that need to be done while the machine is down) and *external* (the tasks that can be done off-line, while equipment is running). We also look for ways of simplifying steps and removing the old faithful Lean wastes. The 5S method is a big player. It is a technique for creating layout changes that make tools and parts more accessible."

"Won't this level of analysis make the employees nervous?" asks Chuck.

"Possibly. It creates the same issues as introducing any changes. SMED can worry folks that we are looking for job cuts, which is not the case—and we have to make that clear. No one will willingly work to take away their own job."

"We include the operators and engineers in everything we are doing. We explain the need for the improvements and, where possible, have them find the issues that need to be fixed. We also explain that the changes and successes are all theirs. Honesty and involvement are the best tools we have."

"Much of the acceptance will be down to you and your management team. If they buy in, promote the changes, actually practice what they preach, and reassure their people, a lot of the acceptance we need comes naturally. Your guys need to communicate the purpose: why we are here and why the eventual outcome will be good for everyone."

"I believe the best technique to find the key issues is the Big Picture map, the one we explained at the meeting in corporate. It takes a bit longer, but we get more information as the managers discuss the big issues. We don't stop at knowing what the issues are. We go one step further and estimate how much each issue costs us, standardized over a year. This is important, since lots of small issues can cost more than one or two big ones. When we have found the biggest offenders, we can evaluate how much they cost and how easy they will be to fix, prioritize them for solutions, and go for it."

"Each issue to be resolved might need to be mapped in detail to look for process issues. We cunningly call this 'process mapping.' There will also be issues everyone knows about but never bothered to fix. They have chosen to live with these issues—along with their associated and recurring financial loss."

"In either case, we need to fix root causes—not symptoms. We need to ensure that the problems don't return. This usually means that new procedures, training, or checks have to be put in place, like a maintenance procedure or a KPI to be monitored. We must avoid or anticipate any repeat failure."

"Remember, we need the folks to be willing to help us identify and implement the necessary changes. We also need them to follow any new standards or procedures. If the teams are uncomfortable during the analysis stage, we will have an uphill climb from the get-go. Management must be seen to be supporting the implementation at all times. There must also be two-way communications with Jeff and Hamish at corporate. We will need some support."

"For today, though, it's just you and I having a chat. And, maybe, if there is some time, we can take a walk through the workshop and chat with a few folks."

"The other types of studies tend to be data or information driven. We look at your reports, efficiencies, die-change times, maintenance and breakdown records, absenteeism, and labor relations. These types of studies are less obtrusive. We work with teams of people with the most relevant knowledge, who explain the points to us—highlighting any issues and answering any questions we might ask."

"Should we decide on a Big Picture map, it will be created by the senior management team and will be specific to Next Automotive. It has the added benefit that it gets all the managers onto the same page as they openly discuss the issues."

"Sounds like a lot of work," says Chuck.

"It is a lot of work. But consider it like preparing a metal surface before we can paint it. Get the groundwork right, and the rest is a cinch. The conclusions from the map will set us on the best path to improvement. Are you OK with the approach?" asks Richard.

"Mostly," Chuck says. "Let me tell you what I think."

He starts to talk freely, largely answering every question Richard would have asked, and the consultant takes notes. Sometimes he likes to stick to key words to remind himself of the flow of thoughts and ideas, but for more complex ideas, he takes proper notes. In a discussion, like one with a doctor, it has been reported that the patient only ever remembers 30% of the consultation.

Chuck expresses his main area of concern. "Our most obvious issue, what did you call it, our *burning platform*, is premium freight—the cost of special deliveries to our customers, whether by courier, special truck, or air freight."

"As you know the automotive industry works on the principle of just-in-time delivery. Perfect when it works, but very unforgiving when it doesn't. It reduces the cost of carrying inventory all the way down the supply chain to the original equipment manufacturer, where the vehicle is assembled. The assumption is that any supplier will be good enough to deliver the right product at the right quantity and quality on time, every time. Being able to do this is the price of entry to the game."

"In reality, there are many suppliers our size that haven't as yet reached the required level of sophistication. Many of the businesses, like ours, started as Ma and Pa shops with a tool-and-die maker being the founder and original owner. Some of the biggest parts suppliers in the world started that way, but we have all evolved at different speeds."

"We now have sales of $70 million and make 3% profit. We don't have much room for error, and yet we squander $300,000 per year on premium freight, of which not one single dollar is budgeted. It is all a straight loss to the bottom line."

"Basically, our product takes longer to make than we promise—or plan for. This doesn't happen simply because parts get lost in the warehouse. The cause or causes must permeate through the whole business: everything from sales to planning, through setup, quality, production, and shipping. I've involved all my guys, at various levels, working on this for the past 12 months and, although we made some headway, the run rates for the cost of premium freight is still the same!"

And there it is: the final realization. Chuck looks relieved. He's said it, and he's asked for help. Not to put too fine a point on it, Richard guesses that the plant is running out of control—a fairly common issue.

"You know, Chuck, everything happens in its time. I'm very glad that you have been so open. You are correct that the freight cost is only a symptom. Something stops the goods being ready to ship when promised. We need to find out what the cause or causes are."

"One measure I like is OTIF—On Time and In Full. It is a two-part measure that requires the entire order to be completed on the date promised. In another life, I used a measure, not sure where it came from, but basically, for every 1% of goods not delivered on time, it cost us 1% of sales. We used to stop at 5%, for some reason that I still don't know, but on a $70 million turnover, 5% amounts to $3.5 million. How much did you say you were wasting on premium freight?"

"You must be joking," exclaims Chuck, "but even a part of that would be a real bonus."

Richard explains, "The point about late deliveries is they are the sum of all the errors and wastes in your processes. By identifying and actively working on fixing the issues, we should be able to win back some of this amount. The biggest barrier we have is time."

"We need to select willing teams to work on improvements and yet ensure that we still meet delivery times. Fixing issues will create the time we need for more teams. It will not be easy. Meanwhile, I would ask you to draft a communication to the floor but don't send it out yet. Hamish and I would like to see it first. Emphasize that our objective is to find ways that we can improve and grow. Explain that, more than ever before, we need their help. Once we have what we believe to be the right content, each group's foreman and leader should communicate it verbally, all within the same time frame, to avoid surprises, rumors, or misunderstandings."

"There is one difficulty, though. Our meeting with Ronson was a bit of a problem. Hugh packed at least 40 people into the conference room for a meeting that was planned for only Hamish, Hugh, and myself. Now they all know that the corporation has given us a deadline. Secrecy is probably not an option any longer. Maybe that will work to our advantage, though. We truly have a burning platform for our employees to work to resolve."

"Anyway, we still have a lot to do. Could you please make a list of the folks you think I should talk to? An organization chart will also help; it lets me know who's who in the zoo. If you could set up a schedule allowing for 30 minutes each in the conference room, I will be able to speak to most of them in one day. I'll feed back to you everything I find out—but, if you don't mind, not who gives me the information. I would like to keep the trust of the guys."

"Right after that, Michael and I will begin the observations, the data analysis and, most likely, the construction of the map. We have to have this before we can identify any disconnects and start working on improvements."

11

Chuck Nothis

I was surprised to find I was inspired by the meeting with Richard and wanted to know more. I jumped into Google and searched for "Lean Mapping Books." In the top three was *Strategic Lean Mapping* by Steven Borris. Clicking on it, I was taken straight to Amazon. Within a couple of minutes the e-book was downloading onto my tablet. I read the first chapter before getting back to work.

My first action was to wander down to the production line and see what was going on. As soon as I entered the floor, Ralph was charging toward me. "Hello, Chuck, how are you today?"

We chatted a bit over a coffee in the office. I updated Ralph on some of the points discussed with Richard. I noticed that Ralph seemed worried that he might not be doing his job properly and that is why we are bringing in an outsider. "Ralph, do you mind me saying how pleased I am that you are my production manager? We would be nowhere near as successful without your driving things forward."

"Things could get worse before they get better," I say reassuringly. "We will need to set up teams to find and fix problems and yet still make our deadlines. I have been advised the first couple of fixes are the worst because we need to sacrifice man-hours but, as we win back time, it will become easier. I guess that is one of the main reasons we have never gone this route before. I want you to be involved in all the improvements, starting with the Big Picture mapping exercise to find our best opportunities."

I explain about the process and tell Ralph I will pass on the book when I have finished reading it. "The engineers will need a mentor, and I can't think of anyone who could do it better than you. Would you be OK with this?"

Ralph thinks a bit and accepts the offer, feeling much more secure.

We walk around the factory, almost in step with the *whump* of the presses. An operator is standing by, waiting at his machine, so I decide to stop and chat. I feel strangely nervous! "How are things today?"

The engineer, who has been working on the press, smiles back and replies "Great." Without any prompting, he adds, "I'm just waiting to find out what my next job will be."

"How is the machine performing?" I ask.

"Pretty good. I still have that leaking piston, but it is not causing any serious issues yet."

"If you can get a bit of time, would you mind updating Ralph on the problem? We might need to arrange to get it fixed soon."

The engineer nods and smiles. "Nice to chat with you; we should do this more often." I have to admit, it feels good; my first social, information-gathering chat. Richard called it a Gemba visit: talking to the folks on the line. I like it.

While chatting to the engineer, I was aware of the operator at the next machine hunting through his tool cupboard and box. He was looking for something. He even checked the tool cupboard at the next machine. I had just read about Lean wastes, and already I was spotting them—without even trying. Just think of the improvements we will see when everyone has been trained.

Ralph and I chat about current issues as we move our way through the plant, occasionally stopping to chat with a painter or a welder or an assembly technician—anyone we thought might be interesting. When we get back to the main entrance, I thank Ralph for taking the time to show me around. I tell him how much I enjoyed it and that I hope we can do this more often. Ralph agrees and makes his way back to his office.

I have a memo to write, one I would rather avoid.

***

Standing on the mezzanine, looking out of the upstairs observation window at the plant, I notice the shop floor is quiet. I wonder, "Why aren't the presses running?" Just a few minutes ago, I was sitting at my desk writing reports. That was when I became aware the familiar *whump whump* of the heavy presses had stopped.

I look back at the row of offices. There is no one there, either. Yet my watch says it's only three in the afternoon. I start to investigate and walk downstairs to the plant, but when I get to the bottom of the stairs, all the lights are out. It is pitch black—so dark that I can barely see my hand in front of my face.

I glance back upstairs, and the lights have gone out there, too. I feel my way forward, following the curve of the wall, scanning with my hands to find a light switch. I slip and fall into a body of water. There must be a leak that has killed the power! Before I know it, I am covered in water. It is over my head. But there is no sound. I can feel the cold of the water, yet at some level I know it's the swimming pool in my backyard. I am thrashing my arms around, trying to get my head above the surface. Is the cover on the pool? I'm drowning! I gasp and sit bolt upright.

I look around, trying to get my bearings. The room is still dark but familiar. A hand touches my shoulder. I turn and look in the direction of the hand and stare blankly at my wife. "Chuck, are you OK?" Jenny, my wife asks, switching on a light. Disoriented, I slowly come to my senses. "Yeah, I'm fine, just a bad dream." I had seen folks jumping up like that in the movies. It never occurred to me that it happened for real—to real people!

"You have had a couple of bad dreams recently, but this is your worst by far," Jenny says, not at all reassuringly. "Is there something troubling you?"

We chat about the state of the business.

On a normal night, I usually alternate between periods of sleep and lying awake, sometimes getting up to watch television—which is pretty awful at that time of the morning. My preference is Discovery or Science-type channels. Some of them help me to fall asleep on the sofa. The problem is that I tend to wake up tired every morning and I lack my usual drive. Because of these poor sleep cycles, I often drift off to sleep in the evening while watching television. The consequence is that, when I do go to bed, I am no longer tired—Catch-22.

My mind is constantly active, thinking about the issues of the day. My morning shower tends to wake me, but I am still a bit sluggish heading off to work, usually arriving late. No one complains, as I never go home early. I guess, if anything, I work way too many hours.

I have never quite gotten used to being the senior guy in the division, responsible for the whole company. Although I know a lot—well, pretty much everything—about the automotive business, I tend to carry my uncertainty around with me as to whether I deserve to be president.

I came up through the ranks, starting as an apprentice tool-and-die maker. Always ambitious, I applied for many different positions within the plant. All were for sake of gaining experience, but some sideways steps, even those with lower wages, boosted my prestige and enabled upward moves. I planned my career like a chess game—always thinking a few moves ahead. Eventually, I made it all the way up to the corner office, with the associated advantages and, unfortunately, the disadvantages.

There is a lot I don't know about management and leadership, and I'm always afraid that someone will find me out. Remarkably, self-analysis is the very quality that keeps me striving to improve, buying book after book to learn new skills. I am no longer the little kid at the back of the class in school who doesn't know what he's doing. My desk is at the front of the class, where the teacher sits.

***

CLARITY

Today, Hugh Greenlees has invited me to lunch at The Dog and Duck. I remember the comment Richard made about his meeting with Hamish and Hugh, but I still think it is best to attend lunch with Hugh—just to see what it's all about.

I arrive exactly at 12 noon. Somehow, I usually manage to be on time for lunch. Hugh is already there, sitting in a corner with a pint. "Hi Hugh, been here long?"

"No, just about half an hour. I didn't want to be late to see you," Hugh chuckles.

We settle in and both order the steak pie. "What will you have to drink?" asks Hugh.

"I'll just have a Diet Coke, thanks."

Hugh orders the drinks from the waitress, "A Diet Coke for my friend here and I'll have another pint of Heineken."

Straight to the point, Hugh asks, "So, Chuck, have these two consulting boys been into your plant yet?"

"Yes, they've been in a couple of times. They're busy little beavers, aren't they?"

"Be careful what you tell them," says Greenlees. "You don't know what they'll do with the information."

"What would make you say that, Hugh?"

"Well, they have to justify themselves to corporate—to find someone at fault. What makes you think that won't be you? You can't trust consultants; you can't trust anybody!"

I am shocked at Hugh's attitude. I don't know what to say.

"Don't tell me you've been going along with them," says Hugh, "answering all of their questions and showing them your dirty laundry. They'll string you up."

"If I don't work with them, there will be no end of trouble. I'll be seen as a blocker and be removed."

"Maybe, but why would you help them take your job away?"

"They have been fair with me so far, and a lot of what they have done has been really good. I considered what they were offering and decided I could use the help. I'm taking it … Sorry, Hugh." I get up to leave, having completely lost my appetite.

"Of course, of course, just trying to help you," says Hugh. He waves goodbye as I leave.

Driving back to the plant, I say, "Awkward!" and think, "Did I say that out loud?"

That was incredibly uncomfortable. If I was to be honest with myself, I have probably been sitting on the fence as to how I was dealing with this entire change initiative, but no more. This last little interaction has made me decide: I'm in!

As I drive back, I now see exactly what Richard and Mike mean when they talk about the need for a positive culture. Without one, failure is guaranteed. I wonder if Hugh's actions could drag the whole corporation down with him.

12

Independent Pharmaceuticals

Lucie Bell meets Michael and Richard in her office. It is a particularly nice, tastefully decorated space. At the risk of being sexist, it has a woman's touch: woven carpeting setting off a glass desk and conference table. She likes wall decorations; there is a picture of her family—Ma, Pa, and her brother and sisters, another one of her on a tall gray horse and, in pride of place, her framed PhD in science. Lucie is dressed in a white lab coat and flat shoes. She shakes Michael and Richard's hands and then leads them over to the round conference table. "I'm very glad you are here. I've been looking forward to this," she says, "and what a delight, I get both of you!" Michael and Richard return her smile; she genuinely seems glad to see them. A nice change from Ronson.

"I don't think my business is massively complicated. Oh sure, it has lots of high-tech equipment and rules and regulations, as you would expect when the product is popped into someone's mouth, but in truth the science is already established."

"We are a generic pharmaceutical company. We have all the same controls and responsibilities as the companies who develop new formulas and products, but we don't have the huge research departments. We make our money through supplying pharmacies with drugs that are no longer under patent protection. This means we are not dependent on research teams developing the new breakthrough drug that will cure cancer or Alzheimer's. Rather, we supply tried and proven drugs that help combat cholesterol, high blood pressure, gout, and so on."

"This means we will never be a multibillion dollar business, but we will be a profitable business, and the degree of profit will be dependent on our good reputation and efficiency. Our customers are mainly within our own state, but we have a great opportunity to expand nationwide. Our marketing is very professional, with good pricing, attractive packaging, and eye-catching displays for the sales teams because we also have a range of nonprescription products." Lucie thinks and then adds, "But we must ensure consistent high-quality product and reliable customer delivery times."

The two consultants nod their agreement, both of them liking how Lucie has put lots of thought into the next steps of developing her business. "So tell me, Lucie," says Michael, "what do you think are the most likely improvement opportunities facing your business today?"

"Well, its horrifyingly straightforward," says Lucie, "in principle, that is. It's in the expansion of our client base, but it seems to be blocked to us."

"I think we have a good working environment here. We benefit from cross-functional teamwork, and we meet every week for a business health check and planning session…" she pauses. "But it seems that the same old problems plague us for months and sometimes years. We have become expert in finding ways to work around them. We expect them, when what we really need to do is solve them."

Both Michael and Richard laugh. "I'm afraid that's not uncommon, Lucie, and yet recognizing this issue is the first step to improving—and a big step it is at that," says Michael. "A friend told me a story once about a house-proud old man whose favorite piece was the Persian rug that sat, pride of place, in front of the fireplace in his sitting room. A hot coal landed on it and burned a small hole; it drove him crazy! The carpet repair guy made constant dates to come and make the repair, but he always seemed to have a reason to miss the appointment. As time passed, the old man's anger and frustration lessened; he simply got used to the situation until finally the new look of the carpet became part of the furniture!"

Proud woman that Lucie is, she looks around her nice office as Michael recounts the story. "It's true," she says. "I wouldn't accept it in here, but it looks like I've been accepting it out there," and she waves at the door leading to the factory. "Do you think that all problems are solvable?"

"Probably," replies Mike, "given we have the skill and knowledge in the factory or we hire it in. We can even run targeted training courses. But we need to consider the cost of the fix to the cost of the problem. If it costs more to fix than we will ever get back, then we would need to decide what the other benefits are—to the employees' morale, for example. Does the issue drive them crazy? If it is a safety issue, then it must be reviewed in a different light. But most issues are tolerated because we don't know how much they are costing us. Sometimes we just don't realize it is a problem that *should* be solved, like having an idle machine waiting for materials or instructions or for a breakdown to be fixed."

Lucie considers Mike's answer. "We have one product we produce here that far outsells the volumes and profit possibilities of all the others. It's a lemon-flavored, powdered drink called Flu Gone, and we can sell everything we make, in this state alone! It's every bit as good as the best competitor's product and, because it's generic, our pricing is way better. We could potentially sell this product all over the country. The problem is that we can hardly make enough to meet current demands."

Lucie anticipates the "Why?" question. "It's the packaging equipment. It's always down for adjustment. We get leakers at the top end of the foil package where the machine rollers close the glued end after filling. It seems like this problem has been around longer than fire! It's not just the lost production time during the constant readjustments of the machine, although that's bad enough. We have to hold back lots of production for extra checks. We simply can't allow leaking packages getting to the pharmacies or the final end users. The leakers result in very high levels of scrapped product and rework time, with the associated increased labor costs—all of which finally translates into late shipments to our customers."

"Just as *we* would replace a supplier that was consistently unreliable, our customers, the pharmacies, sometimes will decide to do the same. As you can imagine, we have no monopoly on this product, so once a customer has been lost, they might never come back. I once estimated that these issues cost us at least $2 million per year. And there are probably a pile of hidden costs that we don't even see."

"Lucie, we believe we can help you get rid of this hole in your carpet and, maybe later, even consider a long-term maintenance strategy—like TPM (Total Productive Maintenance). This discussion has been remarkably helpful. Do you have any thoughts as to how you would like us to spend the rest of today in getting a really good overview of your business?" Richard waits for a reply.

"Yes," says Lucie, "I've given it some thought. I've asked our production director, Kevin, and our quality director, Rajiv, to join us here in my office. We can bring them up to speed and then have them take you both on a tour of the facility. I've already explained to both of them that I believe you can work with us and help us systematically resolve some of our biggest problems, and maybe even more importantly, help us achieve opportunities that we haven't even had time to pursue due to our constant firefighting."

Lucie walks to the phone and adds, "While you're spending time with these guys familiarizing yourself with the business, they will introduce you to the workforce: the operators, supervisors, and managers—in fact, to all the key players in the company. This should allow you to determine what you would like to delve into deeper. OK?"

Michael and Richard nod their agreement, and Lucie calls Kevin and Rajiv into the office. They seem like nice men, fresh in starched white lab coats, big smiles. It's contagious: Michael and Richard find themselves grinning from ear to ear as they all shake hands.

"We're glad you guys are here." says Rajiv. "We've heard brilliant things about you from Lucie. You can really help us!"

The consultants are both a bit overwhelmed by their expectations, and yet they feel good about it. They look at Lucie as if they are all newfound friends; she is beaming from ear to ear, too. "Pop in to see me when you finish the tour. We can discuss next steps," she says.

The tour is an eye opener; Rajiv and Kevin are very familiar with everyone they meet. The operators greet them as friends, and yet the respect they receive due to their positions is obvious. The whole experience feels balanced. Everyone is friendly to the consultants too; they welcome them. In the offices, they meet the staff and managers. The quality-control folks are busy in the labs and out on the floor, working with the operators and technicians, who go quietly and confidently about their business. At first glance, everything seems to be running just fine. There is no sign of the issues Lucie mentioned.

Gradually, some opportunities spring to light. In one lab there is a huge focus on measurement: The walls are covered in graphs and charts; they are everywhere. "What do you do with this data?" Michael asks.

"Nothing, really," says Rajiv. "But we need it for compliance. We track everything in case we ever have any problems with our products. So far we have had perfect performance."

At last, a lightbulb moment: "Have you ever focused on just a few key measures that represent the rest, and use those for directional guidance?" Michael asks.

"Not really," says Kevin. "What kind of things do you mean?"

"Data are like the leaves on a tree. There is so much of it we can hardly tell it apart. Sometimes we need to see through the leaves to see how the branches connect, to see how the various leaves are connected. Yet, just as the brown leaves tell you something is wrong, we need to know what that color change is telling us, and the sooner we spot the problem, the more damage we can prevent."

"What we need to do is find what the current problems are likely to be and then identify the key measures that will help us to both monitor *and* control the issue. These are known as Key Performance Indicators, KPIs."

"I'll start thinking about that," says Kevin. "In the case of the cold medicines, the main worry is about them being underweight. But the only way we weigh them is through the quality checks."

"Don't make it too complicated, Kevin," Richard suggests. "If we are doing all this work to avoid selling product that is underweight, think about what we can measure that will directly tell us the weight. If there is not an obvious online measure, then we can determine if we can we use the quality-control samples. Or, if that is not an option, is there something upstream in the process that is proportional to the weight, or do we need to introduce a cheap weighing system?"

They finally arrive in the main hall where the powder-filling equipment is located, and it's not running. Both Rajiv and Kevin look perplexed. "We started running a new batch this morning and it looked like today would be a good day, but we are down already!" says Rajiv.

"Don't worry," says the quality inspector. "We are just checking the fill weights on the packets from each sealing head; you know we have to do it every hour."

The consultants can see the operators making adjustments, and there are pallets of product with holdout tickets all around. "Why every hour?" Mike asks. "Does the variation in weight fluctuate that fast?"

"The machine seems to have a large variety in its fill weights pocket to pocket. We can't afford the possibility of underfill, so we must check and adjust—a lot!"

"Rajiv, Kevin, how would you feel if we taught your guys some basic SPC, Statistical Process Control, and problem-solving techniques, and then work with them to see if there is a solution? You know, just like the tree trunk and the leaves?"

"Definitely," says Rajiv. Kevin's head is nodding in enthusiastic agreement. "Can we do it sooner rather than later?"

Kevin chips in, "The operators will love that; they love to be a part of something."

Richard takes his phone out of his pocket and taps the Calendar icon. His week is full of appointments. He thinks for a moment. "Right, how about Sunday morning at 8 a.m.? If we do it in four-hour sessions every weekend and get half of the operators each session, it'll only take two formal training sessions per team and we will be off and running."

They all agree. Kevin and Rajiv are happy. Richard makes two entries in his calendar: one for Sunday and the other for tonight—create an SPC course. The rest of the tour is uneventful, but the consultants already believe that they can do a lot here. They stop at Lucie's office on the way out and update her.

"Good," she says. "I'll be at the Sunday sessions. We can determine what comes next at the close of day one on Sunday."

13

Lucie Bell

I am sitting in my garden with a chilled glass of white wine, updating my journal. I like to sit facing the sun. The seat position and the white parasol in the center of the table make the laptop screen easier to see. The other three chairs are stacked in a matching wooden cabinet at the far corner of the deck. Behind me sit two wooden sun loungers with soft padded cushions.

I am staring at a blank page with the day and date at the top, fingers poised, ready to type. Noticing the sun glinting on the glass, I take a sip of wine and begin to type. "I'm a happy girl—everyone knows that—chirpy, considerate. I'm even considered good at what I do. My life looks easy to the outside world. I've got it made." I take at look at the bottom of my garden, where the river flows past, meandering through the silver birch trees, then continue. "Well, I have to admit, my life has its good points—some very good, indeed."

I want to update my current work issues and pick up on a new paragraph. "I suppose I must enjoy solving problems. Every day brings something different. I must feed on the challenge of being a company president. To some, it might seem like an easy life, though, right?"

"Well, it can be. Millions of folks hate their jobs. We all have problems, whether we are a cleaner, an operator, an engineer, or a manager. Even a small company like mine has its bad days."

"We are doing pretty well as a company, but my boss has suddenly told me that we need to do better—much better. Yep, I have a boss, too, just like all other employees. Even he has a boss, the board. Even the board members have bosses, and the path loops all the way round to the customers, the fuel that keeps all businesses running. Without them, businesses would be nothing."

"I try and keep a balanced perspective. I have not been unhappy with the profit levels. I even want to improve them but, I guess, I am not as driven as I thought I was. The truth is my company has problems we have all taken for granted. There's no end of production line stoppages due to quality and equipment issues, and the workforce must be exhausted. They work six days a week as the norm, just so that we can keep up."

"But what about me, though? I am always nice and chirpy." I look at the empty chairs and sun loungers and know I could—probably—spend less time at the office. But I love my job and, besides, I chose this life.

"My time with my family is precious, but I do like a bit of 'me' time, too. I am lucky to be able to afford a nanny, and tonight, the kids are out with their dad."

"I guess I do need more help at work, and until now I have not been getting any. But again, to be fair, I don't ask for it either. I could easily have hired my own consultants, but I never thought about it. Hamish, the new COO, hardly ever visits. He must be reasonably happy with what we are doing or we would see him more often. But, I suppose he has even bigger problems than mine to deal with."

"My managers are doing their best, but their best isn't solving our problems. We must find out what we need to do to get better—to consider all our problems and our deficiencies. We need to take some of our own medicine."

"Occasionally the other three division presidents and I get together to talk about the state of our businesses, but quite frankly, that hasn't proven to be of any help either. Hugh, Chuck, and Elizabeth are in much the same boat as me, probably worse. Their businesses are all slightly broken—I say slightly because they all still manage to eke out small profits. Sadly, small is suddenly not enough!"

"How do they deal with it? It seems as if they are all waiting for something to happen that will do it for them: maybe a fairy godmother hovering in the shadows with her magic wand. There is little that is proactive going on. At the last meeting, the four of us sat, with coffee and doughnuts, and each took our turn to complain. We complain about everything: the CEO, the COO, the economy, the equipment, and our employees. Mind you, I am pretty happy with my employees on the whole. The meetings are not productive. Certainly not positive or supportive; to be honest, they pull a person down. There is a general macho attitude, even from Elizabeth over at the call center, but I think behind it all there is real fear, a real sense of desperation, and it's contagious."

"Maybe Richard and Mike are just what we need. Maybe they are our fairy godmothers." I laugh at the image that appeared in my mind. I check my watch. The kids will be home in about an hour. Clicking on the Save icon, I close the laptop lid, pick up my wineglass, and sink into a sun lounger, still admiring the view.

I reach over and pick up a poorly bound pile of papers from the small table between the two chairs and read the front page, *Les Miserables*. My interest in acting has never faded. The amateur dramatic society is the one weekly appointment I make sure I never miss. Opening at the bookmark, I find my lines and start to repeat them aloud.

Yep, life isn't all bad.

14

Phonethics: The Call Center

Richard was impressed by Elizabeth Golden the first time he saw her. She carried herself well and seemed to have an easy way about her. Today, Richard and Michael meet Elizabeth and her team in their conference room. It is spectacular. Immediately, their eyes are drawn to the outside wall: It has floor-to-ceiling windows overlooking the ocean. It's a breathtaking view. Richard is reminded of a similar view from a training room in Scotland.

This is a true equal opportunity company. Of the 12 people from Phonethics in the room, all but one is female: five senior delivery managers, three managers from training, one from quality, and another from IT. Then there is Bridgette, who leads workforce management. The project manager, Nigel, is the only male.

"I can't help but notice the call center seems to have a preponderance of females in the senior ranks," Richard comments.

Elizabeth laughs and explains. "It seems to be the norm in the call-center industry, and we have a policy to promote from within where possible. The team has all worked in operations. They, pretty much, all began here as agents on the phones, working their way up from team leaders to their current positions. Agnes, who runs our IT department, is the genius of the group. She keeps everything running from a telephony perspective. She joined us from Active Sources, who as I am sure you are aware, is a large insurance agency. Elsie, who manages training, and Nancy, who manages quality, are homegrown, as is Bridgette. Nigel started in IT and moved into project management six months ago."

The door bursts open and in flies Griselda, all of a hurry and aflutter. "Sorry I'm late everyone," she says, smiling. "We've been having the devil of a job trying to recruit another 50 agents to make up for the ones who left us." She sits down and looks intently around the table.

Elizabeth formally introduces Michael and Richard and then has everyone else introduce themselves. She launches into the current state of the business. "For the past three months we have not been making any money. It's horrifying. We are an outsourced call-center company; we answer calls on behalf of our clients. Currently we represent an automotive company, a telco, several banks, and two financial services companies. The calls we handle are mainly customer service in nature, with some 'level one' technical assistance."

"Generally speaking, we are paid by the call. Of late, our incoming call volumes have dropped off, which reduces our earnings. Call rates oscillate from very quiet to very busy, so we find that our average 'calls per agent' tends to have peaks and troughs. There's no consistency. It's all very random. When there are few calls, we find ourselves a bit overstaffed, which means we are spending more than needed on wages, and then we might get really busy an hour later and not have enough agents—but it does improve their utilization."

"Also, we frequently have a lot of angry customers calling into our centers." She looks directly at Richard and explains, "Richard, in case you are not aware, we have two call centers: the one here in Littletown and another in West Playing Field." She glances down at her notes and back to the table, "We also need to admit that our recent inefficiencies have been causing difficult relationships with our clients. They keep telling us they can get just as good a service offshore, for less money than they are paying us. They repeatedly want us to justify our rates." Elizabeth looks lost. "We really have to step up our performance from a quality perspective before the clients act on their threats. We all know that if they go, we lose the business."

The managers join in the conversation and contribute lots of interesting comments. They help to paint the overall picture, which is largely in agreement with Elizabeth's view. The situation is serious.

Richard looks at his notes:

- High attrition with lots of people leaving.
- Morale is low.
- Many of the callers are angry.
- The clients bully us.
- The average time it takes to handle a call is too high.
- We never seem to have enough people to do the job.
- The client insists on more staff.
- In general, call volumes have gone down.

The consultants thank the team for their frank and open, if not uplifting, performance update, and they join the team for a tour of the facility. Once again, Richard is drawn to the sea view. "It must be very relaxing to have such a nice view of the ocean."

"Yes, isn't it quite beautiful?" Griselda says as she leads Mike and Richard on the tour of the facility.

The call center is on three floors of a high-rise building. The workstations are on rows of long tables with no dividers between each one. The agents are generally busy taking calls. It is an unusual environment, with some agents standing as they answer, making grand gestures with their arms like an orchestra conductor. Occasionally there is a burst of applause when the sale of a supporting product or a service contract is made. Other agents just sit at their stations and chat, smiling as they talk to their clients and sourcing information from their monitors.

As Richard looks around, he notices there aren't many team leaders apparent. All the operators are working alone. It seems no one is receiving any support. On asking why, it is pointed out that the team leaders and managers have lots of admin work to do and tend to come out for emergencies only.

"The team leaders are very busy," Nancy, a senior delivery manager, explains. "They calibrate their agents' quality scores, work on sickness and absenteeism issues, payroll and, you know, all the usual things."

The training suite is vast and nicely laid out, with all the current audio-visual technologies. New recruits can spend weeks here before being let loose on clients. They need to be properly trained in all of their products and on how to use the PC systems and databases. The wall planner shows a very busy program.

After the tour, everyone goes back to the conference room, and Elizabeth asks Michael and Richard what they feel the next steps should be. "Well, we would like the use of a small office and access to the managers as required. Also, we will need to spend some time listening to calls alongside the agents."

Michael adds, "Can you provide any data on the incoming call volumes per client per half-hour period? Can we can do this for all open hours?"

Mike goes on to itemize the initial data needs:

- The average handle time
- The standard deviation
- The percentage of first-call resolutions
- The number of referrals

- The quality scores by team
- The attrition level by team
- Any information regarding current client sentiment
- KPIs (key performance indicators) or charts used to track performance

Checking his calendar to schedule the next visit, Mike asks, "Could you get all of this together for us by, say, Monday, and have it put into the office we will be using?" He gets affirmatives from Elizabeth, Bridgette, and Agnes.

Elizabeth shows them to the door. "Thank you for being here, guys. I'm afraid I'm running out of ideas!"

"It's our pleasure, Elizabeth, and we look forward to seeing you again on Monday."

15

Elizabeth Golden

"Where is that salad dressing?" I scan the refrigerator, even checking behind the piles of ready-made meals, but can't see any. Then I remember the bag next to the door. I lift it onto a table and sort through the cans of soup and vegetables. Yep, there it is. It's been another busy day, and the last thing on my mind is making a meal, so it is another chicken salad tonight.

I turn on the television and look for something funny. *Two and a Half Men*—perfect. My condo is not unlike Charlie's beach house, if you overlook the fact that I live in a high-rise. But it overlooks a marina and has a good-sized balcony where I can sit outside. I love the way the lights reflect off the water. Just as well, as it is usually dark outside when I get home from work.

This was once my idea of perfection. I bought it as the ideal condo for a single woman, or rather a divorced woman. I guess I just never expected to live here for so long after my divorce. I'm just 38 and have been divorced for eight years now. My marriage lasted for eight years. It takes a bit of settling into living on your own, but gradually it becomes the norm. At least my original decision not to have any kids has worked out for me, but I do find myself thinking about the possibility now before the batteries in my biological clock time out.

In the last year I found a new boyfriend, or rather he found me. This was my dream man: good-looking, smart, funny, well dressed, working—and married! It is true to say that I was taken with him from day one.

No, he never told me he was married for a few months. The problem with dream men is that they can also be nightmares! I could have avoided any feelings developing if I knew when I met him. I would never have dated a married man.

He waited a long time, as if waiting for me to fall in love, before he told me he was married, but unhappily so. He explained that he was waiting for the right moment to tell his wife he was leaving. It's been a year now, and guess what? The right moment has not come up.

My friends warned me of the risks, but I was in love and *knew* he would eventually make the leap. After all, statistically 50% of marriages fail. In fact, when I last checked the reports, 41% of first marriages fail; 60% of second marriages; and a whopping 73% of third marriages end in divorce. So, the odds are good. It is funny, though, that I never gamble or play the lottery—I only seem to gamble with life.

Since this is his second marriage, I have a better than fifty-fifty chance their marriage will fail—if he keeps his word. But rationality has no place in this situation. I still get annoyed—even jealous—at holidays when he chooses to spend time with his family. At least he tells me he would rather be with me, and sometimes I get a call.

I guess I also get annoyed when I have to settle for random visits, when he has "business trips" or "works late." I know that he lies to his wife routinely, at least a couple of times a week, and has done so for a year that I know of. I know how convincing he is: I have been in bed with him while he tells his wife he is having dinner with a boring client.

What if his mold is set? Why would he suddenly start telling the truth now? I guess all men lie.

I have been the boss at Phonethics for the past four years. Initially I liked it, but after the first two years, it started to drive me crazy. I know the industry really well, and I should—I've been in it all of my working life. It used to be simple in the old days. The client paid for a number of FTEs (full-time equivalents), or people to answer their calls. Now the situation has become much more complex; they pay for the number of calls handled, and the staffing levels are my problem. It has become an incredibly demanding industry, with intense competition from countries where labor is cheap. Sadly, corporate has not kept up with the level of change required—no investment and no room for change.

I tried to tell Jeff Lincoln, the CEO. I worry that we are on the approach run for the edge of a cliff, but he simply wouldn't listen. Then, when Hamish arrived, I gave him a full update of all the issues the industry is faced with, and he wouldn't listen either. It seems we will have to go over the edge before anyone listens!

The phone rings. It's the operations manager from the call center. "Hi Elizabeth, sorry to bother you, but the calls are coming in way above forecast—the volumes are through the roof. The clients' workforce management is onto us constantly about long waiting times for their customers."

"Ask people to stay back on overtime after their regular shift and call in the next shift early," I advise. "Also make sure your agents are taking calls and not tied up with after-call work or training, or for that matter anything else. Just make sure they are on the phones. Make sure both you and the supervisors are on the floor, making sure the agents are where they should be and doing what they are supposed to be doing… Anything else?"

"No, I'll get right on it. Thank you, Elizabeth."

This is how it's been of late, with knee-jerk reactions to every little thing, and the calls at home are constant—no end to them. It has become a 24-hour job in this industry, with no room for a personal life. Hell, even the mobile phone makes sure you can't get a break.

Recently, two consultants have arrived at my door—to help me. Help me? "Hello we're from the Internal Revenue Service and are here to help you.…" Sure you are!

The profits from the business are sinking to almost zero, and I'm going down with them. Where is the support or patience from corporate? Now, consultants have been hired to get to the bottom of it. I've told my senior management everything that's going amiss, but it seems like they need to hear it from consultants before they'll do anything. I'm close to the edge, pretty much done with this!

There's a nice analogy in a parable about a man who gets trapped in a flood. He is struggling to stay afloat and prays to God to help him. "Don't worry," says God. "I will save you."

The water carries him close to a tree. There is a man on a small raft, clinging to the tree. "Give me your hand," the man shouts.

"No, it's OK. God is going to save me."

The current sweeps him on. Then a boat comes by and offers to take him to safety. Again he refuses help. "No, it's OK. God is going to save me."

Next a helicopter flies overhead, and again he refuses their help.

The man drowns.

When he arrives in heaven, he meets God. "Why did you not save me?" he asks.

"I sent you a raft, a boat, and a helicopter.… I thought you had changed you mind."

The moral: Help comes in many forms.

The phone rings again. This time it's my boyfriend, Bill.

"Hi honey, I can't make it tonight. I can't get out of the house. We've just had a terrible fight and the kids are crying. I'm on lockdown."

I slam the phone down, and it immediately rings again. It's the operations manager at the call center!

16

The Project Plan

Hamish walks into the boardroom. He seems happy. Michael and Richard are already there. It's hard to imagine it has been less than three weeks since they started this project. Urgency sets its own timescales. Today they are going to work on the project plan and, as Hamish is the third musketeer, he has to be here.

"So what do you think of progress so far, Hamish?" asks Michael.

"I'm good," says Hamish, "but it is taking a long time to get moving! Three weeks and you still haven't started making any improvements."

"I understand your frustration," says Richard. "We are actually further forward than you might imagine. We have had several meetings at corporate, one training course, and we have visited all four companies to meet and greet and get a feel for the issues. It has been a fairly hectic timetable."

"All the steps we have taken so far were necessary. We had to assess the extent of the problems, understand the mandate from Jeff, and see where you stood on things. Also, we had to get the high-level view on each business from the division presidents: how they saw the issues. Later we will find out how others see them and see if there are any management disconnects."

"We need you to stay with us on this. It might even get a bit worse before it gets better. We can work out the overall timelines and deliverables now and, God willing, this will make you more comfortable with our progress."

Still not convinced, Hamish reluctantly nods his agreement, and they begin. Michael fixes a row of flip-chart pages onto a wall. The objective is to map out a rough plan.

Richard turns to Hamish. "Project management is just a tool like any other. And it's the right tool for us now. It will give us an initial overview of the entire project from start to end. Before we start, we need to consider a few essential elements:

- A project statement, which will ensure that we are in agreement with what we will have as an outcome of the project

- The expected timeline
- The project objectives as major tasks

"Later we will break these tasks down into their component parts, so that we can sequence them against the timeline and monitor their progress.

"When we have a first-pass plan, or as much of it as we can define at the moment, we can assign responsibility to each major chunk of work. It is very important that tasks be allocated to specific people and not to groups. So, only when we know the tasks, can we identify any resources we need to complete each element."

Richard visualizes the process in his mind and adds, "We can then do a *back pass* to ensure that our plan is valid. The breakdown of the work elements is designed to ensure the meeting of the individual objectives and, most importantly, that the achievement of these objectives when combined will meet the original, targeted outcome of the project."

"If we detect any issues, we can make changes or add steps that will support them. Overall, it is just a more complex variation of the Plan-Do-Check-Act process." Richard is watching Hamish's reactions as he speaks, knowing the COO is still sensitive to the presence of the consultants. "We need your help with this, Hamish. We can't do it without you. When complete, we will all be on the same page and can promote the project with a unified front."

Hamish knows that these are the early days, and he does feel more comfortable about his place in the process. He also realizes that his inputs are essential to the success of the plan. "OK, let's go," he says.

Michael facilitates the meeting and begins by drawing a triangle on the chart. "This is the project management triangle. I am certain you will have seen one before, but it helps me get my mind into gear." Michael always assumes that the opposite is true—that no one has seen it before and, further, that no one will want to admit it. He has found that this technique works well; besides, it is a nice refresher. So he continues, "The triangle has three sides, the length of each being dependent on the others."

At the top of the triangle he writes the word *outcome*; on the right-side apex he writes the word *timeline*; and on the last corner he writes the word *cost* (Figure 16.1).

"Based on what we know now, Hamish, the outcome is a run rate of $36 million earnings before interest and taxes." Michael writes *$36 million* on the triangle next to the word *outcome*.

"We also know that this objective must be achieved as the run rate for the fourth quarter of the coming 12-month period. So we have nine months

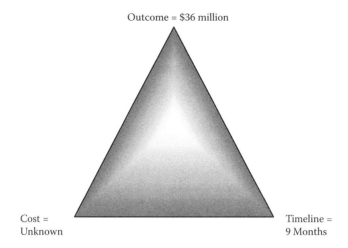

Outcome = $36 million

Cost =
Unknown

Timeline =
9 Months

FIGURE 16.1
The project management triangle.

to achieve a stable rate." Michael writes *nine months* on the triangle next to the word *timeline*.

"Because the three goals are interdependent and the first two sides are absolute, the only variable factor is the cost. It will determine if we achieve the outcome in a nine-month period."

"If we want to increase the outcome, for example, we might need more time and so need to increase the timeline and probably also the cost. If we wanted to reduce the timeline, we would need to increase the resources, which would increase the costs, and so on."

Michael gathers his thoughts. "At this point in time, we have no idea about the amount required to achieve an improvement of $27 million in profit. It will depend on what we find in the divisions when we analyze them. However, we realize that people solve problems—not money—so capital expenditure (Capex) will be a last resort. The biggest cost will be in people."

"As part of our diagnoses, we will estimate how much each problem is costing us and how much it will cost to fix. We should be targeting the gains through productivity improvements, which will include quality improvements, reduced reworks, improved uptimes for equipment, and reduced material wastes. If any major spending becomes apparent, we will assess the facts and take them together to Jeff and the board. The project statement will therefore read as follows:"

"We will achieve a run rate of $36 million in earnings before interest and taxes (EBIT). This is to be achieved in nine months' time and be maintained during the fourth quarter of this coming fiscal year. Any required major expenditures discovered during the business analysis will be presented to the CEO and the board for approval."

"My God," exclaims Hamish, "you're hanging me out to dry! How can we possibly go from $9 million in profit to $36 million in nine months? It's like taking a car from zero to ninety miles an hour in 20 seconds! It's impossible!"

"Not for an Aston Martin Vanquish," says Richard whimsically, and with the vague image of a dream in his eyes.

"You've triggered him now, Hamish. It's his favorite car. Now he is probably imagining he's James Bond—again!" jokes Michael.

"I'm not kidding around here," says Hamish. "How can we promise the impossible?" Hamish looks disturbed. "On top of that, even if it were possible, the board will think we are a bunch of donkeys for not achieving it in the past. … And, another thing: I don't like the promise that we have to maintain the performance over the fourth quarter: We have to maintain it forever! That's the problem with you consultants—no ownership. You want to appear with a flash, and then, after demonstrating your magic tricks, you disappear in the same dramatic flash as you arrived. What about me? What about my authority? Don't I have a say on what spending can be applied to this change process without running to the board?" Hamish goes on to explain his long-term concerns in some detail.

"Oops, Hamish, was it something we said?" Mike teases gently.

"Our reputations are on the line, too," interjects Richard. "The project statement is not a promise of performance improvement—not yet. It is simply an attempt to encapsulate the expectations of the project sponsor. The outcomes have been set for us already by Jeff and the board. We restate them as an achieved end to trigger our future endeavors during the project. We do this to ensure that we are taking the appropriate actions to hit their target."

Richard could see the tension in Hamish's jaws relaxing—a bit. He wanted more clarity. Even Mike doesn't like the appearance of a definite promise of success, but Richard is always very positive, perhaps too positive, sometimes. So Richard offers a compromise. "Perhaps we could amend the statement to include something like '…we will evaluate the improvement potential, and if found to be feasible, we will achieve a run rate of $36 million.…'"

Hamish agrees. Mike prefers this, too. It is, after all, a very big task.

Richard continues. "Regarding the potential requirement for spending, Hamish, an estimate will become apparent during the analysis, and it would be you who would approve it and decide whether or not to recommend it to the board. We will be working as team—the three of us, together."

"Michael and I will manage most of the overall project along with you. We will also work with your teams to ensure the results, but you are the true project leader, and *all* the credit will go to you and your team. This is exactly as it should be. You must be involved at every step and with any decisions about costs."

"Regarding your thoughts on maintaining the results forever as opposed to just over the final quarter, we completely agree. You are making a really profound point here. We are starting a process of continuous improvement, not a one-hit win. We won't just disappear in a puff of smoke, like Houdini, either," Richard says in reassurance. "We will ensure that the project is sustainable by working with your people to design and install management and production-level control processes to ensure that you and your team will continue to make the gains achieved by all of us … forever."

"It will require a serious commitment from your employees and you. It will require a culture change for many, if not all. It is exactly like losing weight; it takes a lifetime change in eating habits to keep the weight off. All these special grapefruit, banana, water, or high-protein diets will fail eventually. The only solution is real change. If, in the future, you decide to stop eating the right things, the weight will return."

"Our process is exactly the same. It is very likely to collapse if you stop carrying out the sustaining actions—and not only will you stop making more savings, but you will lose all of the gains we have already made."

Richard adds, "Besides, if you want us to pop back from time to time and do some retraining or reinitiate the motivation of your guys, we can conduct wellness audits, say, every quarter to ensure that the controls are still working. And, we will use your own teams to find any new issues and tweak things, where necessary, to ensure continuous improvement."

"It sounds like something bad must have happened in your previous experience with consultants, Hamish. We will not let you down. For us, business is personal."

"Sorry guys, no intention to offend. I guess I've grown up in business with the mind-set that we shouldn't need consultants. Sometimes it seems that it's 'Show me your watch and I'll tell you the time'!"

"Hamish, that can be true," Richard smiles. "Besides, we wouldn't *ask* to see your watch; we would sneak a look at your wrist when you are not looking. But, to be honest, it never ceases to amaze me, or many of my colleagues, that some of the biggest issues—and losses—in a company have been around for years. Surely you would prefer we tried to fix them, too?"

Hamish is a bit surprised at the answer, but he knows that what Richard is saying rings true.

"Judge us by what we do and not what others say, Hamish," adds Richard. "Besides, you are part of the team and will know of all the issues we find before we fix them."

"As for the solutions lasting," Mike says, "we will include the need for continuity of performance improvements into the future and schedule wellness audits into the next element of the project plan, which is the Project Objectives. Besides, it is a normal procedure for us to train an improvement champion in each company. His/her job is to supervise the projects in our absence while also being groomed to take a leading role in the future."

"So, we had best get started, Hamish," Richard says, taking the initiative. "If we are to achieve an additional $27 million in profit over the next nine-month period, it is, of course, necessary that we break this monumental task down into smaller chunks. Once we have decided on the component parts, we then need to identify any associated—linked—objectives. Some of them may be more obvious than others, but the sum of these objectives should give us our targeted profit improvement within the time frame."

"Richard, do we need to know the sequence of tasks at this stage, or can we just brainstorm the ideas and prioritize them later?" asks Hamish.

"Defining the key steps seems like a really good idea, Hamish. If we list the tasks on sticky notes, we can just rearrange them for sequencing as needed." Mike smiles at a new way to use sticky notes.

Richard moves to the flip chart, and the three of them begin to brainstorm project objectives. One idea is written on each sticky note, and they are stuck on the flip chart.

Hamish takes a positive lead and rattles out a number of issues.

- Analyze all four companies.
- Get on the factory floor, talk with the people, and observe what's going on.
- Understand corporate expenses and identify their impact on overall company performance:
  - Sales performance
  - General costs and administration
  - SG&A (Selling, General, and Administrative) expenses, a combination of which leads to an overall cost that must be allocated to each of the four businesses (This will still be paid for through profits from sales at a straight percentage.)
- Consolidate all of our findings from the various analyses and estimate savings from potential improvements so that we can prioritize them.

Hamish picks up a thick folder from his desk. "I have gathered some key reports that might give us some ideas." He opens the file and produces an equally thick pile of documents with highlighted points and sticky notes used as reminders and page markers. He arranges the papers in a semi-circle in front of him. "This reminds me of my college days, working in a casino," laughs Hamish.

Mike speaks: "The employees have to be on board, so we have to communicate constantly on what we are trying to achieve. Planning their involvement is crucial. Although we will initially ask for volunteers or select folks that we know will participate, we still need the right people working on the right things."

Hamish interjects, "We also have to ensure that there is no disruption—or as little as possible—to our current business during the change process. Then there's the matter of ensuring that all gains achieved are consolidated into the business and become the new way we do things around here."

Mike responds: "That should be a standard step for implementing all improvements, Hamish. We always build in a formal management control system to allow for ongoing monitoring of the processes and also to use it for early diagnosis of problems. The technique is called *short-interval control* and can be as simple as the operators graphing a few appropriate KPIs [Key Performance Indicators] and using them to look for trends. This keeps them involved and always improves the control of processes and systems."

Richard summarizes: "I've been taking notes as we work, and the first-draft outline of our project objectives looks like this:"

- Conduct analysis of all four companies
- Conduct analysis of corporate costs and allocations
- Consolidate overall findings and estimate savings
- Ensure effective communications across all levels of organization
- Ensure buy-in and availability of all key people for project work
- Ensure quality and throughput continuity
- Effectively install improvements into the business
- Integrate all improvements into a management control system
- Ensure effective follow-up and monitor and control systems

"But what if we can't find the $27 million in profit improvement?" asks Hamish, still very aware of the commitment he is making.

"Well, that one hasn't been presented to us as optional," says Michael. "So I'm going to suggest that if we can't find it all through margin improvement, then we should look for some of it through additional sales and any other ideas we can come up with. After all, we should be actively trying to increase sales in any event."

"Can you capture that, Richard?" asks Hamish.

Richard tries a few phrases, crossing out the ones he doesn't like and adding new ones. He tilts his head as he rereads the current version. "How about this?"

- Identify opportunities for profit improvement through increased sales

"That will do it," says Hamish. "Let's check if we've got everything."

"Can I just make a point, Hamish?" asks Mike. "Even though we have laid out a clear time for the analysis, there is no reason that obvious improvements cannot be started and can run in parallel. The objective is not a nice report, but making savings." Mike thinks for a bit and adds, "Once we get a feel for the resources you can free up, we will also plan any training needed and, time permitting, get some of the basics started."

Mike creates a quick plan in Excel (Figure 16.2). Initially, the divisions are in weeks, and only the initial three months have been planned. It is during this time that the key issues will be identified and allocated to teams. Any obvious gains will be tackled. A detailed map, with columns in days, will be needed for the breakdown of data and precision planning.

Michael, Richard, and Hamish do another quick back pass and are satisfied that if they meet all of the objectives, then they will meet the business improvement target in the timeline. It's still only words so far, though. The actual work still has to be done.

Hamish gathers his thoughts from the meeting. "So, the next step is the work-breakdown structure? I guess a big part of the success pretty much depends on the way the entire project plan is divided into bite-sized tasks that are realistic and achievable in the time allocated. On paper, it looks quite simple!"

Richard agrees with Hamish's assessment. "The work-breakdown structure, at the level we are currently at, will be relatively simple and high level. Then the project-planning process will be mirrored in each of the locations, with chunks of work designed specifically to suit each situation. For now, though, let's look at the first objective and break it down."

1 Conduct analysis at all four companies
   1.1 Conduct analysis at Next Automotive
   1.2 Conduct analysis at Ronson & Ronson
   1.3 Conduct analysis at Phonethics
   1.4 Conduct analysis at Independent Pharmaceuticals

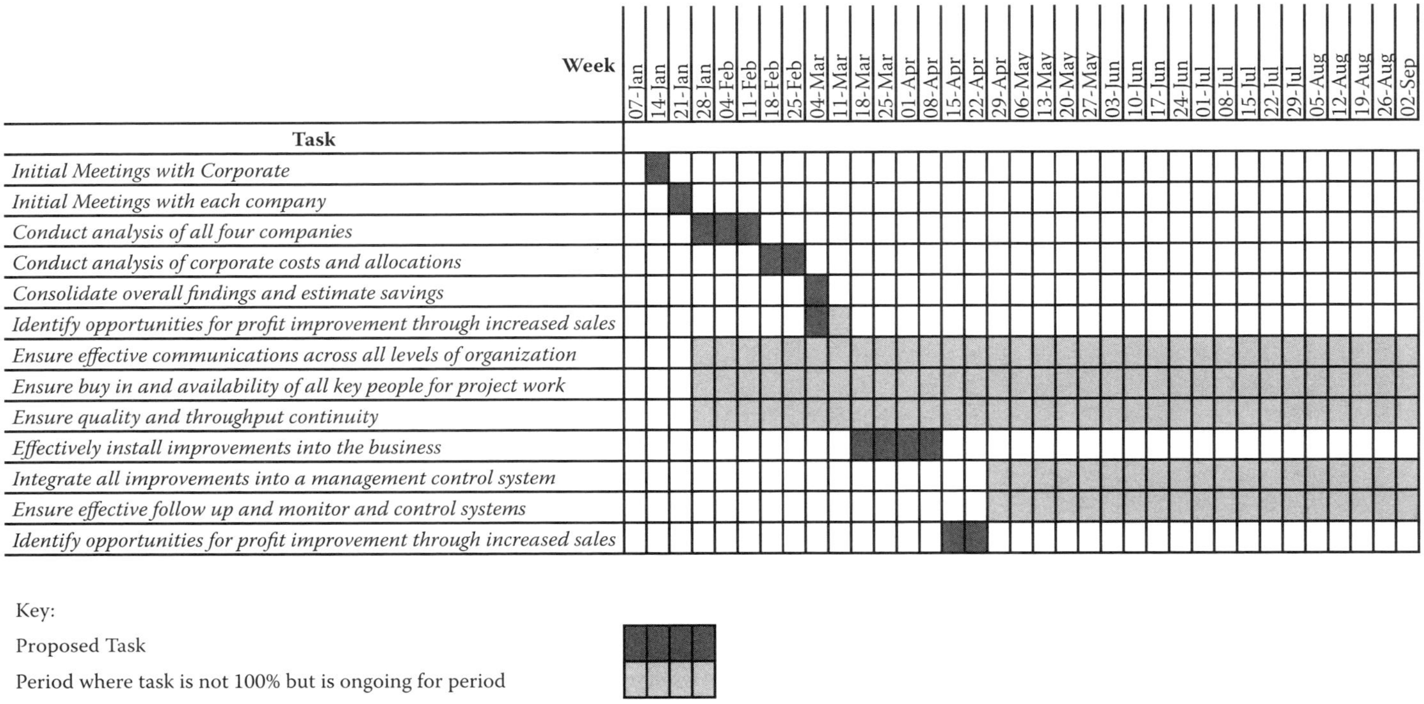

Week

Task
Initial Meetings with Corporate
Initial Meetings with each company
Conduct analysis of all four companies
Conduct analysis of corporate costs and allocations
Consolidate overall findings and estimate savings
Identify opportunities for profit improvement through increased sales
Ensure effective communications across all levels of organization
Ensure buy in and availability of all key people for project work
Ensure quality and throughput continuity
Effectively install improvements into the business
Integrate all improvements into a management control system
Ensure effective follow up and monitor and control systems
Identify opportunities for profit improvement through increased sales

Week columns: 07-Jan, 14-Jan, 21-Jan, 28-Jan, 04-Feb, 11-Feb, 18-Feb, 25-Feb, 04-Mar, 11-Mar, 18-Mar, 25-Mar, 01-Apr, 08-Apr, 15-Apr, 22-Apr, 29-Apr, 06-May, 13-May, 20-May, 27-May, 03-Jun, 10-Jun, 17-Jun, 24-Jun, 01-Jul, 08-Jul, 15-Jul, 22-Jul, 29-Jul, 05-Aug, 12-Aug, 19-Aug, 26-Aug, 02-Sep

Key:

Proposed Task

Period where task is not 100% but is ongoing for period

FIGURE 16.2
Initial rough plan.

"It's pretty straightforward: We go in and we do it. The tools that we will use are the same ones we intend to use with yourself as well as each division president and their key managers before starting the on-site analysis." Mike looks directly at Hamish as he makes the point. "I can't stress enough the importance of senior management support and involvement. For a first pass, we should get in and out of all locations within two to three weeks, the quicker the better when analyzing a business. Anything we miss we will pick up during the later process."

"I think it makes sense for us to continue with the element under analysis to consider the remainder of the steps and how they can be planned into the project. It lends itself well to the exercise," says Hamish. "When we have completed the process on these steps, we can work through the remainder together. Where we feel there is any critical information missing, we can get it off-line. Do we all agree?" Heads nod as everyone agrees.

"OK," Richard takes the pen. "The next step is *precedence relationships*. Basically, it sets the order in which the tasks need to be done." He circles the points with the pen, cap still on, as he asks, "Is there any element from 1.1 through 1.4 that has to be done before any of the others?"

"No," says Hamish. "They are four distinct businesses. We could start them all at once if we had the resources, or start with whichever one we wanted to do first, or maybe we can consider if there is a critical issue we can get started on?"

"Yes, we could do two at a time, Michael in one and me in the other," says Richard. "I'm comfortable with that. What about you, Michael? Hamish?"

Both feel that would be fine. It means that they can finish the analysis of two companies in parallel with each other. Richard says, "I'll do Pharmaceuticals Limited and call centers, and Michael will do automotive and metals distribution, which really also takes care of the next step in the process—*responsibility assignment*.

"There has to be single-point accountability for each work-breakdown structure element, and in this case, Michael will take primary responsibility for 1.1 and 1.2, and I will take responsibility for 1.3 and 1.4. We will do 1.1 and 1.3 in parallel in weeks one and two and 1.2 and 1.4 in weeks three and four."

"There will need to be someone with on-site responsibility who will be able to drive the improvements when Michael and I are off-site. We need to decide on who that will be. Perhaps it will be best to have a preliminary chat with the presidents and see who they recommend."

Hamish has clearly done this before. He raises his right hand to cue his intention to speak. "Regarding resources, each analysis will need the division president and managers to be available for a kickoff meeting on day one. Thereafter, we will need two selected—and hopefully well-respected—subject-matter experts to work with each of you for the duration of the analysis in their locations. We will also need a small conference room to be made available to us as a 'war room' on each site."

Richard notes the points. Michael draws the framework of a Gantt chart, with the work-breakdown elements 1.1 and 1.3 starting on week one and ending at the close of week two, and 1.2 and 1.4 starting on week three and ending at the close of week four.

"How do you feel about the process so far Hamish?"

"I'm good. I've had exposure to project management, as you would well imagine, and I believe it will be an excellent way for us to sequence and complete the work and, God willing, it will minimize the inevitable surprises."

For the remainder of the morning, the three continue to work on the project plan, and they all feel good about the final product. At the close of the day, the remaining project objectives break down to look like this:

2 Conduct analysis of corporate costs and allocations
  2.1 Establish total allocation to each business as a percent of sales
  2.2 Analyze costs by department
  2.3 Determine the percentage that might be saved/reduced and determine impact on EBIT
    – No precedence relationships
    – Responsibility: Richard and Hamish
    – Duration: Lapsed time of one week
3 Consolidate overall findings and estimate savings
  3.1 Consolidate findings with Hamish and divisional heads
  3.2 Estimate savings
    – Precedence relationships:
      – for 3.1: all of 1, 2
      – for 3.2: all of 1, 2, and 3.1
    – Responsibility: Michael, Richard, and Hamish
    – Duration: Lapsed time of one week

The remaining details were planned out in the same way. See Figure 16.3 for further details of the breakdown and Table 16.1 for a summary of the responsibilities.

Hamish looks at the first draft of the project plan. It could look a lot prettier, but the detail is better than expected at this point. "I think I'm OK with it so far. It's a lot to take in."

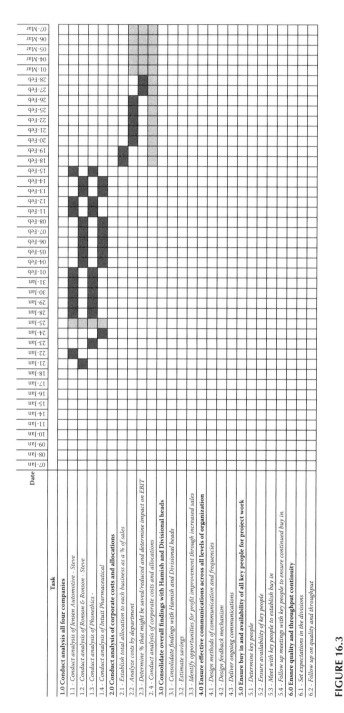

FIGURE 16.3

Detailed project plan—partial.

Effectively install improvements into the business		
7.1 - *Design improvements Automotive*		
7.2 - *Install improvement in Automotive*		
7.3 - *Design improvements steel business*		
7.4 - *Install improvements in Steel business*		
7.5 - *Design improvements in call centers - 2 Sites*		
7.6 - *Install improvements in call centers - 2 Sites*		
7.7 - *Design improvements in Pharmaceutical Business*		
7.8 - *Install improvements in pharmaceutical business*		
8.0 Integrate all improvements into a management control system		
8.1 - *Design management control system*		
8.2 - *Ensure agreement with division presidents*		
8.3 - *Train managers in management control system*		
8.4 - *Install management control system*		
9.0 Ensure effective follow up and monitor md control systems		
9.1 - *Design management control system*		
9.2 - *Ensure agreement with division presidents*		
9.3 - *Train managers in management control system*		
9.4 - *Install management control system*		
9.5 - *Create a written specification for new procedures*		
9.6 - *Train Teams & Operators in new system*		
9.7 - *Identify KPI's and train operators to update and read graphs*		
10.0 Identify opportunities for profit improvement through increased sales		
10.1 - *Identify opportunities*		
10.2 - *Close sales*		
10.3 - *Repeat opportunity cycle*		

Key
Proposed Task
Period where task is not 100% but is ongoing for period

FIGURE 16.3 (*Continued*)

TABLE 16.1

Responsibility Summary

Task Number	Primary Responsibility	Second	Third
4	Hamish	Divisional presidents and their divisions	Hamish, Michael, and Richard
5	Hamish	Divisional presidents and their divisions	Hamish, Michael, and Richard
6	Hamish	Division presidents and their divisions	
7	Michael and Richard	Hamish	Division presidents
8	Improvement team leader	Richard, Michael, and Hamish	
9	Improvement team leader	Division presidents	Hamish, Richard, and Michael
10	Sales teams	Division presidents	Hamish, Richard, and Michael

"It is that, Hamish," says Michael, "but remember, it is only a first draft, so there will be modifications as we learn more. It will be easier to follow when we tidy it up and show the sequence of activities and their durations properly on a Gantt chart. There will also be an opportunity to review and modify it. We will build in project assessments, too. If we use Microsoft Project, or any other project tool you prefer, we can add the arrows that define the precedents and the flow of the critical paths."

"Are you sure it will get us to the targeted goal?" asks Hamish.

"It will if we carry out the plan as defined, making approved improvements as we move forward, and apply the best that every one of us has to offer. And, of course, if we can find the savings, it should get us there, Hamish," says Richard.

Hamish is concerned. "The big limitations are the amount of savings available and how difficult they might be to implement. But how can you be so confident you will find them?"

Mike picks up the question. "Hamish, in my experience, when dealing with a first-time application of Lean and an improvement program, a saving of 10% of sales is usually achievable. So, with a turnover of $300 million, we should expect to see around $30 million. If the savings pan out as we hope, we should do well. And maybe we will even find some goodies we never anticipated."

"OK, guys, when can we review this again?" Hamish asks.

"Close of day tomorrow; we have to keep moving," says Michael. "But, soon, we will need to bite the bullet and take a look at the corporate costs."

17

Corporate Cost Allocations

Michael and Richard are sitting in Hamish's office; it seems like a lot of time has passed since they started this project together, and yet it's only eight weeks and they are *right on schedule*.

In project management jargon, being "right on schedule" means that they are at exactly where they are supposed to be according to the activities on the project Gantt chart—at this moment in time. Richard has heard lots of project managers describe it exactly like that. On one occasion, however, he heard the project manager make this pat comment on a due-diligence project during a potential acquisition. It made him feel uneasy. You see, the manager they were reporting to was not interested in the Gantt chart. He had one objective only, and it wasn't an accurate Gantt chart. His interest was in whether or not they had found anything during the analysis that could jeopardize the acquisition.

Michael and Richard must remember that the processes they are following are designed to identify any issues that need to be considered for remedial action. Some of the issues they discover, though, will not follow a timetable. So, even though it may not be "time" to report, according to the project plan, it is always smart to give a heads-up about any impending or potential problems as soon as possible. A Gantt chart does not replace good judgment. It is just a type of calendar.

Today, they had to make some hard decisions. Following an initial look at the accounts, it was time to address a very delicate issue with Hamish: that of allocating the corporate costs to the four operating businesses.

"Hamish, this is one task I could do without," Richard says quietly and yet being fully aware of the response he is likely to get. "I have had a look at the accounts you gave me, and we have some good news and some bad news from the data. The good news is that, normally, when a fixed amount of funding is given to a department, it will always spend it. Just think about government spends: Each department always seems to spend everything they have been given. If they don't, their next allocation will be reduced by the amount underspent. I remember one company that would request annually that all unspent or unallocated funds be reported to senior management for reallocation—in time to spend it within the year. Another had some 'extra' cash at the end of every financial year. One year in particular, I remember, some of it was used to buy an expensive, state-of-the-art piece of test equipment. It was used once, I believe. The truth was we just didn't need it, and it wasn't even compatible with the other equipment we used. What made it worse was that there was already an identical, older unit sitting, equally unused, in a nearby cupboard. There is a strong possibility that corporate does the same. The bad news is that corporate, just like the four divisions, will need to evaluate their processes and work within reduced funding limits."

Hamish has been in listening mode, taking the odd note and doodling on the pad as he thinks. He is silently digesting what has been said, but he has worries about how "cuts" will affect the performance of corporate. "Listen to me, Richard." Hamish needs to express his opinion. "Corporate costs are a reality in every business in the world! There are fundamental functions that need to be provided, and having a central office saves us a lot of money. We don't just manufacture products; we need to have an infrastructure. Support must be provided for the invisible people that keep the operation running smoothly. They need somewhere to work; staff must be paid. We need sales, human resources, and training departments; we need purchasing, IT, accounting, and all the other hidden functions."

"It is true that corporate doesn't generate revenue or profit from the client, and yet their costs still have to be paid. So, to cover these costs, the board decided that the fairest way was allocating a charge as a straight percentage of sales for each of the divisions!"

Even though Hamish was present when the accounts were reviewed, it is important that Michael and Richard have someone to guide them through the accounts. Hamish naturally feels threatened, and that's never good. He is the major driving force of this initiative and the consultants' key sponsor. He has developed a natural bond with the company and its people, and that makes it difficult to be completely detached and objective. If he was giving advice to another company, he would probably agree 100% with what his consultants are proposing. But he isn't. This is his company, and he knows that the problem has landed right at his front door. Like it or not, now is the time they need to look for cuts at corporate. But knowing doesn't make it any easier.

The consultants have no choice but to meet this head on. Richard goes to the flip chart and turns to a new page. He likes writing down the data, as the time it takes provides a buffer that enables them to absorb and discuss the information.

Richard writes as he speaks. "We need to look at the basic math, Hamish. The corporation currently has $300 million in sales but only $9 million in profits. That is 3%."

Richard looks directly at Hamish, shrugging his shoulders. "The board of directors, including the CEO, has mandated they want a 12% return. That is an increase of 300%, bringing the required profit to $36 million. This is a real increase of $27 million." Richard circles the figure and adds, "$27 million is a lot of money."

Hamish is an experienced manager. He knows they need to find the money, and to do it, they need to look under every carpet. "Corporate overhead is running at 8% of sales," reports Hamish. "This amounts to $24 million, all of which is paid by the divisions. This has been a bone of contention with the division managers for some time now. To be fair, it would be an issue with them no matter how much corporate was charging."

Hamish is not a happy man. Michael and Richard feel glad that they are not facing him on a football field. His guard relaxes as he complains. "Well, what does the board expect me to do—sack everyone at corporate? That *will* save money, but who will do the payroll for the company? Who will work on accounts receivable? What about engineering and information technology? What about all the indirect labor that glues the business together? Maybe they think we should just sack half the employees. After all, who needs a team of people to sell the products? Maybe I should just stay at home from now on! After all, it seems nothing I have done adds value to this company!"

You would think that consultants would get used to this reaction. After all, Michael and Richard have rattled a few chief operating officers before now. They try to be tactful, but going to the front door with the message tends to avoid the confusion of being misunderstood.

Richard speaks: "Hamish, by now you should know us well enough to recognize that we have the greatest respect for you and that we are in this together. You are the single most important member of this team. But who would not feel as you do now, when faced with this situation? Without you, there can be no improvement. You are the leader of this business.

It is because of your job as the COO—responsible for running this entire business and being involved in developing its long-term strategy—that we are here to provide a helping hand and any advice we can offer. Trust me when I say that not every senior manager is as enlightened as you. I know this upsets you, and I understand that. It wasn't my intent, but it was likely to happen."

Hamish responds, "I know you understand the need for the corporate functions, and of course you are also aware of the costs of bricks and mortar. It is probably even a good thing that you don't work for the company. You can stay objective. What we should be discussing is how we can control the amount of corporate cost and how we recognize where we can cut."

Hamish has boxed himself in, and he reframes his argument. "Listen, Richard, I don't doubt that there is room for cost reduction at corporate. But how much do you really think is fair and possible—even realistic? You do realize that if I start a massive layoff at corporate, we could spread panic throughout the company, and some of our key people could just up and leave us stranded?"

"Here's how I see it, Hamish," Richard continues with his explanation. "First we have to look at the high-level profit-improvement options and how they might affect each of the divisions. Our goal is to boost *their* profits and yet not stunt their performance. It will not be easy. At the end of this exercise, if we don't think we can achieve the targets, then that's the message that should be taken back to the CEO and the board, and it would be better sooner rather than later."

Hamish has calmed right down. "So let's lay it out based on what you've seen so far, and then we will see how we all feel about it."

Michael gets up and goes to the flip chart and writes out the numbers, plain and simple. The divisions' profits are significantly reduced by their contributions to the corporate running costs. These functions would still need to be paid for if each division had to provide them in-house. The advantage of a central corporate function should be a reduced running cost.

The following figures are based on earnings before interest and taxes (EBIT):

Steel-processing group
    $110 million sales @ 2% EBIT = $2.2 million
    8% corporate allocation = $8.8 million contribution = 4 times the profit!
       If we reduce the corporate allocation from 8% to 6%, the profit doubles to 4%, or $4.4 million.

Automotive group

$70 million sales @ 3% EBIT = 2.1 million

8% corporate allocation = $5.6 million

If we reduce the corporate allocation from 8% to 6%, the profit moves to 5%, or $3.5 million.

Call-center group

$80 million sales @ 2% EBIT = $1.6 million

8% corporate allocation = $6.4 million

If we reduce the corporate allocation from 8% to 6%, the profit doubles to 4%, or $3.2 million.

Pharmaceutical group

$40 million sales @ 7.5% EBIT = $3 million

8% corporate allocation = $3.2 million

If we reduce the corporate allocation from 8% to 6%, the profit moves to 9.5%, or $3.8 million.

Table 17.1 shows a summary spreadsheet for divisional profits with the proposed changes in corporate allocations. The consultants have recommended reducing the corporate allocation by 25%—a total of $6 million. This takes the 8% contribution from each division to corporate down to 6%. They know that this will be hard to find. But they also might be able to make even greater savings through Lean improvements to the manufacturing plants. However, knowing this should not prevent them from looking for corporate savings.

As a rule of thumb, a 10% saving for a first-time Lean improvement is not unusual. This is equivalent to $2.4 million on a turnover of $24 million—the amount it costs to run the head office. The savings can often be much more, but it is best to avoid overestimating until the data are in. So, they still need to find another $3.6 million in savings.

They have the added problem that the time to make the savings is limited. Table 17.2 shows a summary of the major savings planned.

OVERALL

- Total EBIT from existing operations after corporate cost reductions increases from $8.9 to $14.9 million.

TABLE 17.1

Summary Spreadsheet: Profits with New Corporate Allocations

	Original Sales ($ million)	Original 8% Corporate Allocation ($ million)	Original EBIT ($ million)	Original EBIT (%)	Division Allocation Reduction to Add to EBIT ($ million)	Increased EBIT Including 25% Reduction in Corporate Allocation
Steel-processing group	$110.00	$8.80	$2.20	2.0%	$2.20	$4.40
Automotive group	$70.00	$5.60	$2.10	3.0%	$1.40	$3.50
Call-center group	$80.00	$6.40	$1.60	2.0%	$1.60	$3.20
Pharmaceutical group	$40.00	$3.20	$3.00	7.5%	$0.80	$3.80
Total sales	**$300.00**	**$24.00**	**$8.90**		**$6.00**	**$14.90**

TABLE 17.2

Summary of the Major Savings Planned ($ million)

New Target Profit Calculation	Sales	Original EBIT	Target EBIT	Amount	Cumulative Shortfall
Original sales data for all divisions	**$300.0**	**$8.9**	**$36.0**		**−$27.1**
Profit of turnover (%)		3%	12%		
Corporation allocation reduction				$6.0	**−$21.1**
New sales requirement (as profit)				$10.0	**−$11.1**
Amended total sales for $10 million profit	$83.3				
At current $300 million sales level to make $10 million					
We need to sell $(100/12 \times 10) =$ $83.33 million					
Total estimated sales, including new	**$383.3**				
Productivity savings @ 10% of $300 million				$30.0	**$18.9**

- The gap to achieve new expected performance of $36 million EBIT = $21.1 million
- Additional profit from new sales generated across the divisions = $10 million
- New gap after sales increase = $11.1 million, which must be achieved through efficiency gains
- The potential savings at 10% is $30 million, of which we only need $11.1 million. This gives us a potential buffer of $18.9 million.

Michael sits down, and Hamish stares at the numbers.

"I can't see how we can avoid making a substantial reduction to corporate overhead," Richard concludes. "It's still an unknown as to how much could all come down to the solvability of any production issues we find and the willingness (and capability) of the employees to fix them. Plus, of course, a new sales drive: The targets we are setting are high, and the buffer is necessary considering the short timelines. However," Richard adds quickly, "even if we make all the savings from productivity, corporate will still need to become more efficient."

Hamish is silent. Michael is kind of stunned himself. It's one thing to talk about increasing your profit fourfold and taking on the task because you're a good soldier. It's another thing to look at the numbers in the cold light of day, when you truly understand the impact.

They are all silent. Finally Hamish speaks "… Oh shit!"

They fall into silence again. It's very uncomfortable and yet infinitely more comfortable than speaking.

"Are you guys still prepared to go forward with this? Do you want to? Why would you want to?" Hamish says in a hoarse voice.

"Three different questions," says Michael thoughtfully, and he looks straight at Richard before continuing.

"This is going to be a toughie, Hamish, but we didn't say 'yes' in the first instance so that we could cut and run at the first sign of difficulty. Yes, we will go forward with you, but at this point the bigger question is whether the company still thinks this target is achievable or would they like to adjust it?"

Hamish says, "I'll take it back to Jeff and the board and see what they think. It is not really my decision."

Mike concludes, "Hamish, you never know. They might have set us a stretch target and are prepared to compromise a bit if they see we are making real improvements with future potential."

18

The Low-Hanging Fruit: Phonethics

Michael and Richard have just arrived in the little office Phonethics provided. It is a functional workspace. Just as well, as the data they requested have been laid out on the main table. Some of the piles must be two feet high. The document stacks look like a replica of the Manhattan skyline. Michael is surprised. He did not expect pages and pages of raw data; rather, he thought it would be in the form of usable, readable graphs. But, he muses, "I guess I did get what I asked for."

Michael finds himself wondering if they just collect data, if they actually use it, or if this was a device to conceal problems. It would be easy to be angry and to just simply start plodding their way through the raw data, but there are hundreds of sheets. Thankfully, they do not have the time at the moment! Michael gazes at the piles of paper and thinks, "We need to be more selective about how we use this stuff."

"The problem with information technology is its ability to churn out massive amounts of data at the push of a button," says Richard, flicking through the piles of sheets of tabulated numbers. "How many trees do you think were killed to print this lot? I'm getting scared to drive in forests, just in case I get recognized!"

He walks over to the nearest flip chart, nods at Mike, and the two start to structure, sequence, and prioritize their workload. "What do you think, Michael? What are the keys in this one?"

They have developed a good working process for this: tackling the task in stages. They work together to understand the basic issues and develop the charts. The data enables them to base their decisions on facts. They try to practice what they preach, so they use standard brainstorming techniques for their analyses. In practice, this means that they don't try to prioritize or sequence directly onto the flip charts; it would break the flow of ideas, stifle creativity, and slow them down.

Team sessions should be fun or at least not unpleasant, as that would just engulf the participants in inertia and drive them off looking for a pub and an early lunch. Rather, by brainstorming, they can pull the items that are on the top of their minds, which in turn will suggest some new things to look for. They do this until their thoughts run dry, listing each individual point on a sticky note. They can then use this data later to create Affinity Diagrams, first grouping similar issues together and then sequencing and prioritizing them.

At the end of the process, they review the issues they have generated.

- Business has been in the red for the past three months.
- Average handle time is high for incoming calls.
- Staffing levels are high.
- Demanding clients bully the staff with unreasonable expectations.
- Phonethics is performing in the top quartile of clients' call centers regarding quality.
- Phonethics is being compared to lower-cost offshore alternatives.
- There are two distinct call centers, Littletown and West Playing Field.
- Managers are mainly homegrown.
- Team leaders are too busy with admin work to coach their agents.
- Attrition level is high.
- Clients are telco, automotive, and financial services.
- Call volumes have been falling off.
- Customers who call in are often angry.
- Morale is low.

As Michael and Richard continue working, it becomes obvious that the noise level in the call center is rising. It starts slowly, like the volume of noise in a bar as folks drink more. The workstations are located close to their office door, so they wander out to see what's going on. At first they thought that everyone must be really busy. Looking around the room, they see that the workstations are virtually full, but the agents are not chatting with clients but—loudly—with each other! It seems that there is almost no one on the phone.

"I'll sit beside an agent here," says Michael quietly, looking for one with a customer, "and double jack so that I can listen in on their calls. Why don't you go upstairs and check on the other two floors. Do a quick walk around and assess their staffing and activity levels. I'll see you back in the office in 30 minutes."

Thirty minutes later they are sharing their experience of the call-center floor. It was chaos, with almost no one on a call! They both had to change positions multiple times just to find calls to listen to. They listed possible causes on the second chart and reckoned that it could mean one of two things:

1. That the call volumes are so sporadic that it leaves three full floors of agents idle and waiting—"available for a call"
2. That the workforce management and scheduling is so poor that there are too many people to handle the forecasted call volumes

Elizabeth did mention on more than one occasion that she had problems with overstaffing, but…

"I suspect the answer is closer to the second point; calls tend to fall into some kind of pattern over time," says Michael. "But, whatever the reason turns out to be, it is very much worse than Elizabeth led us to expect. It must be costing the business a fortune."

Richard nods in agreement, "We need to find out if the problem is due to a short-term issue: maybe a negative spike giving a reduction in call arrivals. If so, then the staffing issues could be understandable, but I am surprised the team leaders and managers are not reacting to it. On the other hand, if this is the norm, it suggests a real problem!"

"OK," says Michael, "I will tell the workforce management [IT] guys what we have found and ask them what they can give us that will compare staffing levels with the associated average call volumes."

"Why not just tell them what you want?" asks Richard.

Mike points to the piles of data on the table. He is a proponent of empowerment. "It's always best to get the guys involved. Just asking will make it obvious what we are looking at but does not explain the situation or the possible options. That can start rumors. Besides, we might even get a better response than we ask for. It will show that our intention is improving performance and not staff reduction."

"We can ask that they sample the data over a reasonable time interval, to see if it's an aberration. I will not emphasize the possible scheduling issue, although it might well be obvious, as scheduling is a likely solution. While that's being processed, we could spend the rest of the day on the floor. Between us, we should be able to cover all three floors and ensure that we check out each of the clients."

When they get together again and check the IT reports, they establish that all three client sectors—automotive, telco, and financial services—are equally affected. "Well, it certainly looks like overstaffing and that this is the way manpower is scheduled—mostly unrelated to incoming call volumes," Michael says. "If this data is accurate, we could be running in the region of 30% overstaffed, and no one in management is reacting."

"All right," says Michael, "this will help us prioritize our task list."

They return to the initial analysis and review the points. The first ordered points are as follows:

1. Staffing levels are high.
2. Call volumes have been falling off for a while and this appears to have been a long-term trend.
3. Team leaders are too busy with admin work to coach their agents.
4. Morale is low.

They review the first chart, with all the similar points grouped together, and compare them to the numbered list on the second chart. "Well," says Richard, "those certainly look like the action items we should start with. Because there is no work to do, the agents are throwing paper balls at each other, roaming around the floor away from their seats, and making way more noise than they should. I am a bit concerned that there is no reaction from any of the team leaders or managers. It just looks like it has been happening for so long that it has become business as usual!"

Michael suggests, "Perhaps we should add a new point to our list and find out if there were any reasons for the management inaction?"

Richard writes on the chart:

5. Establish why no action has been taken to the manpower situation.

***

Michael and Richard pull up the Erlang calculator[*] on a laptop. It is time to review the number of phone lines and operators recommended for the current and (planned) future workload. They know the call rates are reducing, so they need to look at the numbers in a bit more detail. After establishing one week's data for the number of incoming calls offered to the agents on each day of the week, they then break down the daily numbers into

---

[*] The Erlang calculator is a tool for evaluating call-center productivity.

half-hour intervals using the average rates of all the workstations. Then, the easy bit, they simply plug in the three key figures to the calculator.

1. Average number of calls offered per half-hour interval
2. Average handle time per call in seconds
3. Expected service level

The output from the calculator is the number of agents required to answer the calls arriving in the period. The acceptable service level (offered to customers) is decided by the client and is contractual. In this case, it means picking up 80% of the calls within 20 seconds.

This is a rough estimate. Because they are working on the average number of calls per half hour, the variation in the number of call arrivals can be high. In fact, it is because they fluctuate so much during the course of the day that the call center's daily agent requirement will also fluctuate and will, or should be, slightly understaffed for the heavier intervals. This means they will not be able to handle the maximum call rate, but will cope for most other times of the day. The goal is to spread the agents, who are scheduled over many different start and stop times, to allow the overlap of onsite agents to be at its maximum during the busy hours. The calculations will, therefore, be close to the actual need.

"Richard, look at this," says Michael. "We are between 20% and 30% overstaffed every day of the week! It seems odd that with this level of staff we get so many complaints, though. Something else is going on."

The consultants delve into the rest of the data in their little conference room and confirm that call volumes have fallen off. It begs the question: Is the call center receiving fewer calls due to a reduction in the total available call volumes, or are their customers simply distributing (redirecting) more calls to the competition? They search over the past six months for trends and variations and, indeed, call-volume movement is only downward, particularly from the telco client, who only occasionally shows a short blip back to historic volumes.

They look at the average "handle time" of the calls: The call center is *allowed* four minutes per call. The average over the same six-month period is 30 seconds longer. This equates to 12.5% extra per call.

Michael flicks though the accounts and sees that salaries are 70% of the overall costs. "Richard, this can't be correct. If this data applies to both sites, based on a turnover of $80 million, subtracting the profit of $1.6 million, we get a cost of sales of $78.4 million" [Table 18.1]. "If 70% of this is the cost

TABLE 18.1

Estimated Extra Call-Time Cost for Call Center

Turnover	$80 million
Profit	$1.6 million
Costs	$78.4 million
Labor costs for agents (70%)	$54.88 million
Extra manpower cost @ 30 seconds extra per call (12.5%)	$6.86 million
Extra manpower cost @ 30 seconds extra per call per site	$3.43 million
Nominal savings	8.575%

of salaries to agents, then it amounts to $54.88 million, and if 12.5% of this is due to the extra work, the cost over both sites is $6.86 million. That is four times the profit!"

Michael considers verification. "I know the savings would never transfer as 100%, but a nominal 8.575% will still translate to a high figure if we can find out and fix the causes of the extra time used in handling calls. I will get the finance folks to get some more accurate estimates. Maybe they can compensate for utilization. But, it will still be a significant saving."

They continue to plow through the data and find that agent attrition is running at 10% per month. This is very high. It amounts to a staff turnover of 120% per year. Looking at the financials, they find that the cost to hire and train one employee is $3,000—and that doesn't consider any manpower inefficiencies during their learning curve, while the new hires are gaining experience. With over 2,000 agents, the high attrition rate is costing the call center $7.2 million per year.

Richard looks at Mike and back to the spreadsheet (Table 18.2). "We need to check this data with finance, too. This is mindboggling; surely these figures can't be right? Perhaps the training estimate is too high? So, if we can save just 50% of that, we are up $3.6 million. And if we add that to the 50% of the call-handling times, $3.4 million, we could save at least $7 million

TABLE 18.2

Hiring and Training Costs for New Agents

Number of agents	2,000
Attrition rate per month	10%
Monthly number of agents leaving	200
Annual number of agents leaving	2,400
Cost to hire and train an agent	$3,000
Annual cost to hire and train agents	$7.2 million
Savings in potential training cost due to turnover	9%

with the possibility of more, up to $14 million! Not bad for the first couple of days, eh?" They are both very pleased. "Well, Michael, what now?"

"I guess we check the figures and then share this information with Elizabeth. She will no doubt want to confirm our analysis, and then she will need to reconvene a meeting with her entire staff." Mike is looking at his calendar, "Probably for next Tuesday, because we have to go to Next Automotive for a couple of days. Oh, yes, and I think we need to ask Elizabeth to invite Hamish as well."

19

Initial Analysis and Morning Meetings: Next Automotive

Michael and Richard are back at Next Automotive, and this time Chuck Nothis is on time to meet them. There is a sense of urgency in the air. They meet Chuck in the conference room, which has been tidied up. Even the cardboard boxes of spare parts are gone from the corners.

"Good morning, Chuck. How are you? You remember my partner, Michael?" Hands are shaken and the formalities are behind them very quickly.

"Glad to see you guys," says Chuck. "A lot has happened in the last two weeks. Right after your last visit, I got *lots* of interest from pretty much everyone in the business. All of the managers and support staff either trooped into my office or stopped me in the plant and asked me what was going on. We had preplanned the communication strategy, and so I was able to present things in a positive way and that you and Michael were going to help us focus our efforts to reduce premium freight costs."

"And this caused a bit of a stir?" Richard asks.

"A bit of a stir!" Chuck appears to be holding back a smile. "Most of the managers jumped right into defensive mode and explained that they were on top of it. They claimed the breakthroughs were just about to happen, and that no help was required! I think they might be concerned about your uncovering their dirty laundry."

"It's a natural reaction," says Michael. "It even has a scientific name, the Hawthorne effect. Basically, people make improvements in their behavior when they believe they are being studied. It will give us a nice short-term boost, actually. The concept has been around for centuries. There's an old variation of the story about the days of conquest during the reign of Attila the Hun. Attila was so feared, due to his reputation for brutality, that most of his enemies would much rather make friends than fight him—so much so that he capitalized on this by sending out spies to every city he intended to conquer. They posed as simple travelers. The spies told stories of the fallen cities and of the horrors they had witnessed. They exaggerated Attila's brutality to the citizens, explaining how he would kill all the men and rape all the women. They stressed how anyone would be lucky to escape with their lives. Then came the punch line: how it would have saved everyone a lot of misery if they had just left the gates open and greeted him in friendship."

"Are you two guys telling me you use the management techniques of Attila the Hun?" Chuck asks with a grin.

"Far from it," Richard laughs. "However, the very thought of any scrutiny can cause proud people to clean up their act before a visitor arrives. There is even a TV commercial that sells a brand of toilet cleaner based on the cleanliness rating a visitor might award their host: Use 'this product' and get a 10. Pretty much everyone wants to be seen in the best light possible. This tends to lead to a kick start in most improvement processes. Besides, they are pleasantly surprised when they discover that we are the exact opposite of what they expect and realize that our objective really is to help them solve the problems. 'Focus on it and it will move' is one of my favorite maxims," Richard says. "Remember Uri Geller?"

"Who?" asks Chuck, scanning his memory. "The guy who bent the spoons? I remember … clever trick. He pretended he was just focusing his attention on them as he stroked them until they bent."

"Can you stroke a spoon and make it bend?" asks Richard.

"That is exactly what happened here," said Chuck. "Straightaway, we saw an improvement in production, higher volume off the presses than ever before, breaking records. The welding area is producing about 5% more parts than average, and everyone is looking busy. Stores and warehousing even started early on their inventory counts. Everyone is tidying up their areas and offices; all of it was very encouraging."

"You say *was* encouraging," says Michael.

"Yes and a lot of these improvements are still in effect. However, just two weeks later, the run rate of premium freight has actually gotten worse. Year to date, we are still at a run rate of $300,000, but the last two weeks annualized would be nearer $400,000! I'm close to the end of my tether, and Hamish is all over me."

"Right. Then we had best get at it," Richard says. "What have you got for us?"

"You and Michael can work out of here; use it as a war room. These are the organizational charts you asked for, pretty much what you would expect in a company of this size, with all department heads reporting directly to me."

Michael and Richard look at the chart and see the top center box: "President: Chuck Nothis," with a single line of eight boxes below feeding into Chuck's. There is a department head for Production, Engineering, Quality, IT, Production Control, Finance, Human Resources, and Sales and Client Services. Feeding into each of these, in turn, are their direct reports: quality inspectors, payroll, salespeople—pretty much as would be expected. They comment to Chuck that tool and die report into engineering and the press setters report into manufacturing.

"Yes," agrees Chuck, "this could be a bit of a disconnect. Maybe we could look into that. But isn't there always going to be some level of that? Engineering designs the tools, and die repair keeps them tuned up for the next production run, so coupling them up makes sense. The setup guys are integral to production, so isn't it natural that they should report there?"

Mike thinks a bit and asks, "It is good logic, but what if the engineers prioritize a new tool over one needed for current production? With two departments, who decides?"

***

Chuck shows Michael and Richard the interview schedule for his direct reports, which starts at 8 a.m.—right now! That's what Richard asked for. He looks over his shoulder, and Ralph Fines, the plant manager who met him at the beginning of his last visit, is standing at the door.

"Come in and sit down, Ralph. We were just wrapping up this discussion, and nothing secret is going on here," he says.

Ralph walks in and takes a seat at the table. Chuck briefly explains the rest of the interviews and that, as requested, they are each 30 minutes in duration, and that the folks will come here. "Will both you and Michael be conducting them?"

Michael shakes hands with Ralph, and Richard explains that he will be doing most of the interviews and that Michael will visit the shop floor and make some preliminary observations—if that's OK. Chuck agrees that will be fine.

Richard says, "The three of us should meet back here at 12 noon and discuss our initial thoughts."

Chuck says he will arrange sandwiches. Richard likes that. Apart from being hospitable, there's nothing like a nice sandwich or two for lunch!

The morning's interviews pass without any fuss. Everyone pretty much has their own viewpoint, interested more in talking about their specific areas of responsibility than in the business's performance as a whole. This is, of course, perfectly normal. Here and there, there is a little bit of finger-pointing, but nothing massively overt; generally speaking, there is a good team here. When they do the group mapping exercise, they will verify the situation and see if any one department causes unforeseen problems for any other.

Michael had a good morning too. The people on the floor, during the Gemba as it is known in Lean, have been helpful and courteous in explaining the types of problems they encounter. There has also been some useful activity on one of the heavy presses due to the need for a die change.

Michael and Richard finish their mornings a few minutes after 12 noon, just in time for Chuck and lunch. They get right to it on a couple of flip charts and brief each other in real time, which is brilliant, because Chuck sees that there are indeed no secrets. Chuck is hearing and seeing exactly the same information being consolidated by the consultants.

The developed flip charts look like this.

Data from interviews

- Silo working is a problem.
- Department managers see their departments in a vacuum, as if their performance stands on its own.
- The attitude is generally positive; they believe they are winning.
- Most departments have no clear measures to tell the difference between a good day and a bad day.
- There is some finger-pointing regarding the cause of late shipments/premium freight.
- There is a general feeling that die reliability is a problem.
- There is an expressed willingness to accept help.
- Despite the feeling they are winning, overall the feeling is that if the consultants came back in one year's time, everything here would be pretty much the same.

Data from the floor observations

- Die changes are time consuming, causing long delays in production runs through reduced availability.
- SMED is required.

- Repaired dies are unreliable.
- They often need excessive rework in the actual presses from the fitters and setters before they will run, further reducing the machine availability.
- This rework is not seen as an issue needing to be fixed.
- Die setters have to hunt for tools to fasten the dies into the presses— again reduced availability.
- Simple 5S will help.
- There are lots of buffer stock/work in process (WIP) between the workstations.
- There is a lot of expediting of orders due to potential late delivery, causing an increased number of changeovers.
- Every *interrupted* production run requires double the number of changeovers, one for the "expedited" product and then another just to get back to where they were before the schedule changed.
- A lot of unnecessary downtime.
- The employees on the floor are afraid that they will be made redundant and lose their jobs.

"So what's your overall impression?" asks Chuck.

Michael answers first. "Well, looking at the responses from the interviews, the overriding feeling I get is that the department managers think they are doing a good job and that, if left alone, everything will be OK. However, it looks like they are open to a bit of help. They know they are under the spotlight. There are few production measures. Without data, I don't feel a management-level Big Picture map would really help at this point. I think the interviews are enough to get started. We should delay the map until we are ready for it."

"But what about the value stream calculations?" Richard asks. "Will it help to know how much time we can save?"

Mike replies, "I don't think so. We already know that SMED is needed, and some of the other observations show there are serious wastes leading to time losses, so we can just make an estimate from any process maps we do."

Chuck is thinking out loud, "I didn't realize that departments were concentrating more on their individual outputs than on the outputs of the business. That's a little concerning."

"That is not unusual," says Richard. "We tend to put our efforts into what we are recognized and rewarded for. For example, as I said earlier, building a new die might be prioritized over fixing one needing repair for production. After all, someone else is responsible for production. To change the current focus, we will have to introduce new triggers to replace the old ones, and new consequences to ensure the behaviors we want to see."

"And what would those behaviors be?" asks Chuck.

Mike responds, "The managers and the employees need to see how their actions might interfere with each other. At the moment they are blind to that. The problems will show up on the process maps of the worst-affected areas. We can maybe identify them if the interviews are clear enough. But we can gather information as we go."

"What I want the managers to *see* is the fact that they don't have the right data. I want them to understand how *useful* data helps rather than hinders and how their priorities can create delays for others." Mike thinks for a moment and then explains, "They need to recognize the importance of the unreliability of parts to creating late deliveries. If we just tell them the problem, it won't work. After all, they have not recognized it so far. If they do the analysis themselves—with our help—if they make the measurements, they will see the production delays that fitting a faulty or incomplete die creates. Then we can ask why it was not ready, and they will become directly motivated to get it right the first time."

"And, we need to be aware that it might not be their fault but, rather, a purchasing, supplier delivery, or warehousing issue. They need to work together and recognize there is a need to change. At the moment, all they see is that they are working as normal and not bad."

"So how are they going to see what they could do better?" asks Chuck.

"The teams need to be shown what kind of issues to look for and that there are ways to fix them. By working in cross-functional teams, it will be possible to estimate the time losses, quality issues, and lack of production predictability. Couple this with letting the teams come up with some new ideas of how to solve the problems, and it will help immensely."

Richard adds, "We need to focus on total business success as opposed to individual departmental success: the way product flows through the factory. We need to consider the capacities of equipment and the departments, reduce batch sizes, introduce Kanbans*, and get stuff moving better by eliminating as many constraints as possible. As Mike has suggested, we need to get everyone working as a team to achieve clearly stated business results."

---

* Kanban is a scheduling system for just-in-time production and delivery.

Michael continues, "What I saw on the floor suggests that the actual production time might be around 60% to 70% of total lead time. But I am only guessing at the moment. We will establish how long specific actions should take from the planning folks. Then, we can measure:

1. How long it takes from parts being released from inventory to the finished parts being produced;
2. Then, because the measure in item 1 is not truly accurate, we also need to find out where advance preparation will help, for example, if there is any lost time waiting to find out what parts we need before we even get to stores.

"Most of these issues are basic Lean wastes and can be fixed. So, knowing where they are and how to recognize them is essential. I'm not basing this purely on the die change I saw today. It also comes from the chats with the operators and some of the observations made, plus I had a look at some of the production and die maintenance and setup records. The same changeovers can take significantly different amounts of time. They should take around the same time. We need to get accurate data to confirm this but, again, I have to stress this shows an opportunity."

Chuck looks unhappy. "I don't get that," he says. "Every company has to have setups and quality checks, and there are always the other delays that we really can't foresee."

"Chuck, have you ever heard of the *hidden factory*?"

"No."

"Basically, it refers to rework times and the hidden losses that drain the resources in a factory," Mike explains. "Imagine we make 10 units and have them ready to ship. We assume the time taken was as planned. But what if 5 of them are faulty out of every 10 made, and they needed to be dismantled and reworked? We could be adding 50% extra to the lead time. So, we plan for a six-hour job because that is how long it takes, and not the four-hour job it should be, losing two whole hours."

"Because the rework is not recognized as wasted effort, indeed is seen as essential work, no action is ever taken to correct it. And what if, due to some miracle, we can make a major reduction in any lost time we are experiencing? Do I have to trigger a major layoff? Wow! That is a big leap from where we are now," Mike says.

"But we should try to answer it," Chuck presses.

"We sure don't recommend layoffs," says Michael. "Not because we're softhearted: It simply doesn't work! We can't expect the guys who help us with productivity gains to keep helping us if the reward is the loss of their job or the loss of those of their workmates."

"So what's the alternative?" asks Chuck.

"One alternative is to do nothing," Mike explains. "But imagine you had 20% more production time right now—would you be looking for more work or just call it a day?"

"More work," replies Chuck, nodding his head.

"So, if we can improve things and we recognize that the change is not intended to be a one-hit wonder, we can go on to plan to help you create a culture of continuous improvement. What we are doing now is just the start. Our immediate plan is to make the new targets. We will try and eliminate the cost of routine premium freight and likely all sorts of linked overtime costs due to rush orders. Also, time gaps will appear in your process that will allow you to take on additional work, which I'm sure happy customers will be more than willing to give you."

"If, after all of this, you still feel overstaffed, it is likely that it will be taken care of by natural attrition over the coming year, so that you simply don't have to rehire, replace, or retrain. It looks as though you have a 4% annual turnover of your workforce right now. So, if you became 10% more efficient and did not replace those folks who leave, then in a few short years you will have a stronger, even more experienced and secure workforce. The 'extra' folks can be used to help find new savings or be cross-trained to support absences or work on new products or whatever you need."

"So now what?" asks Chuck.

"Well, right after lunch, let's get the management team together and present these initial findings to them—that is, if you agree with them." Richard waits for a reaction before proceeding. There is none.

"Then, we will get their buy-in to the next steps, based on what we have found so far. It will be composed of two major elements that can happen simultaneously, if the resources permit. Firstly, we start to develop a quality culture: one where problems are no longer acceptable. They will be formally identified and recorded for resolution. We can start almost immediately by introducing meaningful morning production meetings. This creates a prime area of focus where the cross-functional management team will review all issues—new and old—and the progress of their resolution."

"Then, running in parallel, but taking second place behind the work of the morning meeting teams, we run the mapping sessions we have just discussed. Depending on the type of maps we create, they will take a few days each but will provide a number of advantages we can discuss later. You should lead the morning meetings, Chuck, supported by one of us. The problems we address will all have a positive downstream impact on the rest of the business."

Richard explains that there will be several steps to the process. The following points can double as the generic meeting agenda:

1. We will monitor day-to-day production issues.
2. Identify how many incidents of premium freight happened the previous day along with the associated costs. Shipping and production will give us that answer.
3. Formally identify *all* specific issues and reasons for the delays—everything that contributed to the premium costs being required.
4. Next we ask what we can do to ensure that this does not happen again today.

"We consider whatever answers we get from any of the team members. We want team participation, but not to the exclusion of the department head where the shortfall in performance occurred. The solution might have two parts: a temporary fix for containment and a root cause solution to eliminate the issue forever."

"The next steps depend on the issues chosen for correction. When we know the issues, we need to prioritize them for resolution. We can do this based on the costs that we get from point 2 and the production time lost, converted to a cash equivalent through man-hours. We also need to make an initial assessment as to how difficult each will be to fix: the amount of resource needed and the cost of materials. Simple issues can be dealt with immediately. The bigger issues need to be prioritized first. We then proceed to Step 5."

5. Identify the permanent solution. What is the root cause of any deviation from the daily target? These are the issues to be addressed immediately.
6. Record *all* issues on a whiteboard or similar. Repeat issues will be given priority attention. The more often the repeat, the higher the priority.

7. Each issue will be allocated to a relevant person who will be responsible for solving the problem.
8. A completion date will also be agreed upon.
9. We will follow up on results every day at the morning meeting and allocate support as needed.

"Everyone will be surprised at how quickly we start to improve. The 80:20 rule will have a major impact. As we fix a few key issues, the bulk of the delays will disappear. Not only that, but there will be a renewed perception that the whole business is improving. Everyone will want—not need—to come prepared for the 9 a.m. meeting, so prior to it they will be focusing like crazy on the next layer down, and that focus will act like the links in a chain right down to where the action is."

"I'm happy to give that a try," says Chuck.

Richard adds, "Any unknown issues identified in a process map can be introduced to the group and be included with the list of issues at the morning meetings. The maps will also show where we perceive there are disconnects that we can review together as a team. If we decide to create future state maps, they will become living documents, displayed on walls for all to see and always open to advice on change and improvement. How do you feel about that, Chuck?"

"I'm in. It makes perfect sense! Let's get the team together and begin."

20

Theory Becomes Practice: Next Automotive 3

It's been two days since Michael and Richard had the interviews with the management team and conducted their on-the-floor observations. Chuck tells them that his people are on edge.

"What exactly does that mean, Chuck?"

"Well, there's been an endless stream in and out of my office, everyone thinking that they are the center point of the problem and, without exception, believing that this is unfair. Mostly, they just want you to go away!"

"And what do you think, Chuck?"

"It would certainly be easier on everyone if we continued as we are, being content with gradual improvements."

"Is that what you want Chuck?" Richard asks. "We have to get to the bottom of this!"

"Let's see how the first meeting goes," says Chuck. "If it goes badly, I might have to pull the plug on the exercise."

"Well, is it going to go badly? Were there any late shipments yesterday requiring premium freight?" Richard asks.

"I don't know. I tend to get that information weekly."

"Not anymore!" Richard says. "Let's go in and get this started. Sooner or later, we have got to make a stand. You know that the first few weeks will be the worst ... right?" Richard says, smiling.

They walk into the room and most of the managers are already seated, with a couple of notable exceptions. It is 9 a.m.

"Good morning, everyone. Let's get started," Richard says.

The plant manager chirps up that the die repair manager is not here yet, and neither is the shipping manager.

"Give them a call," Richard says. Chuck is looking nervous already. The calls are made and they wait five minutes, during which time the shipping manager appears.

"We'll have to start without die repair," Richard says, and the meeting begins. "Would you mind if I open the first meeting, Chuck, so that everyone understands the ground rules?"

"No, that'll be fine, Richard, go ahead."

"Thanks for being here, guys. I know you have all read the e-mails we sent out or have been told the purpose of these meetings by your line managers, but I just want to clarify the situation again while you are all together. We will hold this meeting at 9 a.m. every morning until we are all comfortable that premium freight is under control. After that, we might reduce them to every second day, but the frequency won't become more extended than that."

"I have to express that the way we are running is not OK. If anyone does think it is, then that person is at the wrong party!" You could hear a pin drop in the room.

"Nothing ever changes unless there is a discontent with the status quo, and there is most certainly discontent at corporate. Now it is imperative that this same discomfort is felt among us in this room. No change is not an option."

"It's going to get hot in here over the next few days and weeks. Please don't take anything personally, and try not to feel shaken up. I know that will be much more difficult than it sounds. The questions that we will ask are meant to find and trigger change, and we all know that change is never comfortable. However, there is absolutely no need for anyone to take it personally. Our goal is to find the problems and allocate them to selected folks to fix them."

"From this point forward, we need everyone to be on board: no exceptions. We need you to answer the questions as best you can, even if you feel you are being asked the same questions every day. The thing is, as well as asking the questions about the problems, we will also be asking for solutions and the follow-up will be ceaseless."

"It is possible, maybe even likely, that some people will leave this meeting a bit unhappy or upset, and the temptation may be to bitch about it with each other and on the floor. I just want to remind everyone that this initiative is companywide. It was triggered by Jeff Lincoln, the chief executive officer of the company, and the results from its implementation are squarely in the hands of Hamish McIntyre, the chief operating officer.

Here at Next Automotive, the results are in the hands of Chuck Nothis, your president. So if there's any bitching and complaining to be done, that's the chain of command you should follow."

"Michael and I are going to support you every inch of the way. We will help you to do your best work. No one can do more than their best, but remember there is no one other than you and us to solve the problems!"

At this point the die repair manager walks in, wiping his hands on an oily rag. Richard asks him to take a seat, but other than that, he just moves right on.

"When I say that there is no one else, I mean that the organizational chart shows where the buck stops for each function in the business. There's only one quality manager, one plant manager, one die repair manager. The organization is flat, with all of the key functions having its respective head."

"It goes a bit further than that, though. Although everyone is busy, it would be quite pointless if we only concerned ourselves with our respective functions. An 'I'm all right Jack' attitude will hold us back. The company needs you to focus on the output of your respective function, but it also needs you to play a part in the overall team. We need you to treat this business as if it were your own, because it truly is. Unless you are one of the lucky few who do not need to work to support your family, then you need this business to succeed."

"What we sell are automotive parts. This means that they *must* go out the door in the right volume, at the right quality and, of course, on time. Individual departmental success can also be counterproductive if it leads to a bottleneck or creates any issues up- or downstream. Let me ask a question: Does anyone disagree with the logic of what I just said?"

"No, but you could have said it a lot more gently," said the die repair manager.

"Yes, I could have," Richard responds. "And I'm sorry about that. I'm a bit dramatic. But in truth, I'm in this boat with you, and we really don't have a lot of time: around seven months. I'll do my best to be more considerate. All I ask for is your best work during this process. Are you on board?" asks Richard.

The response is better than he expected. There's a lot of nodding in the room, and a few people actually verbalize their support.

"I'm going to ask the questions today, Chuck will do them tomorrow, and by the time the week is out, one of you will lead the meeting each day.

It's not rocket science; the questions are very simple." Richard goes through the list.

- Were there any shipments yesterday that required premium freight?
- How many?
- Which parts?
- Why did they require to be sent by premium freight, what was the cause?
- What was the cost associated with each premium freight shipment?
- What do you intend to do to ensure this cause does not happen again tomorrow?

"We need to deal with finding root causes and eliminating them in a short-interval fashion. We should consider three days to be a lifetime! We will take everyone involved through a problem-solving course, starting with all of you here. Most of you will know how to do it; some might be thankful for the refresher; but all of you need to be on the same page and be able to work with all the teams."

Going through these questions, they discover that there were two incidences of premium freight yesterday. They discuss and capture the causes.

1. The lack of available tools to install a die in the press
2. Parts being unable to be found in the warehouse

They discuss the use of *shadow boards* being located at the tools. Only the tools required for the change will be located on the board, and they should be in good, usable condition. No damaged tools should ever be replaced on the board. Responsibility will be allocated to a designated person to ensure that the board is always complete and the tools are usable.

It is also suggested that the shadow board should look professional, just in case a customer visits the factory, but for the prototype, functionality is the priority as long as it is improved as soon as possible. The boards should be mounted in full view, and the silhouette of each tool should be clearly painted to highlight any tools that are missing at the end of each shift.

The plant manager is assigned to undertake this task. The design, tool content, and locations are up to him.

The discussion moves on to consider possible ways to ensure that no time is lost looking for parts. The first step is to identify the specific issue: Is the part out of stock, in goods-in, not in its location, or in the wrong location? Stored under the wrong part number? They needed to find out what was the problem, and then why, and then what they were going to do to stop it from happening again. The warehouse manager is assigned responsibility for the issue.

The shipping manager accepts responsibility to ensure that a staging area will be set up in the warehouse to hold all parts due to be shipped. They must be located in advance, and any last-minute rush orders must be highlighted. It is also advised that the staging area be marked out using sticky tape and not be painted until the best functional layout has been identified. The discussion also includes the possibility of having the staging areas located next to the loading area and the floor laid out in bays, numbered to correspond to the shipping schedule. But the solution was up to the shipping manager. Both of these points were recorded on the whiteboard for follow-up the next day at 9 a.m., and the consultants thanked the management team for their support. The entire meeting was over in 30 minutes.

"What do you think, Chuck?" Richard asks.

Chuck is pale, with slight beads of sweat on his brow, but he seems ready to lead the meeting tomorrow.

Next day, it's the same routine:

- Task number one is to ask if there were any late or premium shipments.
- Why?
- What are we going to do about it so that it doesn't happen tomorrow?
- Follow up on the previous issues:
  - Where are we with the tool boards for die changes?
  - Have the staging areas for the next day's shipments been completed?

At each meeting, Michael and Richard go on and on—repetitive, demanding, unbending, supportive, determined, and highly successful. Everyone wants to succeed at what they do; no one wants to do a bad job. Everyone has a level of pride, and no one wants to be embarrassed about not knowing what's going on.

The 3F's principle is explained to the managers:

Floor: Don't solve from a distance. Talk to the people involved.
Fact: Intuition can help fault-finding, but not without the basic facts.
Find: Be systematic and logical, using any resources you might need.

The level of focus evolves. It completely changes and intensifies. The managers are on the floor every morning at 7 a.m. getting their facts right for the 9 a.m. meeting, and they are still on the floor at 7 p.m. if necessary to ensure that the last shipment makes the truck.

To know what's going on, they have to be there, to look and to ask questions, and so their supervisors have to do the same thing. The operators and mechanics have to know the answers too, because the supervisors are there looking, asking, and following up. It is the epitome of active management: Manage from the front and empower the employees to ask questions (nicely). No more sitting in the office waiting for problems to come to you!

The 80:20 rule is proven again. Within five weeks there are no late shipments or any need for premium freight. The managers are running the meetings and asking the questions of each other. They rotate the lead and work as a single team. Chuck, Michael, or Richard is always there, and the team very much wants to show them that they are on top of things and, by God, they are!

During the five-week period, all sorts of problems and potential problems came to light, and remarkably, even the most difficult of them are either resolved on the same day or a work-around is found that allows all of the current business expectations to be met. However, a lot more than this is happening. The eyes of the management team are being opened wide regarding every weakness in the business across all functions. It's very much like the water level in a tank being gradually lowered with the improved performance, and every time it is lowered, the next peak or limitation breaks the surface and they address it.

The process map shows the main disconnects in workflow through the business. The main needs are:

- To eliminate the Lean wastes
- To improve equipment reliability
- To ensure proper supply of all necessary tools and materials from outside vendors, using incoming quality control as required
- To optimize the flow of product through the facility by reducing batch sizes and the impact of delays due to bottlenecks and "waiting" wastes
- To ensure customer satisfaction with their required product mix and delivery

The frequency of the issues is included in the estimated loss, as is the cost to production. This helps with prioritizing the solutions. With the map, they can *see* where they have delays or poor quality or delivery shortfalls in incoming raw materials or subassemblies from their suppliers.

The map highlighted that there were die-quality problems from one particular supplier. The poor quality was causing them long setup times and ongoing adjustments in the press. This happened even with new dies, but the issues were never permanently fixed. Instead, they accepted this quality and service as normal and lived with regular adjustments. Some of the dies are three years old and they are still fixing them before use. All of these things have to be fixed.

They have a right to expect the same quality and reliability from their suppliers as their customers expect from them.

When they map the flow of product through the facility, they include everything they considered to be problems: downtime for maintenance or setup, the cost of buffer stock, the need to change production schedules, the necessity and location of quality-control stations, the method of measuring performance—everything, across all functions.

Lead time became a key measure. Simply by increasing the amount of time spent in actual processing of the right orders through the facility, they gradually reduce buffer stock, process time per order, raw goods in inventory, and finished goods in the warehouse. All of this in turn will reduce their costs and increase their throughput capacity for the business.

At the close of month two, since the first 9 a.m. meeting, everyone is sitting together in the conference room—all of the managers, Chuck, Michael, and Richard—as they review the current state of the business and the progress made so far. And when they consider the road that is laid out before them, there is confidence in the room.

This is the same group of people who first came together two months ago, but now they are one team.

21

Chuck Nothis: Curriculum Vitae

It's funny how you try and summarize a life's experience down to as few pages as possible, so that someone might take the time to read it. You would imagine an employment agency has one task, and that task is to find good employees. And yet, from what I read, all they do is scan a few lines of a résumé, and even that happens only if a computer program sees keywords and then flags the résumé as a possible.

"Chuck Nothis: Curriculum Vitae" is written at the top of a page in a 14 point, bold font. I find myself wondering if the font used is important. I am sure someone will say it is. But there it is: my working history reduced to two pages. I don't want to find a new job. My family is settled now, and yet I feel the need to dip my toes in the water and see what might be out there. I feel a need for a safety net. And, if I am thinking that, what are all the other folks who work here thinking?

I scan the wording of my CV, just in case there is a spelling mistake, which is apparently unacceptable these days. Or, what if I've used a wrong word or if the spell checker has made an automatic correction that I might have missed. I can't stop my mind from wandering from good to bad to cringe moments that embarrass me, even now.

I admit I do find myself feeling much better overall since standing up to Hugh Greenlees. "How could I have been so stupid?" I wonder. But I did—do—owe Hugh a lot.

Scaling the organization from apprentice to division president was not easy, but I did it. There were lots of people wanting to get ahead, every-one looking for a bit more money or security, and yet I was the one who found it. Looking back, I remember telling my foreman that I wanted to be a foreman someday. I remember him scratching his stubble beard and saying anything is possible, but I would need to work hard and prove my determination. "After all, Chuck," said the foreman, "someone is always watching what you do."

And work hard I did. While my workmates waited expectantly for the horn that signaled the coffee break and downed tools faster than Wyatt Earp could holster his gun, I worked until I finished off whatever job I was doing—not artificially longer, though. Then, when the horn sounded again at the end of the break, my workmates stole a few extra minutes and ambled back to the job, but I was always back at my bench first. It wasn't so much that I had something to prove, but that I had a pride in what I did. To say my ambition cost me some friends would be a gross understatement, yet I saw it as a way to escape from my poor background. Besides, my real friends knew the real me.

I suddenly feel flushed and worried, "What if working for only one company is seen as a bad thing by employers?" I guess it's too late to worry about that now.

We were from a working-class family but, like Billy Connolly recognized, poor people never saw themselves as underprivileged. We had the same living standards as our friends and neighbors. I suppose it was only as we got older we became aware what the advertisements said we should have—all the material things we never really needed when young but apparently do now. And of course, I did need money to take girls out on dates.

My commitment earned me increasing responsibilities. My managers knew they could depend on me. Then came my first promotion—to team leader. I even deputized for the foreman and stood in at a few production meetings. Eventually, I reached my first milestone: becoming a foreman.

I guess I was never satisfied with what I had, though. The goal was always the next step, and to be honest, my strategy worked well. So I kept on working hard and going the extra mile. I scanned the job advertisements looking for anything that might boost my career. A sideways step or even a salary reduction would be considered—if it boosted my status and my CV. But I never had to change companies. There were enough opportunities here.

I had an insatiable desire … no, it was more of a curiosity as to what the next job up the ladder entailed. So I would select role models and ask their advice: the production superintendent, the plant manager. I watched what they did and how they did it. Any books on management were high on my list of priorities. I borrowed books from my mentors and bought even more. I would read the books time and time again, my head filled with all the knowledge and, sometimes, conflicting ideas I was digesting.

I was relentless. More often than not, I chose my career over my friends. During lunch breaks I would talk with the production foreman, the maintenance foreman, the quality foreman, the shipping and receiving foreman—anyone. I wanted to learn as much as possible about the entire business, and over time I did.

The promotions came as I fought my way up the ladder. If I was passed over, I would find out why and actively correct any shortcomings. What's more, I was happy to do it. Climbing rung by rung and even changing ladders, I believed that true learning only came through doing.

My hunger for knowledge blurred with my goals, until I finally reached the top. I became division president. Even today, I wonder why my goal stopped at president! It was not like me at all. So what went wrong? How could I have become so insecure?

In all honesty, I really am not very sure, and yet somewhere at the back of my mind, I had a niggling feeling that somehow it was all too good to be true, that someday it would all come toppling down around my ears. I no longer felt that there was anyone to join for lunch and learn from. The decisions were mine to make, and I would survive or fail by them. There was no one to discuss my fears with. Thinking about Mike and Richard, I remembered being told once that consultants were useful to chat with. They have nothing to gain, and conversations are confidential. Besides, I liked them.

***

I am outgoing and encourage personal development. I would be the first to recommend everyone should have a mentor and, as there was no formal mentoring program at the Bow Corporation, I found my mentor by default. I found Hugh Greenlees.

Hugh was the longest-standing division president in the company, and he willingly took me under his wing, training and molding me. But Hugh, like everyone else, was not perfect. His dark side was mood swings; fine when the business was performing well, but when performance leveled off—or, worse, dipped—he became very negative, and it rubbed off on everyone around him.

He was also a tad underhanded and could easily play the bad guy in movies, the one who sets up colleagues he didn't like. He was always nice to all his own bosses and did everything asked of him. But he would complain immediately once their backs were turned. He would tell me of folks he grilled in one-on-one meetings behind closed doors—to keep them under control. How he would ignore folks he disliked in group situations or stop any training programs they were on. There were cases where he neglected to tell folks about new policies or plans, so they would look bad, and those he made promises to and never kept.

He was not all bad, though. He supported his favorites, and I was one of them. He would take the time to help folks who asked him for advice and then followed his counsel. I was invited to all the prestigious business functions, attended the new training courses, and was given excellent references. Yes, he was good to the people he liked as long as they supported him as he expected.

The recent drop in business performance had a different effect on me. It manifested more as indecision and lack of confidence. I began second-guessing every decision I made. Hugh had a major influence on me. It could have been destructive, but recent events eventually caused me to see him in a different light. I am still grateful for the mentoring and, I suppose, will remain loyal within limits, yet at the last lunch, where Hugh was seeking revolution, I wanted evolution.

It was truly a kind of epiphany, a recognition that something new was needed. It was like the cliché where a light goes on. Suddenly, there was clarity: no more indecision. I knew what had to be done—and more than that, I wanted to do it.

The old Chuck was back!

My newfound confidence has been clear to all. "I've noticed you are sleeping better, Honey," my wife would say. "Hey man, what's up?" the plant manager would quip. "You're in here in the mornings before I am!" The guys on the floor would smile and say "Hi," as I did at least two walk-abouts every day, always stopping to talk, and laugh, with my team.

Everyone commented on the new me—or was it the old me? Jeff and Hamish said it looked good on me. Life was better, and I could feel the glow as if it shone through me. Ladies and gentlemen, Chuck Nothis is in the building!

And yet, I still updated my CV.

22

Understanding Data and Basic Statistics: Introduction to SPC

Not a normal Sunday morning, today Michael and Richard have a special training course. They arrive at 7:30 a.m. to get organized, but find Kevin and Rajiv are already here. The room is set up exactly as requested: The seating is arranged in a large, open-mouthed, U shape, kind of like a horseshoe for horses with legs pointing the wrong way. Richard likes how it invites an easy and close interaction with the participants. At the open end of the horseshoe, the consultants have positioned four flip charts on their easels.

Richard likes flip charts—in addition to overheads—as they facilitate learning by freezing an important point. The charts allow them to show four extra pieces of information in sequence at any point in time. It also lets the folks know which step they are at in the learning process and how it relates to the previous and next steps. The flip charts also allow extra information to be explained if there are any questions. It's not so easy to do this with an overhead presentation of facts alone, as the moment one moves forward to the next slide, the previous one is lost to sight and, possibly, also to mind.

The consultants have pre-prepared materials, which they place at each chair. The participants begin to arrive early and then flow in as if the floodgates have opened. They are surprisingly happy for their day off: laughing, smiling, and chatting with each other. As they gather around the coffeepot, they seem genuinely excited. Richard suspects that the chocolate and jelly doughnuts are helping, and he is excited by those too! Lucie joins them, along with Kevin and Rajiv. She chats with her people.

"All right folks, it's 8 o'clock," says Richard. "Let's get this party started!"

The folks take their seats around the table. Richard and Michael had expected good attendance—a group representing the various areas of the powder-filling department and some support folk, but the room has

40 participants—everyone has turned up! They had intended to do this session over two weekends with half of the folks each week in an effort to minimize any adverse impact on production, but everyone is here!

"Sorry folks," says Richard. "We only expected to see 20 of your smiling faces this morning, so we only have training materials for half of you. We will bring 20 additional sets in tomorrow, but in the meantime, would you mind sharing?"

"No," they all shout and laugh good-naturedly.

Lucie walks up to the consultants at the front of the room. "Would you mind if I said a few words to kick this off?" she says, beaming from ear to ear.

Returning her smile and with deep exaggerated bows Richard and Michael express their delight. "Madam, the stage is yours."

"Good morning everyone," says Lucie.

"Good morning, Lucie," the assembly chirps back.

"I'm very happy to see all of you here this morning. I know that of late you have been good enough to work every Sunday morning just to keep up with our customers' needs, and now that we are coming into flu season, that need is ramping up. I'm sure that it's no surprise to you to see Michael and Richard here, as you saw them tour our building late last week, and Rajiv and Kevin have told all of you why they are here."

Richard can't believe it, but everyone starts to applaud! Lucie turns to Michael and Richard, and it's her turn to compliment them with a very dainty curtsey!

Lucie continues, "Richard has told me he thinks you are a highly skilled team, but I already knew that. He has assured me that he and Michael will do everything in their power to help, starting with sharing a technique with us that just might help chase away this constant stop-start-rework cycle in the powder-filling department. I know some of you don't mind the overtime money; after all, we have to pay the bills! I also know that everyone is getting tired and would like to be able to take a few vacation days and spend time with your families. Don't worry, when we fix this, there will still be plenty of overtime for anyone who wants it and, God willing, we might even be able to create some new jobs. Have fun!" she laughs.

Now, it's Richard's turn to wax eloquent. He loves it; it's his favorite bit! He has wondered why he never joined an amateur dramatic club, like Lucie. It would have suited him—the heat from the footlights, the smell of the greasepaint melting on his face. He thinks, "I was born for the stage: God help me, I may have missed my vocation!"

"Good morning everyone. I'm Richard, and I'd like to introduce my partner, Michael." Both take their bows. "The first thing I want to say is that we don't solve your problems: you do." The employees look around at one another, slightly surprised. "Folks like us come along with our magic wands and the answers to all your problems. Then, when things start to get better, it might look like it was us who did it. Yet we all know better. The power to revolutionize how things are done around here is in the hearts and minds of all of you."

"Our part is to be a catalyst: to show you some new techniques and help you move forward with an idea, a concept, or a process that you have possibly not used so far. Indeed, most of the techniques we use have been around for more than half a century. They have survived the passage of time because they work."

"The first lesson is simple. Any process is just a tool. It's just like a hammer or a screwdriver in a toolbox. It is just a tool, a series of steps, designed to achieve a specific objective. It's really important to use the right tools to do good work. If we try to put a screw into the wall with a hammer, it might go in, but it will be extra work and will create a mess. It probably won't achieve the objective either. It might not hold up the picture. The trick is to know how and when to use each tool. It also helps to remember that a fool with a tool is still a fool. So experience is the true skill."

"The people in this room have the knowledge and ability to run this process more than anyone else ever could, and it's obvious that you are a team. Sitting here today, we have all the people who operate and maintain the equipment, those who ensure quality, and those who supervise and lead. And believe me, folks, leading is a lot different than managing. This room is full of leaders."

"I've noticed more than a few of you taking a sneak peek at your participants' materials and then stifling the occasional yawn. This is going to be fun! There will not be any tests to pass at the end of the class. It will take a bit of time for the ideas to sink in. But we will be here to help put the ideas into practice."

"By the end of the course, you will have a graph to plot data on that will help you to predict whether the equipment is performing as it should. All you will need to do is add points and check a few rules—if we go for a manual chart—or just add the data and let the computer do the tests if we go for a software solution. My preference is that you go for manual first. Actually handing the data helps you to better understand what we are trying to do. We will also try and fit in a couple of fault-finding tools that you can use to fix any issues you find with your processes."

Richard has regained their attention, and they're happier. "I will need to include some quite complex theory, but this is only to help you understand what you are doing. You won't be tested on it, so don't worry. Nor will we try and catch you out with hard questions. We know how hard it was for us to learn. It might seem hard initially, but over time, it will become second nature and something that some of you will want to learn more about."

"This particular tool, this hammer, is called Statistical Process Control (SPC). It may not be the newest or most glamorous technique, but it works just as well today as it did 60 years ago. Some folk even argue that it is old hat and that it can cause folks to see problems that don't exist, but they usually can't offer anything better to replace it with."

"I don't agree with them. I believe we are smart enough to see the warning signals and become alert to a real *potential* problem, only taking action if the situation gets worse. But, to be honest, what do we have to lose? Either way, what we are going to show you and the data we use will only be beneficial in the long run. Any questions?"

Nothing, so Richard proceeds. "Let me give you a bit of a history lesson. At the end of the second world war in 1945, the world was faced with tremendous devastation. In Japan we witnessed the first use of atomic weapons, and they left a wasteland; the Japanese economy was devastated and had to be rebuilt. An American scientist, I don't know how better to explain him, Dr. W. Edwards Deming, accepted the task of teaching Japanese companies SPC. He found a willing audience. A country with many issues will willingly accept help, guidance, and new ideas."

"These principles and ideas were so sound that they helped raise the Japanese economy from destitution to one of the most advanced and powerful in the world. If they can be applied to an entire nation, they can be applied to your business, too."

Richard has their attention and explains the teaching process they will use. He is using the flip charts now to ensure understanding and make ideas visible. "We will teach you each concept and how to apply it. We will make the key points visible on the flip charts for reference. Seeing the information makes a huge difference to learning. Hearing the lesson can get lost, blown away like words in a wind, but both seeing and hearing, together, reinforce each other."

"We will look at an example to solidify our understanding, and then we will do a simple case study so that you have an opportunity to practice each technique in a safe environment. It's like having the picture in front of a jigsaw box to help you build your own picture."

"You see, learning comes from doing, not from simply understanding. It was that way for everyone here, including Lucie, Michael, and myself. Of course, we have all studied to gain knowledge. That's a good starting point, but it's not enough. We have to apply what we have learned so that we can turn knowledge into know-how."

"So, once you have practiced on the case study, we will split you up into natural groups to work together on what you have learned and apply it to the problems you are currently facing in the department. You'll be working as rcal teams—just like you always do—helping each other. If we have picked the right tool from our toolbox, which we believe we have, then the teams can present to Lucie what they have found. Then it's only a short step from there to implementing the fix, making the changes, *and* being recognized for your genius!"

The participants look bewildered. They are wondering what is coming next. Richard explains that they are going to have a look at Statistical Process Control, and all the faces in the room look shell-shocked. And so they should. Richard remembers the first time he was exposed to SPC; back to statistical calculators, back to math. It's a wonder anyone would choose this.

Michael steps to the fore, understanding how the participants feel. He tells them a few jokes, and then he listens and laughs with the participants at their jokes. He does this because he cares and not to curry favor. It's a wise program leader who knows that relaxed and happy participants are successful participants.

Their goal was not to teach a lot of statistics, although they wanted to give some basics. As always happens, as soon as they mention probability, someone shouts, "Will it help me win the lottery?"

"Well," says Mike, "there is some good news and some bad news here. The good news is that I have only a limited understanding of statistics. I only use the bits I need to do what I need to do. We can use calculators, Excel spreadsheets, or software programs specially designed for statistical analysis. The software I prefer is called Minitab®, but there are others on the market. We could teach you more, but learning statistics is not the goal here—understanding and learning how to apply SPC is."

"We will do a bit of simple game playing using dice to give you an idea about probabilities, but we will not be doing anything complicated."

Again, the voice chirps, "Will it help me win the lottery, though?"

Mike looks at a smiling face at the back of the room, grins, and says, "That's the bad news. Do you know the odds of winning a lottery that uses six balls?"

"Yes, they're really high," says the smiler.

"What we will do, if that suits, is talk a bit about statistics and probability, and then we can have a look at the lottery calculation."

The group agrees, and Richard and Michael get out the coins—not very high tech, but great as an introduction to probability. "If I toss this coin, what is the chance it will land as a head?"

In almost perfect unison, they get a response of "50:50." So everyone tosses the coins a few times, and some folks get only heads, some get only tails, and some get more of one than the other. Only one person out of 40 actually got 50%. It was only as they did larger numbers of tosses that the heads-to-tails ratio got closer to 50% for the participants.

The group discusses how each individual result could not be predicted, but the average result would settle at 50%—if enough throws were made. Richard explains that, although there are two possible outcomes, any individual result will be random. The same goes for any measurement in a process, including the weight of powder to be added to a package or to make a pill, or anything else, for that matter.

The consultants then switch to a single die as a teaching aid and talk about the probability of getting a specific number. "Easy," they all said, "1 in 6." And, just as before, it was rare if any specific number would appear every six throws. Then, just to complicate matters, they introduce a second die and ask the same question. "What is the chance we would get a given number on any throw and a chosen number on a second throw?"

"If we choose the number 2 as being the outcome from each of the dice, we still have the probability of 1/6 from each die, but the total number of possible outcomes is no longer only 6, as for one die, but 36. The probability of throwing a 2 is 1/6 for die #1 *and* for die #2. The math bit is that the probability now becomes $1/6 \times 1/6$, or 1/36. If we added a third die, it would become $1/6 \times 1/6 \times 1/6$ or 1/216."

"So, what does that tell us about the chance of the powder measure being perfect every time?" Michael asks.

At first there are no responses until Richard asks what the total weight depends on. It turns out that there were eight separate ingredients. Then Richard asks if each weight was perfect. They realize that there would be a variation in each measure and that the total weight would be related to the accuracy of each measure, and the more measures, the bigger the final error could be.

Then they discuss how the variations could be reduced. The group lists accurate scales, accurate dispensing equipment, the skill and accuracy of the operator, leakage from the packet, and a few other issues. But, more to the point, the group sees that the more interactions with the product, the bigger the error is likely to be.

Michael speaks up, "Before we do any more stats, we should have a look at the lottery, as promised."

"There are 49 balls and we draw 6 of them. After each draw, the ball is *not* returned. So what is the chance of selecting a given number from 49 balls?" The answer is easy: 1/49, then 1/48, and so on. They develop the following equation:

$$Probability = (1/49) \times (1/48) \times (1/47) \times (1/46) \times (1/45) \times (1/44)$$

$$= 1/10,068,347,520$$

Then someone from the class shouts, "No it's not! It is only about 14,000,000 to 1."

Mike asks the class to recheck the calculations, but they get the same answer again. "So what have we done wrong?"

The group looks back at the dice example and sees that the 1/6 × 1/6 was to get a *specific* answer number each time. This would be the same as predicting the order of the balls as they were selected.

Mike waits for the answer: "We don't need to do that—any order will do," shouts our smiling friend.

So they do the calculation again. This time they need 6 numbers from 49, 5 from 48, 4 from 47, 3 from 46, 2 from 45, and only 1 from 44. The new equation becomes:

$$Probability = (6/49) \times (5/48) \times (4/47) \times (3/46) \times (2/45) \times (1/44)$$

$$= 720/10,068,347,520$$

$$= 1/13,983,816$$

which can be rounded up to 1 in 14 million.

"The thing is that someone eventually wins it," says Mike. "People hope that they will be the lucky one. They don't realize the immense magnitude of the number." Mike looks around the table and adds, "We are more likely to be attacked by an alligator or are 150 times more likely to be struck by lightning, and yet we never leave the house wondering whether we will be struck by lightning or hit by a meteorite. We know the probability is so unlikely as to be virtually impossible—and yet we still hope we will win the lottery."

Mike checks his watch and, to the relief of the attendees, says, "Time for a break."

SEEING THE NUMBERS

The first stage after they return is to show the class how to make a data table and draw a bar graph. Michael likes to assume that no operators know how to do this, which he has found helps save embarrassment. It only takes a short time to give the extra detail, and it pays off more often than not. Many folks will never admit they don't know something, so it is best just to do it and apologize for going into too much detail.

The two consultants pick one set of results and use this to make the first table for the group. It is easy to read the numbers, but not so easy to visualize the differences. So, next, they simply draw a horizontal line (mentioning that it is also called the *x*-axis) and write the two outcomes: Heads and Tails. Next, they draw a vertical line at the left side (calling this the *y*-axis). They explain that this axis will be the scale of the histogram, just as we get a scale in a map.

Michael explains: "Looking at the data, we can see the highest number of outcomes (heads or tails) was 13, so we want to make a scale that would show all the possible numbers up to 13 and be easy to read." Since the highest number was 13, which is hard to scale, they ask the class to decide the best scale. The group chooses 0 to 14 to make 7 divisions, where each division represented two counts. The graph is shown in Figure 22.1.

Michael and Richard then ask five of the participants to summarize their experiments on the heads/tails coin-toss experiment and create a data table that shows the name of the tester and the number of heads and tails recorded. The objective here is to show that there is a *range* of results. Once more, none of the data tables show the 50:50 or the 1/2 result expected.

To draw the graph, they needed to create an *x*-axis with two sets of data: the name of the person and the number of heads and tails for each person. The vertical (*y*-axis) had to include the highest number or

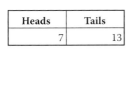

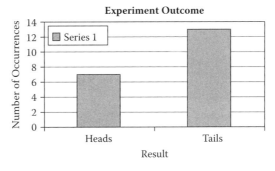

FIGURE 22.1
The coin toss as a histogram.

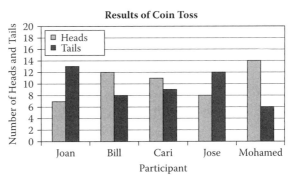

FIGURE 22.2
Summary of five different coin-toss tests.

outcomes—heads or tails. In this case, they had 14 heads, but chose a scale with a maximum of 20, with 10 divisions of 2 counts each (Figure 22.2).

Michael faces the room and says, "Now that we can see the data on a graph, it is easy to see that the range of heads is 7 to 14 and the range of tails is 6 to 13. Quite a difference when we expected the number of heads and tails to be the same! It is worth noticing, however, that if we average the five sets of results, we get 10.4 heads and 9.6 tails. Very nearly 50:50."

In answer to Mike's next question, "Do all of you understand what we mean by the average?," everyone says "yes."

"So, for a few minutes we are going to discuss some basic statistics—measures and names for groups of numbers. There are a few that will be worth remembering, but you don't need to remember them today," Mike jokes. "What you will remember is that there are two ways to get to sleep: one is counting sheep; the other is thinking or reading about statistics."

THE CELL PHONE BATTERY EXAMPLE

Mike asks the class to consider a scenario where they all have the same cell phone, and the manufacturer says it has an average standby battery time of 100 hours. He then asks, "Now imagine that no one has called or texted you for 100 hours—you are in mobile hell. All of your phones have been sitting in standby for the specified 100 hours. Out of the 40 of you here, how many of you think you would be able to send a text after the 100 hours?"

There is a bit of discussion, but they come up with "mostly none," and a few "some of us," because "some batteries last longer than others." "Most of us" is the wrong answer. By the time the *average*˙ lifetime has been reached, half of the batteries will have failed. This is what the average means. The winners recognized that battery life varies, so they need to work on the concept of *averages*. The average is also known as the *mean*.

"Could I have a phone with a battery that fails in, say, less than 10 hours?" asks Mike.

Many agree that this is a possibility. Some have had phones with lives that don't get even close to the average time and they had to return them. They go on to discuss the issues of quality and the need to design the batteries so that *most* last as close as possible to the average.

Mike's next questions are "How close would we need to be?" and "Who decides?"

The group resumes discussion of the issue. No one complains about getting extra hours, and lots say that they should all last for the 100 hours. The discussion now turns to the extra costs in making a battery that would last longer: It might cost more, weigh more, and might be bigger in size, making the phone less desirable. There is also an option not to use the average time as the specification. By having an average lifetime longer than 100 hours, more of the products will meet the spec.

The group also discusses the extra cost to the company in returning and exchanging faulty batteries. They also consider how rework and scrap are both wastes that directly affect the bottom line by reducing the company profit. Then there is a potentially bigger problem: It might impact the reputation of the company—depreciate the brand.

Through discussion, the group decides that if it was a cheap phone, as the 100-hour lifetime would suggest, they might accept a 95-hour battery life.

˙ Technically, the "middle" data point, where half the values are above and half are below, is called the *median*, but I don't want to complicate matters.

This means, for the average to stay at 100 hours, the "range" of life would have to be from 95 to 105 hours. But what is the best way to measure this?

"We need to carry out tests," says Mike. He produces the data from 40 measurements. "I don't want you to get bogged down with this detail. I will explain again later and remind you all how to use the information on what we produce today. In essence, you just need to learn how to draw a graph, add points, and ask a few questions about the data. Easy! But I suspect that some of you will probably know it all pretty soon—because you want to."

"You might imagine the hard part is turning the 40 bits of data into a graph that will tell us the mean and something about how the battery life is distributed about it. Actually, it is quite easy."

- Sort out all the 40 numbers in order, low to high. *This will give us the range of the data.*
- From the range, decide the scale of the horizontal (*x*) axis.
- The data ranges from 97.4 to 103.3 hours or 5.9 hours.
- What we want to know is how the data is distributed. It is a good guide to have between 10 and 20 points, but there is only one value for most of the readings.
- Sort the data into groups.
- Think of a mailman sorting letters. He has bags for each city, then for each area, then for each street and, finally, he has boxes for each house number or group of house numbers.
- So we choose to sort the data into 30-minute intervals. 97.26 to 97.75 hours; 97.76 to 98.25 hours; 98.26 to 98.76 hours, and so on until we reach the top of the range: 103.26 to 103.75 hours.
- "Add" the data point to its "box."
- Count the number of points in each box.
- For example, we find that we have eight batteries that lasted between 99.76 and 100.25. The range helps for sorting but it is often easier to mark the horizontal axis using the average value of each group. (99.76 to 100.25 being 100)
- Select the scale for the vertical (*y*-axis).
- Since the biggest number is 8, we can set up nine divisions on the vertical axis and label them 0 to 8.
- Plot the number of points in each box.
- Represent them as a rectangle from the *x*-axis to the number, as shown in Figure 22.3.

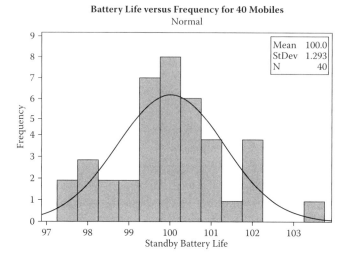

FIGURE 22.3

First set of random data: 40 points with data range in 0.5-hour increments.

"I want to give you a bit of an explanation about the shape of the graphs. It is a very important shape in statistics," Mike says apologetically.

"If we have a process, like making batteries or filling packets with powder, we will have a target (an average value) we want to achieve. But no process will ever produce batteries that last exactly 100 hours because there are too many things in the manufacturing that change the possible outcome. There is the size of the electrodes, the strength of the electrolyte, the quality of the insulating material used, the quality of the solder joints, even the temperature of the room where the battery is tested and the condition of the test equipment. There will be some variation in every step of the process."

"Remarkably, we will find that, in production as in nature, the process variation is most likely to follow a bell-shaped curve, as we can see in Figures 22.3 and 22.4. Notice that the 'bell' is the same on both graphs. It is symmetrical about the average, where most of the points lie. Also note that the bars of the histogram don't line up exactly with the curve and that the two charts of data produce a slightly different looking chart. This is because the two sets of data were chosen at random."

"The bell curve is also known as the binomial or normal distribution. (Mathematicians like to have lots of choices when naming things! I wonder if their pets also have multiple names?) An added beauty of SPC is that the graph does not need to follow a normal distribution to work."

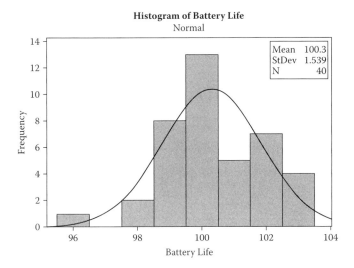

FIGURE 22.4

Second set of random data: 40 points with data range in 1.0-hour increments.

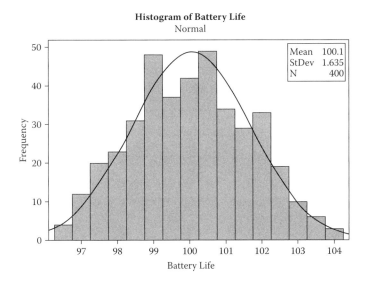

FIGURE 22.5

Third set of random data: from Minitab using 400 points.

Mike wants to explain in a bit more detail how more data points enable a more accurate graph that fits the bell curve, so he also graphs 400 data points—10 times more than the number of people in the class (Figure 22.5). "Notice that the alignment of the curve and the midpoint of the bars are much closer. The more data we use, the more accurate the graph becomes."

"What we need to do with our battery is to limit that variation—the range—so that the worst we get is 95 hours and so, being symmetrical, the best would be 105 hours. Remember, we chose the limits we wanted; we set a product specification based on what the customer—we—wanted."

"But what is it that decides how wide the range will be? Is there a measure that will guide us?"

"Notice that in Figure 22.5, the range is 96.5 to 104 hours, but in Figure 22.6 it is 87 to 110 hours. The range has increased from 7.5 hours to 23 hours, and all that has changed is the *StDev*—the standard deviation. It has increased from 1.635 hours to 3.355 hours, an increase of 1.72 hours."

"We can also see the range is a bit wider between Figures 22.3 and 22.4, but it is not as big a change because the standard deviation has changed by only 0.25 hours."

"Figure 22.7 shows very clearly that the standard deviation and the variation in the process limits are linked. The means (averages) are almost the same, but the graph with the higher standard deviation is wider and has a lower peak, even though they both have 400 data points. The wider graph demonstrates more process variation, which results in a wider range of battery life."

"The main point to take here is that, if we want to limit the battery life to most being above 95 hours, we need to reduce the variation, which we do by reducing the standard deviation."

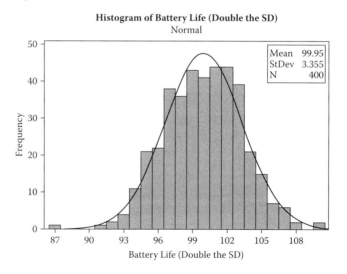

FIGURE 22.6

Fourth set of random data: from Minitab using 400 points.

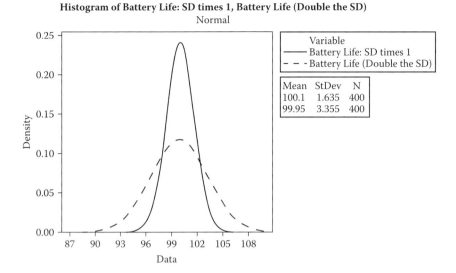

FIGURE 22.7
The graphs from Figures 22.5 and 22.6 shown on the same scale.

WHAT IS THE STANDARD DEVIATION?

Mike continues, "We know that the average of all 400 values for battery life is 100 hours. So, we can safely assume there are close to 200 batteries on either side of the average, excluding any that are exactly equal to 100 hours" (Figure 22.8).

"If the average/mean line was a target and we were shooting at it with a gun, any 'points' to the right or to the left of the line would be misses. Those misses will be a measurable distance from the mean. At each distance we might have a number of hits" (represented by the height of the curve).

"If you have remembered, the histogram has an interesting shape: We can see that most of the 'hits' are closer to the mean, and the number decreases the further away we get. So, if we have 200 hits on any single side, we must have an 'average' error distance."

"I have not used all the standard mathematical symbols, as my hope is to simplify the explanation as much as possible. If we call the mean x and then number the shots x_1 to x_{400}, we can subtract each shot *position* from the mean, add then all up, and take an average."

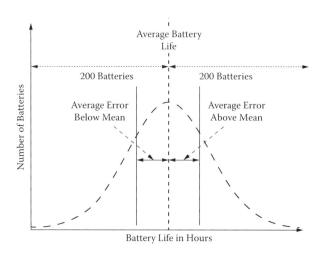

FIGURE 22.8
Just what is this standard deviation?

$$\text{Mean} = x = \frac{x_1 + x_2 + x_3 + \ldots + x_{398} + x_{399} + x_{400}}{400}$$

"Now, to calculate the distance of each point from the mean, we do the following:"

Average distance $=$

$$\frac{(x_1 - x) + (x_2 - x) + (x_3 - x) + \ldots + (x_{398} - x) + (x_{399} - x) + (x_{400} - x)}{400}$$

"But we find when we do this that the answer will be zero. This is because the misses to the left are negative and the misses to the right are positive, and they will both cancel each other out. We need a cunningly clever math trick to get us out of this hole—and complicate everything!"

"It turns out that if we square* each number, they will all be positive, because a negative times a negative gives a positive. So we now have

$$(\text{Average distance})^2 =$$

$$\frac{(x_1 - x)^2 + (x_2 - x)^2 + (x_3 - x)^2 + \ldots + (x_{398} - x)^2 + (x_{399} - x)^2 + (x_{400} - x)^2}{400}$$

---

* We call it *squaring* because we multiply two sides of a square together to get the area. This means 2×2 is the same as 2 squared and 2^2.

"We call this (average distance)^2 the *variance* and represent it by the symbol σ² or sigma squared. So we now have

$$\sigma^2 = \frac{\left(x_1 - x\right)^2 + \left(x_2 - x\right)^2 + \left(x_3 - x\right)^2 + \ldots + \left(x_{398} - x\right)^2 + \left(x_{399} - x\right)^2 + \left(x_{400} - x\right)^2}{400}$$

"Why do we need a term called the *variance*? This is a measure I tend not to use, but some folks do. The variance is a more sensitive measure. If the mean has the value 2 and there is an observed point 3, the distance from the mean is 1. The variance is 1^2, which is also 1. But if we have a second observed point 4, the distance from the mean is now 2, but the variance is 2^2, which equals 4. So, doubling the distance from the mean increases the variance by 4 times. It is very sensitive to the distance."

"A more important value, the single figure that tells you the distribution you can expect to see, is known as the standard deviation. It is given the symbol σ or *s*, the difference depending on the number of samples—a small sample, less than 30, is an *s*."

"All we need to do now is fill in the values, do the calculation, and take the square root of the result and we have the *standard deviation*. So, what do we know about the bell curve or normal distribution?"

"We know the standard deviation controls the *variation* in error. It is the single measure that tells us how close we are to the target. If two people take the same number of shots at the target, the one with the lowest standard deviation is the most accurate."

"If we plot graphs on an axis with the same scale, a small standard deviation gives us a narrow peak and a large one gives us a wide peak. We also know that if we want to reduce the *range* of the error and get more results closer to the target, we need to minimize the standard deviation."

"There is one more fact about the normal distribution that I feel would be nice for you to know. If we have a normal distribution of data—one that looks like the graph in Figure 22.9—there are some nice statistics and probabilities that can be applied to it. If we have 100 data points, we can expect 68.26 of them to land in the range ±1 sigma."

"If we were counting the shots that landed between the mean and one standard deviation to either side, we would expect to see 68 hits. If we look at the wider range of ±2 sigma, we can expect 95.46 of the data points to be found. If we add one more increment, to ±3 sigma, we will now find that almost 100% of the data points land: 99.73 out of 100."

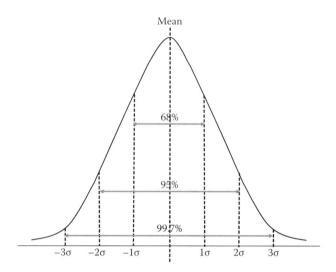

FIGURE 22.9
The bell curve of a normal distribution.

The training so far has turned out to be a success. It has given Michael and Richard a chance to assess the team. They like what they saw: people helping each other in their teams, working to achieve understanding, acceptance, and know-how.

Michael asks the group, "So how do you all feel about that? The right answer gets you a lunch break."

"Fantastic," they laugh. "Who would have thought it would be so easy?"

"It's only proving to be easy because you are so willing," says Lucie. "You guys are the best!"

And with that, they are halfway through the session and break for lunch. "After lunch, we will work on the powder issue."

23

The Powder Analysis

Richard addresses the group after lunch. "Why do we have processes? The answer is really simple: We do it so that what we make turns out the same way every time. If someone offers us a cup of coffee, we might specify milk or cream or how much, how much sugar or sweeteners, whether we like strong or weak, and maybe even if we can have decaffeinated. We do this because we know what we want and because we know what it will taste like, within limits. Processes are no different. A good process gives us a reliable and a reproducible output. What we get at the end will be what we expect to get—within predetermined limits."

"However, if we just wait until the product is ready and then test it, we might find it is not as good as we expected. And if it is not, how will we know what we did that caused the change? Then, if we don't know why it was different, do we just make a new batch and hope that it will be OK? What do we need to know that will enable us to fix the problem and make sure that the product turns out as it should?"

"When we put it that way, the answer is obvious, and yet so many folks don't follow the basics."

1. Develop the process to get the product you want.
2. Set measures and quantities where possible. Even better, give the quantities error limits.

    Richard remembers a bakery "where the butter was just cut and weighed to see if it was 'roughly right.'" The same happened with the other ingredients.
3. Set standards for the materials used and equipment quality in a manufacturing setting. This includes the quality of materials as supplied.
4. Collect data on the process.

    "We don't just want to know if a task was done (a check in a box is not enough) but what the material was, the diameter of the tube, the weight of the sugar, the time of the inquiry, how long it took to answer, the setup parameters, the name of the operator, the workstation ID, the shift, the time, etc. We want details that we can refer back to if we have a fault we missed. But, most importantly, we also want to measure, where possible, the state of the process while the product is being made. We want to take measurements that will confirm the process is working and that all the previous steps are still working."

5. Analyze the data.

"Data is not just for historical records. It is to be used—graphed. It should be looked at to ensure the parts are correct and within the tolerances set and to see whether there is a 'trend' developing. Maybe, the length of a component is increasing or the sugar is not as sweet as it should be. The sooner we spot the problem, the sooner we can do something to correct it."

6. Take action based on the data.

"This does not mean you must do something. Indeed, if everything is correct, you can 'decide' that no action is needed. You should even record the decision to show that a decision was made. In a risk assessment, for example, you might decide there are no electrical risks. But in an external audit, the assessor wants to see proof that it was considered: 'Electrical hazards—not applicable.' But if there is something wrong, we need to know if we should stop making the product or if we can make a temporary fix. We need to use our data to be sure our solutions are working."

"So, every process needs to have data recorded; the data should be used in a proper analysis, and the results of the analysis need to be used properly and turned into a corrective action if needed. In the case of our powder problem, we have to get the team to decide if we are collecting the right data and then the best way to use it to help. This latter will be harder for the group to grasp."

"We have already started to discuss variation, but at this stage we want to expand it to define two types of problems: *Common cause* is the first. It defines changes that happen at random in a process. If we drill a hole, for example, and then measure the diameter of the hole, every hole will be slightly different in size. If we don't cool the drill, for example, the hole might increase in size as the drill gets warmer, or the cuts might not be so accurate if the drill becomes blunt."

"We also have *special cause* errors. These are seen as spikes or dips in a graph. They are caused by a preventable issue: a train being late because there was no driver available or a signal failure; the wrong size of drill being used; whole milk being used in place of fat free; an unskilled or untrained operator making a mistake; the wrong material being used; names being incorrectly spelled; or the equipment developing a fault. In general, these are the issues we fix first."

"We asked the quality controllers to bring us a selection of the most recent powder data. But we quickly found there was an issue with the way it was recorded. If there was a preprocess check and the test failed, the data point was *not* recorded. The problem was fixed, and only when the 'pass' was achieved was the data stored. This did not have any effect on the product seen by the customer but hid the setup issues and complicated any fault-finding analysis. Imagine a car rental company that believes all their cars start with no issues because faults were not recorded."

Richard looks around the room and continues. "Strangely enough, I have seen this tendency to only record 'good' data before. I remember one situation where two different production tables were used during a process to manufacture computer disks. As it turned out, one of the tables had a fault and so, depending on the table used for the test, it could take two readings to get a 'pass.' The bad news was that during production, both tables were used alternately, and so 50% of the production had a very high risk of being faulty."

"The problem was magnified by a secondary problem: The faulty disk also attracted dust particles, and so test wafers would fail the dust count. As before, only the passes were recorded, and it was a while before anyone complained about the number of final test fails. So, again, half of the product would be contaminated with particles."

"The moral of the story: Record *all* data points—particularly the fails. If the fails had been plotted on a graph, the problem would have been visible very quickly—with readings oscillating up and down in sequence—even assuming that no one questioned the high particle count. The amount of potentially lost product was staggering."

Richard and Michael push on and use the powder data as a standard example for how to build a control chart, with 25 groups of numbers made up of subgroups of 5 numbers each, so there is a total of 125 numbers representing measures.

POWDER DATA

Richard takes the lead. "We knew that there was something wrong with the process. One issue was a problem with the packet seals. Although the costs are yet to be confirmed, it was roughly estimated to be a couple of million dollars. But there was also another concern, an issue that the company chose to live with."

"The packets had a minimum weight specification. The weight can be more than 5 grams, but not less. And, because of a high degree of variation, the fill weight is set at 6 grams, which basically ensures a *huge* financial loss. The extra contents will cost *at least* 20% more than necessary:"

$$[(6 - 5)/5] \times 100\% = 20\%$$

"And that is before we even start to make cost savings. This can be seen more clearly in the graphs that follow. But if we consider that almost 40% of the profit is made on this one product, that accounts for $1.2 million. But we know we overfill by up to 40%, so we are throwing away another $200K to $300K in lost profit."

"Figure 23.1 shows the 125 data points QA provided. We had the option of analyzing the data manually by sorting and dividing the data into 'bins' and repeating the earlier calculations as shown this morning (Chapter 22). But we decided to save lots of time and use Minitab®, a statistics analysis program."

"The data from the list represents the outcome of a process where each ingredient is weighed and mixed to obtain a specific amount to be added

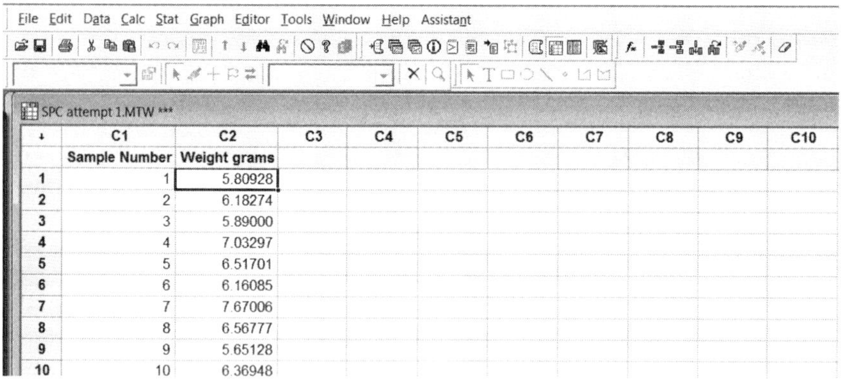

↓	C1	C2	C3	C4	C5	C6	C7	C8	C9	C10
	Sample Number	Weight grams								
1	1	5.80928								
2	2	6.18274								
3	3	5.89000								
4	4	7.03297								
5	5	6.51701								
6	6	6.16085								
7	7	7.67006								
8	8	6.56777								
9	9	5.65128								
10	10	6.36948								

FIGURE 23.1
The 125 data points entered into the program.

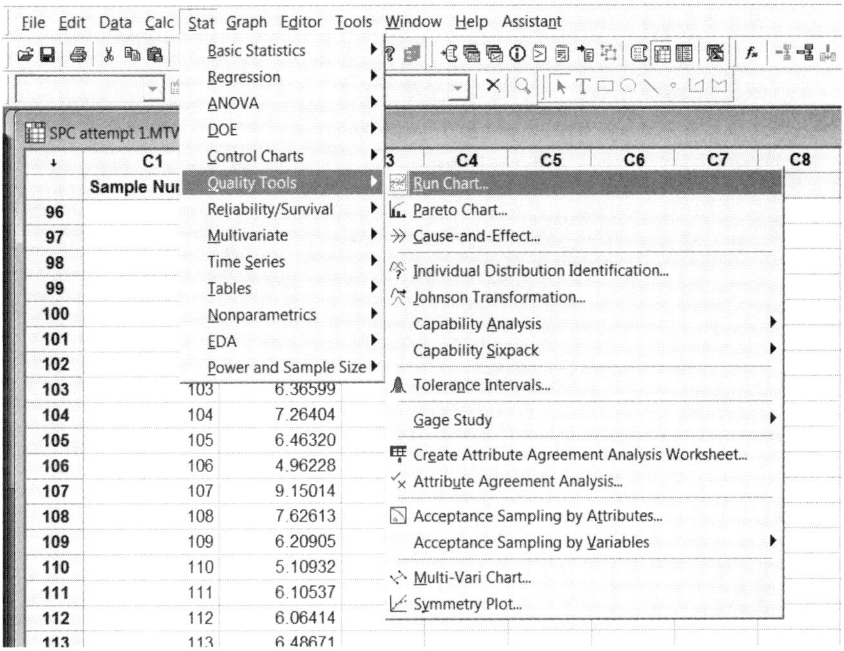

FIGURE 23.2
Selecting the Run Chart option.

to a package for use as a drink." The data was entered into the second column (C2) of the Minitab worksheet. The sample number was entered in column C1 (Figure 23.1).

"The first thing we wanted to do was have a look at the data. So we chose a simple graph that would let us see all the points. We chose a standard run chart" (Stat–Quality Tools–Run Chart, as seen in Figure 23.2).

"As you can see, upon selecting Run Chart, the data-entry box is displayed (Figure 23.3). We select a single column, as all the weights are in C2. We want to see every point, so we choose a 'subgroup' size of 1, to show every point. We have also requested the data mean to be included. When happy, we select OK to get the graph."

"The run chart in Figure 23.4 plots every reading. The odd thing about the chart was that it looks fine. There are no signs that anything is wrong, just a really wide range—probably due to the data being 'passes' only."

"It is relatively easy to convert a run chart to an SPC chart by adding the lines for the standard deviation levels. Indeed, I regularly get criticized for promoting manual tasks, but it is a really good way to learn and get used to working with charts."

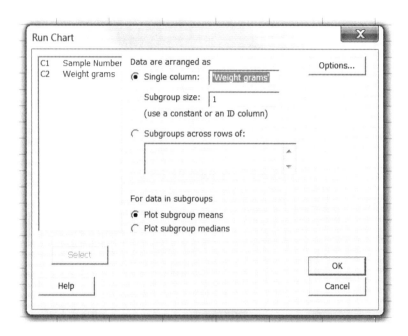

FIGURE 23.3
The data-entry dialogue box.

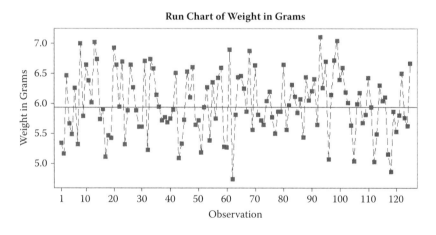

FIGURE 23.4
The run chart.

"We can see that some of the points are still below the 5-gram level. To get a better feel for the data distribution, we draw a histogram, just like we did with the cell phone battery data" (Figure 23.5).

"We know that the packet weight *must* be 5 grams or greater, but with a range of points from below 5 to just over 7, the operators knew that

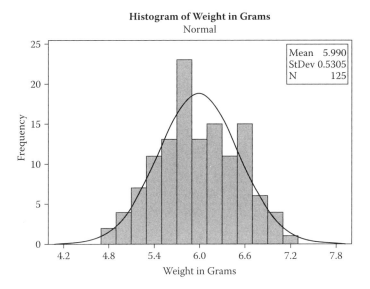

FIGURE 23.5
The data as a histogram showing fails below 5 grams.

setting the target at 5 grams would have meant 50% failures. So a *safety* target was chosen at 6 grams. The company set a product specification of, basically, a minimum of 5 grams—with no real maximum and, as we will discover later, with no reference to the capability of the equipment or the process. Following these limits, at least 90% of the packets would be acceptable. But this meant that we were also overfilling the packets by the same amount—a lot of waste."

SO, WHY BOTHER WITH A PROCESS LIKE SPC?

Richard surveys the room. "It took me a while to get an understanding of how SPC worked. Fortunately, not understanding does not prevent use. We can still use it if we just follow the rules. But one day it just clicked."

"If production follows a 'normal distribution,' then we can expect certain data to appear at an average frequency. With dice, we can expect, or predict, a 3 to appear around once every six throws, for example. But what if we found the dice never landed on a 3? Or what if we got a 3 every couple of throws? It would tell us there is something *not* normal with the dice. It would tell us we might have a problem."

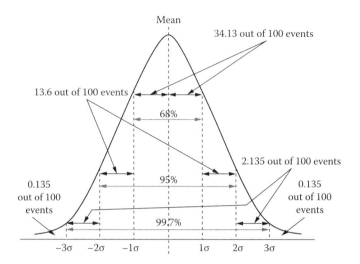

FIGURE 23.6

Number of events within ranges for any 100 data points.

"In a more complicated process, one that follows the bell-curve distribution, we can actually calculate accurate expectations for how data will fall" (Figure 23.6).

"We also know that, although the scale is in sigma units (standard deviations), they relate to real numbers above and below the mean. Now, deciding the likelihood of one number following a previous one, we could just as easily work out some rules for patterns of numbers we would expect *not* to see." (By the way, when I say '*we* can work out,' I don't mean me, but a real mathematician!)

"These patterns became known as the Western Electric Rules. Although I will list them, Minitab® will even do the analysis for you and tell you if there is an abnormal trend. I have explained the logic behind the first few tests as a guide."

1. Any point outside the ±3-sigma control limit: There is only a 0.27% chance in this occurring, since 99.73% fall within ±3 sigma.
2. Nine consecutive points in a row fall on one side of the center line: The logic here is that there is a 50% chance of a point falling on either side of the mean, just as in tossing a coin. The likelihood of nine heads or nine tails in a row is very slim, but not impossible, so it flags a warning.
3. Six points in a row all increasing or decreasing anywhere on the chart: This is the same logic as in item 2, but we would expect the

data points to oscillate above or below the previous point, not all move in one direction.

4. Fourteen points in a row alternating up and down: Again, although we expect an oscillation, such a pattern is abnormal.

5. Two out of three points (on the same side of the mean) fall outside the +2-sigma limit or two out of three points fall outside the −2-sigma limit.

6. Any four out of five points in a row fall outside the +1-sigma limit.

7. Any 15 points in a row lying within ±1 sigma.

8. Eight points in a row outside +1 sigma or −1 sigma. They can be on either side of the mean or split between both sides.

"In SPC (Statistical Process Control), we use control charts like the run chart, but we take a few test samples and calculate an average. It is the 'averaging' part I don't particularly like, but many see it as more realistic. The chart we used is known as an Xbar-R chart" (see Figure 23.7).

"As explained previously, the Xbar chart represents a group of samples, in this case groups of five. The average of the five samples is taken and the value plotted, which is why we see only 25 points on the graph and not 125 as we can see on the run chart at the top of Figure 23.8. My concern is that taking the average smoothes out the variation, so we now have none of the 25 points falling below 5 grams, which we know to be wrong. However, the 'error' is within the quality standard. In the lower graph of Figure 23.8, the Range, we can see that Point 24 has a corresponding point sitting at the mean range of 1.2 grams. We know that some points must be lower, but not how many or by how much. We must also consider the test results as part of our analysis."

"The data is displayed in two diagrams: the top graph being the data distribution about the mean (Xbar) and the range at the bottom (R). The data is sampled in groups of five, and the mean calculated, as is the range (max-min)."

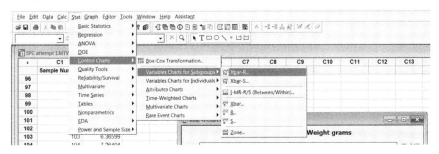

FIGURE 23.7
Selecting an Xbar-R chart.

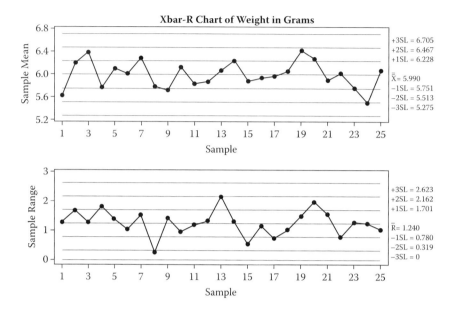

FIGURE 23.8
The Xbar-R chart.

"I like to see all the data on a run chart. Fluctuating data can have an average in the control range while having points out of spec due to the distribution of the range. In short, some of the points can be less than 5 grams, but the average is acceptable."

Richard and Michael know that they need to find out why the fill variation has been so high and then set a reliable target much closer to the required fill levels. So they spend a bit of time discussing problem-solving techniques with the group, focusing on the 5 Whys and the Fishbone diagram. The goal is to find the root causes and not only the symptoms.

The group quickly picks up the 5 Whys, as all this involves is asking why a symptom exists and then repeating the same question for each symptom. Normally, the "whys" will solve most problems. It does not always take five questions, though. It can be fewer or more.

The Fishbone diagram is a bit more complicated (Figure 23.9). The consultants draw the skeleton of a fish on a flip chart, indicating that the problem to be solved is written at the head of the fish and that each bone is headed by a possible cause that is normally grouped under a set of key generic categories, based on the 5 Ms (Man, Machine, Methods, Materials, Measurement). Recently a new term has become popular, "Environment" as it covers the surrounding area and allows for green issues to be considered.

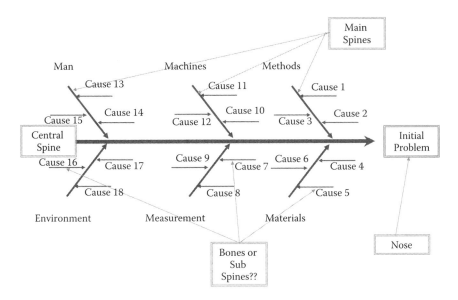

FIGURE 23.9
The Fishbone diagram.

"Although these are the names given for the most common options, we can choose any names that the team might find more relevant to their analysis. But, we would recommend the team sticks to the standard options as it ensures more possible causes are considered," says Richard.

Lucie, Rajiv, and Kevin join Michael and Richard at the front of the group, and they explain together what the next steps will be in solving this problem: "We would like you, during the coming week, probably on Wednesday, to create a Fishbone diagram and use the 5 Whys to see if we can get closer to a cause. Michael will be there to help, but you guys will be doing the hard bit! Before we start, we will need you to agree on a cross-functional team to work on the issue: operators, process engineers, maintenance technicians, and engineers."

"So," asks Mike, "what are the main issues?"

As the group brainstorms and calls them out, Lucie captures them on the flip chart:

- Powder leakage from the packets
- Delayed production due to quality fails
- Downtime of filling equipment for repairs
- Constant adjustment of package weights

- Ongoing adjustments to the glue application and sealing heads on the packets
- Late on production runs—OTIF (On Time and In Full)
- Unhappy customers

Mike continues, "We have a pretty full list of issues. What we don't know is how many are related." So the next step is to discuss Deming and the 80:20 rule, which posits that 80% of the problems are created by 20% of the issues. In Lean, this 20% is known as the *Vital Few*."

"Now," Michael says, "we will all get together again next week to help each other wrestle this sucker to the ground, but in the meantime, each group should work independently to save time. Use the specifications in the equipment manual to find out what the expected accuracy of the filling machine should be—*not* what you are currently getting. We also need to have a look at the recommended maintenance and the expected availability of the machine, particularly its uptime. The technical guys should have access to the manuals. If you don't have any manuals, ask the vendor."

"To determine the machine capability, we need to get a sample measurement of the amount of powder that we put into each packet. The SPC technique we will be using takes 5 consecutive samples from 25 random points across the production run. This gives a total of 125 samples. Weigh them and develop a new control chart. See how it matches the one we have just created."

"Establish the upper and lower control limits. Remember that control limits are not specification limits. The control limits are defined by the process: its natural limits. Specification limits are what we choose the limits to be. They are the quality we decide is best suited for the customer's quality needs. For example, the size of a plastic carrier bag for a supermarket does not need to be accurate to thousandths of an inch. However, the thickness of the plastic must be a minimum size—as it partially determines the weight the bag will carry—but it must not be so thick that it increases the cost."

"The objective is that the control limits fall within the specification limits. Then, as we improve the process, we can reduce the variation in the control limits. This has the effect of improving quality and costs, but we do not *need* to reduce the customer specifications, although this can be advantageous if it reflects the improved quality."

"So, I would like you to add the specification limits and the control limits to the diagrams to see how they compare. I recommend that the members of each team help one another with this. Remember, we are one big team, and we are in this together."

Someone in the group asks, "Are our control limits not the same as our specification limits?" Mike answers the question and then asks her name. He writes it down to ensure that she is included in the analysis team.

"Next, you should play with the Fishbone diagram. We will use the biggest issue, so write the problem as 'leakers in powder filling' at the head of the fish. If you can, gather data to make the problem definition more detailed. This can become part of the definition or be added below the summary in a box. You will find that the more accurate the data, the better. Graphs can also be used to define the problems. Treat the problem statement in such a way that anyone would be able to read and understand it, not just someone who is involved. Having data also shows whether the problem is being resolved."

"Then, brainstorm possible causes and write them on the bones under each of the categories. Keep your work on flip charts, and we will review it together on Wednesday."

"Are we all good with that?" asks Lucie, and she gets a strong affirmative from the team. "Don't be shy in talking to your managers and quality control teams. Asking for help is good and, as you all know, my door is always open for a chat."

Lucie glances at the clock on the wall, "We are finished half an hour early. Go home and enjoy the rest of your day, and thank you for everything. You're the best."

There is actually applause from the team, the best reward anyone could ever expect.

24

Hugh Comes Around?

"Richard, I got a call yesterday from Hugh Greenlees at Ronson & Ronson. Remember his line, 'Don't call us, we'll call you'? Well, he's calling. He's had another bad quarter, and I think his team promised him it wouldn't be. Are you ready to go back in?" asks Hamish.

"Yes I am, Hamish," Richard sighs. "I can't say it would be my first choice of joyous things to do, but I'm ready. Are you coming?"

"I am. I have to come at least for the opening meeting. Can you meet me at 9 a.m. in their office?"

Richard agrees, and they are off! When he arrives, Hamish is already waiting for him in the conference room, but no one else is there.

"Is Hugh joining us?" Richard asks, looking at his watch disapprovingly.

"You would think he would be here, wouldn't you?" Hamish agrees.

They sit down and wait. Fifteen minutes pass. Hamish is clearly a very patient man! Finally the conference room door opens and in walks Bobby Thompson, the plant manager. He looks over at Richard and then he spots Hamish. Bobby looks as if he's frozen in time.

"Mr. McIntyre, sir, I didn't expect to see you here! Is Mr. Greenlees aware you are here?" he says, looking around as if he expects to see Hugh standing in a corner.

"Well, it doesn't look like it, does it?" says Hamish.

"I'll get him, sir," says Bobby, and he darts out the door, only to return one minute later.

"Mr. Greenlees won't be able to join us this morning. I'm afraid he has an important meeting with a supplier. He says I should go ahead with the meeting without him."

"Right," says Hamish. "Here's what I want you to do. Richard is my guy, and when he is here I want you to know that he is representing me, so give him every cooperation. Is that clear?"

"Yes sir!"

"If I hear that he is being blocked *in any way*, I will be back here lickety-split, and nobody will be glad to see me. Is that clear?"

"Yes sir!" Bobby repeats.

"Wait here a moment. I want a word with Richard before I leave."

Hamish and Richard step into the hallway. Hamish's face is scarlet and he is struggling to control his anger. "I'm no virgin at this game," says Hamish, "but even if Greenlees does not respect me, he should certainly respect the position of COO!"

Richard nods his agreement.

"Take no nonsense here, Richard, and update me at the close of the day. You have my complete support!"

And with that he is gone.

Richard walks back into the conference room, where he finds Bobby seated, his face as white as a sheet. "I'm sorry, Richard ... I didn't realize ..."

"It's OK," Richard says softly as he sits next to him. "Bobby, I need you to know that we are in this together. I realize that politicians say that all the time, but you must realize there are problems that need to be fixed, and any help is better than none."

"We have things we need to do, and we will do them. There is no alternative. But, I will need your complete support and that of your staff. In return, I promise you that I will not harm you or any of your people in the process of helping this company—not in any way."

"I also understand that it is possible that you may feel from time to time that, for one reason or another, it might be difficult for you to help me. If that happens, I would ask you to be up front with me and just tell me it's out of your hands. In any such situation, I will simply pass the issue to Hamish so that he can resolve it between Hugh and himself. This is an agreement that already exists between Hamish and me. Are you OK with this?"

Bobby agrees and guarantees his personal support.

"Good. Thanks, Bobby, I really appreciate your help." Without pausing, Richard goes on, "Here's how I'd like us to proceed. I need to know your viewpoint as to why we can't get the 14 trucks out on time for each day's deliveries, what you think the issues are. We can do proper analyses later." Richard thinks for a moment and adds "Then I want to meet with the supervisors and any other staff who have a major impact on this issue or are affected by it. We have the option of speaking to them one by one or in groups, depending on how many there are. The goal is to find out their thoughts. To be honest, I prefer a single group meeting, but Hugh has created a combative environment, and I worry that a group might not work at this moment in time. Whatever we decide—and I say *we* deliberately, as I hope to include you all the way—will work."

"Don't prompt them in advance other than to ask them to be open. If we channel them down any particular route, we could miss a key piece of information, so let's just let them flow. When we have everyone's thoughts, I will consolidate them without attributing them to any one individual. Then it will probably be the best time for the group meeting. At that point we will discuss the possibilities for change. We will also try and get a feel for where we may be losing time and whether 14 trucks in 24 hours is realistic. A value stream map will help."

Bobby looks as if he has a question.

"Sorry, Bobby, a value stream map simply looks at how long the actual tasks should take—the 'touch' time. Normally when we do a task, we include all the delays and problems in the measured time. It might take 5 minutes to load a pallet, but if you check, the real time might be 15 minutes because we have to wait for a forklift or get a confirmation on the quantity of items. Once we know the touch times—the steps that add value to the process—we can evaluate if the target of 14 trucks is possible. If it is, then all we need to do is eliminate all the wasted time."

"Surely it is not that easy?" Bobby asks.

"It can be, sometimes, but we need to know what all the problems are first and then solve them. As well as the interviews, I will also make time to be on the floor conducting observations. These can be added to the pot of points from the meetings, and we will discuss them as a group. Once we have as much information as possible, we will determine solutions that we can all support. When we have a master plan, I'll kick it up to Hamish, and he will share it with Hugh."

Richard sees that Bobby looks a bit concerned, so he puts his pen down and says in reassurance, "I have no intention of creating any problems between you and Hugh, so during all of this, it's perfectly OK for you to share any information with Hugh as you see fit. It is not our intention to disrupt the chain of command or exclude anyone. All I ask is that you honor your word to continue your support of this initiative, and I will keep my word."

And, with this, they arrange the interview process, which along with the observations, will be completed within the week.

The interviews turn out to be very interesting. Richard and Michael shape the questions to the situation and to the individual. As they proceed, they create a high-level map of the sequence of events on the wall. Where there is a difference in the process, it is added as a parallel step, as if it was an option. They want to find out if there is a process and where the problems might arise. The other purpose, as mentioned, was a basic value stream map, so they could get an idea how much time is lost during the loading process. It also gives them a chance to run through some other options using SMED (single-minute exchange of die) techniques as well as Lean and the Theory of Constraints.

To enable the observations on the floor, the interviews are carried out sometimes by Mike or Richard or sometimes both of them. The interviews are never an interrogation, just a chat. The consultants stick to the same core questions, fitting them into the flow of the conversation. These include a lot of open questions like

- How do you know what to do first?
- Who gives you the information you need to do your job?
- When do you get it?
- Do you have enough time to react?
- What stops you doing what you need to do?
- What other problems do you find?
- How often do you have the same problems?
- How much time does it take to resolve each problem?
- What would you do different?
- If you had a magic wand, how would you change things?
- What do you think of that?

The goal is to encourage free-flowing conversation and gather information. When they hear something they want to verify, they ask confirmation questions, like "I think what I heard you say is ___. Is that correct?"

They take notes. Michael likes detail; Richard prefers minimum notes—key words or phrases to trigger his memory. (You should do what suits you best. There is no point in your having a list of key words if you can't remember what was meant.)

The consultants explain the informal function of the map, and any corrections are listed as options, since the objective is to find the best way. At the end of each meeting, they write the expanded summary in detail, always making sure that the notes are immediately available to all on request, no secrets.

The folks that they interview range from the plant manager to the shift supervisors, to the support staff, to the hourly employees and the truck drivers. They also talk to customers under the guise of making general improvements.

After three days of interviews, they transfer the issues to sticky notes and consolidate their findings on Affinity Diagrams. The first cut of this looks as follows:

- There is no difference between a "good" day and a "bad" day.
- A good day is when the customer complains least.
- A good day is lots of orders going out.
- Trucks are held up for hours on end, and drivers just sit around waiting.
- The main driveway through the warehouse is always blocked with trucks.
- There's lots of waiting for overhead cranes.
- Forklift truck batteries run out, and we have to wait for recharge.
- Trucks delivering new materials to replenish our stock clog up the driveway.
- There are lots of drivers arriving in their own pickup trucks at random for orders.
- Our customers are upset, and no wonder: They wait for hours.
- We count the number of individual picks and end-customer orders as an efficiency measure.
- Some picks are hardly worth the effort, "one length of 3/8-in. steel rod, for example. There's no money in that."
- We can't get the right picks onto the flatbed truck that will be delivering them to specific routes or customers. The truck could be waiting outside due to the gridlock.
- We work three shifts, and on nights we simply stage orders close to the driveway.
- Plate product for the burners (raw materials) takes up a huge amount of space.
- Finished plate (product) from the burners takes up a huge amount of space.
- We never see the foremen or managers.
- When the Lexington plant closed, the work was simply dropped into this one—no thought, no reengineering.
- We need another driveway built at the far end of the building.

- We need new driveways to supplement the one in the middle.
- Sometimes loaded trucks don't get out until the next day.
- Sometimes partly loaded trucks have to be sent out minus a few customers loads.
- We are doing a maximum of 9 trucks a day, but the expectation is 14.
- "I'm a customer and have been for years, but I'm looking elsewhere for a new supplier."
- "I need my order on time, not the day after or three days from now."
- "There's no incentive for me to work harder."

The consultants validate information from the interviews on the shop floor over the 24-hour period and over the three shifts. They sort through the practicality of suggestions and show groups the consolidated information and seek new ideas. They identify the constraints to throughput and work on a hypothesis to determine the merits of various solutions. And finally they develop a trial solution to run past the team. Then it is time to speak to Hamish.

25

Ronson & Ronson Metal Distribution 3

The work of consolidation and brainstorming solutions had been relatively easy. Michael and Richard ironed out most major differences with individual supervisors and managers during the interviews. At the least, they had their agreement to try and make the process work.

Hugh is still being obstructive. In private, he will disagree with virtually anything. "Why ask my opinion?" he would snipe. "You're just going to ignore me, anyway!" Not true: They would always try to include him. But he was right to an extent; they did work around him when needed. They were not being devious, as they had often discussed the need for urgency. Hugh was "nicer" to them in public, but the consultants were pretty sure that he ran them down a fair bit when they were not present. So far, though, their progress is looking pretty good, albeit a bit strained at times.

Changing culture is not like flicking a switch. Change is one of the hardest things for people to do. Proper culture change can take years of effort. Richard has found that the best way to get folks to feel more comfortable with change is not to make them leave their comfort zones, but to expand them slowly to include the new actions that are needed while phasing out the unneeded ones as quickly as possible. But time is not a luxury that Michael and Richard can afford. The burning platform has defined their timescales, and they have to adapt their preferred procedures. Everyone has to change.

One particularly hard-nosed shift manager has tried to block the process and has been totally disrespectful and openly uncooperative during all interviews. If one of the consultants meets him on the floor and asks for confirmation of an issue, he just growls "Rubbish!" and storms away. Usually he does his best to avoid them. Richard once tried to approach him during a lunch break, and the manager complained that the consultant was violating his right to have a work-free lunch break. This is quite unusual behavior. In the course of his professional career, Richard cannot recall another instance where someone has flatly refused to discuss an issue when needed.

It is also the only project where he has been asked by a manager to report fewer issues than were actually found. The request caught him off guard, but he rejected it because it helped no one—except, maybe, the difficult manager, who also seemed to be giving extra work to the folks the consultants wanted to talk to, as if trying to keep them away from the outsiders.

Michael has followed the usual steps, trying to understand the issues, discussing them, and then resolving them one at a time and, to be fair, he has made some progress. But this manager is causing real problems for the consultants due to his position in the company. It is not easy to work around him, and he undoes or simply ignores the new procedures whenever he comes back on shift.

Mike and Richard discuss the problem and decide that the best option is to be more direct. With the time constraints, they simply cannot afford the delay it would take to win him over, particularly when they believe that he is following Hugh's lead and acting in the belief that he is "protected." When they ask the plant manager, Bobby Thompson, for his input, he is reluctant to take a direct stand against Hugh, although he does imply that the issues they have been discussing might achieve the desired result. Mike and Richard flip a coin to see who will play bad cop. Richard loses.

So, Richard invites the recalcitrant shift manager to a meeting and gives him one last chance to willingly work with the consultants. He is uncompromising in his refusal. Richard then invites the human resources (HR) manager to join the meeting, after which he opens the red folder on the table and removes a document—a copy of the company's disciplinary procedure. He had already highlighted the section on not following procedures. He further enlightens the manager by letting him know that his behavior is perfectly fine—as long as he does not expect to continue working here with his disruptive actions!

His response is another visit to Hugh. When he returns, fully recharged and adamant that he will not be making any "undesirable" changes, Richard and the HR manager give him a verbal warning.

"We'll see what Hugh has to say about that!" says the manager defiantly, finally using his get-out-of-jail-free card.

"Would you like me to get you a written confirmation of this warning?" Richard asks. Not waiting for a reply, he continues, "I will even let you choose who signs it. You have two choices: either Hamish McIntyre, Hugh's boss and the COO of the corporation you work for, or Jeff Lincoln, the top man in the organization."

The shift manager freezes, like a rabbit in a car's headlights. He seems surprised as he finally realizes that Hugh is not in absolute command—that he is not in a position to protect him. He backtracks a bit, stumbling for words as his courage slips away. The resistance is over.

Richard ends the meeting. "We have gone to a lot of trouble trying to get your support for this project. Your skills have been recognized, and we do want you to work with us." He pauses, "But, I think you should take a bit of time and think about what we have discussed. As a company, we must improve or be shut down, and I would like you to decide if you want to be a part of that."

Richard makes one final appointment for the next day. He wants the shift manager to settle down, think about things, and come to the party intending to make it successful.

Michael and Richard often debate command-and-control management versus empowerment and persuasion. But both agree that there are times to tread softly and there are times to carry a big stick. Knowing the difference is important. A deadline to achieve a goal or be sold off drastically limits your options. But, so does a manager who openly resists and refuses to follow new processes that have been agreed upon. Having both situations at once is totally unacceptable.

THE PROBLEMS

The improvement group meetings are with cross-functional teams, largely made up of hourly employees and supervisors. Bobby Thomson, the plant manager, is ever present. Richard has grown to like Bobby, who has become a key contributor.

Where necessary, Richard and Michael confirm their assumptions through observation and further study. They develop trial solutions and bounce them around the different teams. The final proposed solution usually has various subelements. Naturally, short-interval control has been implemented at all important stages, particularly on throughput, so that the consultants can monitor and ensure progress.

The entire initiative is designed to ensure achievement of the company's new definition of success, which can now be measured and stated as "14 trucks being fully loaded and on the road by 12 noon." This focus creates the definition of a good day; anything less is now officially seen as a bad day. Every manager, supervisor, and hourly employee must buy into this definition.

The main issues are

- *Pay for performance*: The bonus element of everyone's wages will be redefined, enhanced, and fully dependent on meeting the 14 trucks, in full with no errors, each day. (It is important to ensure that the bonus does not conflict with any other duties that need to be performed. For example, time allocated for improvement teams could be seen as detrimental to productivity and so be avoided by managers whose bonus is based only on productivity. It is best to avoid having an option of doing the wrong thing just because it pays better. So, part of the managers' bonus is linked to the successful implementation of positive improvement in procedures and performance.)
- *Installation of essential equipment updates*: These were to be installed immediately, an example being the purchase of additional batteries and chargers for the forklifts.
- *Accountability for individual work shifts*: Foremen will be responsible and accountable for the targeted throughput of their shifts. Previously, what responsibility there might have been just flowed on to the next shift, which either caught up or didn't.
- *Better coordination between shipping, stores, preloading, and truck scheduling.*
- *Better planning of delivery routes*: The delivery routes will be planned well in advance to enable the materials to be fully organized and synchronized with the order of loading. A truck is not allowed (scheduled) to drive to a loading bay unless it can be fully loaded. Otherwise, it will not be scheduled.
  - Customer orders will be checked before picking. If found to have missing materials (out of stock), they will be scheduled for later shifts. The logic is simple: Trucks will *not* be held up "waiting" for materials.
  - Where missing parts can be sourced, organizing for loading on a later shift gives the company time to get the stock from its suppliers and avoid the loading line being held up, thereby blocking throughput.

- Unless a missing part cannot be delivered to the company in time, and the customer agrees to accept a partial order, nothing goes out incomplete.
  - Out-of-stock items will be flagged as soon as identified.
  - Out-of-stock materials will be reviewed for minimum (and maximum) stock levels.
  - Sales/warehousing communications will be improved to establish processes to confirm reliability of stock availability before committing to a loading schedule.
- *Staging of outgoing materials in the correct bays*: Allocating bays in defined areas to be preloaded with materials for specific trucks (as scheduled) will avoid the wasted time needed to search for materials or move materials stored on top of allocated items while a truck sits idle and "waiting."
- *Efficient storage of bulky items*: Where possible, sheet metal will be stored vertically, like toast in a rack. This enables faster picking and eliminates the need to move materials from above to gain access and then return them, freeing up crane time. New racks will be bought or made internally.
- *Efficient scheduling of incoming materials for restocking the product lines*: Where possible, incoming materials are to be scheduled into specific time slots and not be allowed to block the main driveway through the warehouse.
- *Coordination of immediate delivery in the case of shortfall materials*: Ensure proper information flow between the loading scheduler and purchasing to allocate access to the driveway for the relevant delivery vehicle.
- *Introduction of new drive-through routes and collection bays*: These are to be linked to reorganization of the factory floor layout.
- *Redesign of the building*: This will be introduced as quickly as possible by adding initially temporary, and then permanent, drive-through routes. This includes the possibility of adding low-cost, static loading bays around the warehouse. Both of these improvements will prove to be a bonus, as they will allow for long-term expansion.
- *Accommodation of small-order pickup trucks (customers' own vehicles)*: These customers will be diverted to and served through a metals supermarket-type outlet attached to the end of the main warehouse with its own loading bay, staff, and pricing structure for small orders.

- *Other production considerations*:
  - Need to eliminate delays from the plate-cutting department.
  - The problem of delays during loading and discharge with the flat-roll equipment has been wrongly diagnosed to be at the loading end. The problem causing the bottleneck is at the output.
  - Storage areas must be established for the raw materials and product output from the plate burners. The company's main assets are time- and space-limited. This limitation can be addressed by temporarily storing finished plate, prior to shipment, on flat beds in the yard.

A NEW CULTURE

In addition to the previous list, the final element is contingent on the short-interval control plans that Richard and Michael have developed to identify, prioritize, and eliminate any and all other reasons for throughput targets being missed, as measured by each shift, as they strive to achieve their expected throughput of loaded trucks.

The new expectations are for a three-shift loading schedule:

1. The afternoon shift to load five trucks before the commencement of night shift.
2. The night shift will then complete an additional five trucks and catch up on any shortfalls from the afternoon.
3. The following day shift will load the final four trucks and ensure the day's load of 14 trucks are on the road by 12 noon or earlier.

Michael and Richard are initially worried that a shift might stop working when five trucks were loaded and not help their partners on the next shift by loading a sixth truck, but they figure that self-limiting targets are not a real worry at the moment—but it would have been a nice problem to have!

All they did was simply use a technique from project management: break up a big task into more-manageable sections. This was better than waiting to the end and finding out how many trucks finally made it, as was the current way. So now they have three well-defined smaller targets. This enables individual teams to be responsible for their own workload and yet still be a part of the overall process.

To ensure that all of this actually works requires the agreement of all concerned, from the operators to the senior management, willing or not. The overall approach must achieve this. First, through the use of the high-level value stream map, the actual touch time shows that the "target" of 14 trucks is possible—if most of the delays are eliminated. The belief has to become that the *causes* of the delays are avoidable and are not simply an essential part of the process that have to be accepted. Once the feasibility of the target is understood, everyone has to accept that the 14 trucks per day are a must—not an option—and that the method to achieve this starts with the elimination of the current bottlenecks.

Under normal circumstances, Michael and Richard would approach an improvement program with a more detailed analysis of the issues and the biggest issues prioritized first. In this case, there is a major guiding issue where a number of individual "component" issues all contribute to poor operation. Thus, they still must tackle the obvious big issues first while keeping an eye open for the hidden problems. Normally these will pop up as daily issues or repeat problems, and root cause analysis will enable the problem to be properly identified and resolved.

Why does this process work? Well, because it opens the door to success, and people really do want to be a part of a successful operation. So the consultants involve the employees in finding the solutions and teach them any skills they might need for success. With many issues requiring only basic new skills and a bit of practice, it is a simple concept, but it requires time, commitment, and extra effort to get up and running before the fruits can be enjoyed.

The expectation that any shortfall from one shift to the other must be made up by the incoming shifts and the final deadline being set at midday in the 24-hour period is a powerful motivator, driving high levels of accountability, peer pressure, and teamwork. Any shortfalls on any shift will be seen as letting the entire team down. It all comes back to the simple truth that everyone wants to do a good job, and no one wants to be seen as failing.

At the close of each shift, the outgoing shift supervisor meets with the incoming supervisor and the plant manager to report the actual status against the targets. Any shortfall in this targeted/planned number will immediately flag a cause to be identified and a root cause solution to be found and scheduled for implementation.

It does sound as if a never-ending list of issues is created. However, many of them will have a common root cause, and one solution will eliminate many of them at a stroke. Plus, of course, the 80:20 rule will still play a major part in the results.

To ensure that the process is truly grounded and embedded, either Mike or Richard attend these shift-handover meetings for a while, and they adopt the standard "morning meeting" process as used at Next Automotive, where the two key questions asked daily are

- Why did we not make the targets?
- What are we going to do to ensure it doesn't happen again tomorrow?

To ensure that any shortfall in performance cannot simply be ignored, a written record of the reasons for the shortfall must be recorded along with the actions that will be taken to eliminate it.

Just as at Next Automotive, responsibilities and deadlines will be allocated to specific people. This is known as a W^3. It reminds us we need to define "Who" will carry out the task; "What" the task entails; and, importantly, "When" the task will be completed. The goal, as ever, is a fix within an agreed time span, bearing in mind that the consultants define (an ambitious) three days as a lifetime in a production environment!

Any signs of resistance are handled at a one-to-one level, with the primary goals being understanding and buy-in, just as they promised Bobby, the plant manager. Fortunately, the reality of the burning platform did mean that resistance was less than expected. Add to this the high levels of accountability in finding solutions, and Michael and Richard saw almost immediate improvement.

Around four weeks after this process had been installed, Richard attends a business meeting at corporate. It includes every general manager, vice president, and president in the group. The meeting is interrupted to accommodate Hugh, who leaves to take a call. The others take the opportunity to have a quick coffee.

Hugh comes back into the room after taking the call, grinning like a Cheshire cat. "I've just had some good news," he interrupts. "I would like to take the opportunity to let you all know that, for the first time ever, *my* boys have loaded all 14 trucks, with all customers' orders complete." He openly radiates *his* success, taking full credit for himself and his people. Richard says nothing, looking toward Hamish, who gives him a smile and a wink. It is imperative for the consultants to remember that there is no need to take personal credit for success; after all, it's simply their job. But it does feel good, nevertheless.

Ronson & Ronson went on to success after success due to the power of momentum and the increasing use of the short-interval control mechanism. The mapping exercises highlighted all sorts of potential improvements, so the success was duplicated in other departments: sales and inventory control as well as across all aspects of operations. With high levels of transparency and accountability, Michael and Richard picked off the bottlenecks one after the other—like targets in a fairground sideshow.

The marketing of the small-order users' department did more than just clear a physical limitation caused by the customers' pickup trucks blocking the driveway. Solving the problem led to a new business segment serving the small-to-medium business user. The previous underpricing of small-scale orders was corrected to be more in line with other metals supermarkets, although still bargain basement from the customers' perspective. This easy access for the small-order customers attracted more business, and it became a profit center in its own right, boosting the business's overall margins. Now everything, including the sale of a single length of 3/8-inch diameter steel rod, was profitable!

As throughput increased, profit went up and inventory turns improved. The sales force was also finding it much easier to meet and even exceed their targets. The question was now becoming "How many trucks are possible?"

Hamish was delighted with the continued progress. He had even noted that Hugh's resistance was reducing. Indeed, he once updated Richard on a recent progress meeting he had with the four presidents at corporate. Everyone around the table was positive about the progress, and when it came to Hugh's turn to report, he had a list of successes. At the close of the meeting, during Jeff Lincoln's routine round-the-table session, Hugh commented, "I have to give the devil his due!" admitting, loosely, that the consultants have actually helped.

26

Corporate Update

Michael and Richard have been on the job now for three months, and a lot has been achieved. Clear gains have already been made in most sites, but if they walked away today, a lot of those gains would simply drain away. It's time for a heart-to-heart with Hamish, which brings them to where they are today, sitting in his office.

"Good morning, gentlemen. It's always nice to see you. What's on your mind today?"

Richard responds, "Good morning, Hamish, nice to see you. It's time we updated you on our progress and discussed ongoing plans into the future."

"Our minds are working in sync. I was just thinking the same thing," says Hamish. "I think our progress is good so far, and although I've been involved and supportive, it seems to me that you two have been driving the bulk of the project. I greatly appreciate that, as you have been a great catalyst and have driven real change. You have made great friends in the company and, if you don't mind me saying so—Richard—you have also made the occasional enemy ... as we know, you can be more than a bit *direct* at times!"

"I'm sorry about that, Hamish. I guess we are like politicians: People just take sides based on their expectations of our purpose. They can be either for or against us. Personally, I never mean to be aggressive, and yet I know that from time to time I come across that way. When I am giving a team working talks, I explain that certain behaviors lie dormant in our subconscious; then, at the most unexpected time, something triggers us. A bell rings and Pavlov's dog salivates."

"Are you telling me you're broken, Richard, and that you have deep psychological problems?" Hamish is only half kidding.

"Are we not all a bit broken, Hamish?" Richard uses his best intellectual accent and laughs.

"I'm not sure where this is going," says Hamish.

"Well, it's time to talk about culture and behaviors," Richard says. "As usual, though, I might be getting ahead of myself, and God knows I do like to tell stories. But our efforts are also meant to create a culture of improvement, based on the Lean methodology of customer needs, quality, and perfection."

Richard continues, "If you two fine gentlemen can show a little patience and indulge me, there might be something valuable that comes out of this discussion for all of us."

Now Hamish sits back, too, looking a bit more amused than perplexed.

"Stop me if I start to ramble," Richard says. "You have probably noticed that I tend to use myself as the example in situations that otherwise might seem hypothetical. Interestingly, I do it to avoid offending others by them not thinking I'm talking about them. My plan is that there might be something in the story somewhere that shines a light on the current situation and is relevant enough to make a positive change."

"OK then, recognizing that we are all a bit broken one way or another, I believe we have deep-seated roots and behavior patterns that have a major impact on what we do. Using myself as the example, I want to talk about general management culture and behavior for a little bit before going into the business update."

"Perhaps the reason I seem a bit pushy for a consultant is that, for more than half of my working life, I was running companies. I'm used to command and control—as Michael calls it; I'm used to being the boss."

Hamish interrupts, "Yes Richard, that might well be true, but we pay you to act as a consultant and advise us. The management decisions are ours and not yours—as is telling our employees what to do without our consent."

"Hmm ... Sometimes, Hamish, we have disconnects in our understanding. I know some consultants report out and give advice and, of course, we do that. Primarily, though, my understanding was that you hired us for results first and reports second. I don't see how we can do that without telling employees what to do at times. However, any time we face a serious issue, we involve your management and human resources in those issues. I guess I assumed that when you said we had your complete support, that meant we had your consent."

"Sorry, Hamish, but I was trying to explain my behavior." Richard looks at Hamish and waits before carrying on. Hamish nods, and Richard continues. "I used to be an 'old style' manager. The kind Lean—well, pretty much every improvement methodology—now criticizes. Initially I could be very aggressive. I used the management and process tools I had learned, but also used sheer willpower to drive the results. Retrospectively, I'm not ashamed of how I used to manage. It was how I was taught and, at the time, I thought it was the right way. You can't knock success and, yes, it definitely got results. Which brings us back to Pavlov's dog: People tend to repeat behaviors that work for them."

"For me, as time passed, I found myself constantly in unstable business situations, and my mandate was to stabilize and then improve them. I always did. My work took me all over the world. I witnessed poverty in Asia, South America, and Africa. At times, it was heartbreaking. It has an impact on a person, changes them, softens them."

"When I first met Lean, I didn't really believe the softly-softly treatment of employees would work, but I allowed the consultants to apply it. Over time, I saw it working. I absolutely know now that achieving all of the expected business targets is just as easy through applying kindness and decency as it is through a hard-nosed, unbending business approach."

"I learned in Africa that the mandate can be to shut a company down and still have the people support you through a six-month business wind-down that takes away everyone's jobs. It all depends on how you do it."

Hamish beats Richard to the punch line. "So, if all that was leading to the fact that we have to change our culture, what do you think we need to change here? How do we shape our behavior to get better results in this competitive world?"

Richard responds, "Not everyone will agree with these points, so I will try to argue both sides where possible. But here are a few useful maxims that have worked for me. I will write them down and we can discuss them. They might serve as useful lists" (Tables 26.1 and 26.2).

They talk their way through these points, and it's a good conversation. Finally Hamish asks Richard the big question: "So how do you think I am doing as a leader?"

"Well, Hamish, you're doing pretty well. You have accepted the assistance of consultants you never asked for with an open heart and mind and, believe me, it's not every senior executive who could do that. You are highly visible to your team, and they respect you. That doesn't happen by accident. You allow your division presidents to run their businesses."

"All right, Richard, now tell me the bad news."

"Well, out of your four division presidents, one is an absolute outrage; another has allowed her business to run out of control to the point that it's

TABLE 26.1

Business Guidance on Culture

Make sure the company's strategic goals are met.	Easier said than done.
	Improvements should be in line with the company's goals, so think long term and not just short term.
	Operational and functional issues are not the only ones that need to be fixed.
Respect the organizational structure and chain of command.	This comes down to micromanaging. Structures exist to delegate responsibilities.
	Manage your people and let each tier in the organization's structure do the same. This will create a steel interlinked chain of responsibility and accountability.
Ensure that the responsible people are held accountable for their results.	If someone is unable to do their job, retrain or move them to more suitable position.
	A bad situation left alone invariably gets worse.
Ensure high visibility of the management at every level.	Doors and offices can be barriers; get them out from behind their desks.
	Have them visit the Gemba (where the work is done). Speak to folks; find out their issues firsthand.
Recognize that two or more minds working in harmony will always create superior solutions.	Teams work better than people—but use teams wisely.
	Work within the resources of the company. It helps no one if the team is too busy to meet.
Make sure your team works as a team and that the right people are on the bus.	Always consider who you should involve in resolving business issues. Most folks like to be involved, so involve the right people if you want their commitment.
	If you discover that someone does not want to participate, you can try gentle persuasion or training to allay any fears they might have. However, if they still refuse to contribute, replace them with someone who will.
Recognize performance directly and publicly; be sincere.	Never be afraid to praise, but don't praise bad performance just because you feel you need to.
Pay for performance.	This is a really tricky one. It can backfire.
	If you "pay" for achieving numbers, you might get the numbers and lose quality, for example. Beware of the negative side of targets.
	Many folks are not motivated by money. So find out what they like and give it: a meal with the team or their families, theater tickets, public recognition, a bottle of champagne—even a free breakfast or a certificate of achievement.
	Never make a performance payment to someone who does not deserve it. It undermines the reward.

TABLE 26.2

Personal Behavioral Traits

Be confident.	Confidence is addictive and contagious.
Don't be afraid to be human.	We feel as managers that we must be aloof to a situation.
	Don't hide your thoughts and feelings; but try to keep the positive emotions to the fore.
	Underreact rather than overreact—easier said than done.
	There is enough separation between the leaders and the led. The folks think we live in an ivory tower, so get out of it and spend real time with your people.
Know your people's names.	If you have a poor memory, use name tags or ID badges.
If someone else's idea will work as well as yours, then use the other person's idea and give them the credit.	
Have a real open door, one that people can and will walk through.	
Always be open to new ideas.	
Admit when you are wrong and apologize.	Know what's important and know when to give.
Prioritize your work load.	Work on the most important thing first.
Always do what's right, not what's expedient.	

behind the times; another was sitting on the fence but is coming around quickly; and, praise be to God, you have one really good one."

"Try to be direct, Richard!" Hamish says sarcastically. "Please don't sugarcoat anything; I want to hear your comments warts and all."

They laugh, but Hamish looks a little unsettled. Richard says, "The good news is that you're the man for this, and you can fix it!"

"Let's get a coffee," offers Hamish. "Then we'll do the business reviews and discuss next steps for our strategy meeting with the four presidents and the other executives."

After the coffee, Michael takes center stage, which seems to come as a great relief to Hamish. "First a review of the target and the high-level stuff, then each individual business and their progress to date, then the upcoming strategy meeting with the division presidents and exec team. Then we go forward. OK Hamish?"

"Go for it, Michael."

Mike begins, "The overall target and plan is straightforward. We have to make $36 million in EBIT, and we were making only $9 million. The deadline is the fourth quarter of this fiscal year. Currently, our best chance to achieve this improvement looks like it comes from three distinct avenues we have been pursuing so far."

1. Reduce corporate overhead by 25% from $24 million to $18 million. This will fall straight to the bottom line for a gain of $6 million in EBIT.
2. Increase sales by $10 million, which at the new run rate will equal 12% profit on additional sales of $120 million. However, selling an additional $120 million per year across the company without adding back any selling, general, and administrative expenses (SG&A) corporate overhead will be difficult.
3. Improve productivity in the divisions; move from a current total profit of $9 million to $20 million for an $11 million gain in EBIT.

Michael moves to the flip charts and opens a mini spreadsheet (Table 26.3). "A point to note is that if we achieve a 12% profit margin, then our profit on next year's sales of $300 million will be the required $36 million. Also, if we achieve a 10% productivity improvement, we stand to save $30 million, which will overshoot our target by $18.9 million."

TABLE 26.3

Summary of the Major Savings Planned

New Target Profit Calculation	Sales ($M)	Original EBIT ($M)	Target EBIT ($M)	Amount	Cumulative Shortfall ($M)
Original sales data for all Divisions	**$300.0**	$8.9	**$36.0**		−$27.1
Profit (%) of turnover		3%	12%		
Corporation allocation reduction				$6.0	−$21.1
New sales requirement (as profit)				$10.0	−**$11.1**
Amended total sales for $10 million profit at 12%					
Increased sales amount needed to achieve profit increase	$120.0				
Total estimated sales, including new	**$420.0**				
Productivity savings @ 10% of $300 million				$30.0	**$18.9**

"We recognize that none of this is easy, and yet we also know that this is a mandate from the board of directors and shareholders of the company. It is acceptable to the board if this mix changes at the final count, and these things normally do."

"Moving on to the individual companies, each key point is explained on a slide."

Ronson & Ronson Metals processing and distribution had a preproject EBIT of 2%, and we plan to get them to $4 million. The primary methods are to increase throughput of loaded trucks from 8 to 14.

- This has already been achieved through utilization of a combination of the Theory of Constraints and short-interval reporting, with emphasis on a high level of accountability. Three daily meetings are held, based on our plan to achieve the targets for throughput.
- The target was achieved within four weeks of installing these new methods and is currently being hit 80% of the time, so we are halfway there. We need to make time to further implement the improvements.
  - If we can do 80%, we can do 100%. We have carried out an in-depth analysis of the process and have found a number of areas of waste.
  - Many are due to looking for and accessing stock, but some are due to waiting for support—cranes are a big issue. We believe that some changes in factory layout—Lean calls it 5S—and some different storage methods will help.
  - Waiting for cranes is trickier, as there are a limited number of them. It is a constraint. However, we believe that we can open up some parallel systems to support cranes: Increased use of the forklifts has helped since buying the new batteries. Other remedies include different storage techniques to reduce the number of lifts, different organization and location of loading bays, and alternative internal transport flows. These all reduce the pressure. There might be some need for new equipment and racking, but we believe we have the capability in-house to make much of what we need.
  - Finally, the mapping has highlighted some areas that were not considered to be problems. We can fit them into our improvement plan. The morning meetings will keep the pressure up on real-time problems.
  - Finding all these issues is a blessing and a curse. We have to take care to control the resources, as deliveries must take priority, but

we also must solve the problems if we want to get better—and we will need ongoing follow up.

- There will probably be a need for continued overtime, but this has always been high due to late deliveries.
- The poor performance in the flat-roll division of the business has been quantified.
- Using the simple OEE (Overall Equipment Efficiency) calculation shows that we make only 40% of the amount that could be made on a "perfect" production line with no losses.
- We know that there will be losses due to setups, changeovers, and maintenance, to mention only a few expected losses. But in a world-class operation, this would only be around 15%. So the gap of 45% is due to losses that should be able to be removed, such as unplanned breakdowns, poor setups, and any number of other delays.
- One constraint we have found and already fixed has increased throughput by 40%. This does not mean that we have gone to 40% + 40%, but we now make 40% more product than we were making. We have now gone from 40% to 56% OEE.
- The problem was an error in fault diagnosis. We were fixing a calibration problem at the feed side of the machine input when the error was being created at the output side—the unloading operation.
- James Whitburn, night-shift leader, had the excellent idea of separating small orders from bulk-delivery loading. This evolved to a plan adding a metals supermarket to the end of the existing warehouse.
  - This involved a lot of input from the sales and marketing teams to establish viability and a bit of development money for new loading access and a sales counter. It also took some juggling of staff to enable it to run as an entity on its own.
  - This has increased our market segmentation. We can now compete with pricing for smaller purchases.
  - We found the space by improving throughput plus improving the flow and storage in the plate-burning department, which we will talk about next.
  - As mentioned previously, the metals supermarket allows us to get better margins from our smaller customers, bringing it in line with anyone else in our industry who services the small customers. This idea is proving to be highly profitable.

- It has also eliminated the constraint of small customers' pickup trucks blocking the main drive and becoming a constraint for the main truck throughput: The loss was estimated at 90 minutes each day.
- Lastly, once again, through following basic 5S and the Theory of Constraints, we changed the workflow through the plate department. We had been stuck in the mode of thinking that *this is the way things have always been done around here*, and so finding the constraints one at a time, we eliminated them. As all we really have to play with in this department is time and space, we created more space.
  - The first issue was obvious: the time spent finding and handling materials. This has been common across the site.
  - Starting at the input and storage end of the pre-processed plate areas, we created racks where sheets could be stood up on edge (kind of like books in a library) as opposed to lying flat in bays, separated vertically by blocks of wood.
  - A secondary benefit was increased storage capacity.
  - We have also introduced a couple of rack systems for bigger quantities of material. The racks are designed for forklift access. They work like wood separators, except we don't need to lift the stuff off the top, move it, get the material, and move the stuff back. And we can identify the rack space by customer, avoiding the need to search piles of materials.
  - We can consider automated racking later if the return justifies the outlay.
  - Another advantage is that we can easily access the plate we need for the next order and get it onto the burners in one lift, ready to be loaded, thereby avoiding waiting time.
  - This simple Kanban system eliminates the previous downtime between finishing the run and starting the next run.
  - We did have to work with scheduling to ensure that the operators were never waiting to find out what to run next. That single issue could take 15 minutes to decide. With all the associated downtime to find and deliver the materials, it could cost as much as 45 minutes of lost production time—each and every time!
  - Now we maintain a list of the next three orders.
  - For common sizes, we can allocate storage space by the size and thickness, which again avoids the need to dig through piles of steel to get to the size we need—a process that can take many lifts.

- Next, we moved to the out-feed end of the burners and again increased space through offloading the burners onto flatbeds and storing them under tarpaulins in the yard prior to shipment.
- Where shipping is imminent, it can now be transferred directly to the allocated shipping bay. As well as creating internal space, the flatbeds eliminated double handling at the output side.

"A combination of these factors is expected to more than double the current 2% EBIT performance and open throughput for increased sales from existing and new customers."

Michael having finished his presentation, Richard now steps to the fore. Regarding personnel, Michael and Richard found that Bobby Thompson, the plant manager, proved to be totally committed to and supportive of the change processes. His guidance in team selection and his overall involvement at all times was exemplary. Jesus Armesto designed the racking systems, and the company's own engineers built them over a couple of weekends.

"Now, I guess we need to discuss Hugh." Richard looks directly at Hamish. "I have already discussed this content with Hugh and the need for it to be a part of my report. Believe me when I say that it gives me no pleasure. We have tried to involve Hugh at every stage and, if anything, all of the results we have made so far have been achieved despite his actions."

Richard looks down and to the right. Hamish recognizes this as him thinking. Richard bites his bottom lip and redirects his gaze at the COO. "Hamish, I think we have done really well with Ronson, but I can't help wondering what we could have achieved if the president of the company had been an active supporter, as have the others in their companies."

"Hugh has attended none of our meetings and, if he has shown any support, it has been invisible to us. He, in effect, has given the appearance of an absent leader. I am sad to say that this simply doesn't work—not in today's competitive environment. The longer-term risk doesn't bear thinking about! His attitude, both directly and indirectly, could simply filter down and sabotage the entire process. The projects will need nurturing and support to enable them to sustain and improve. I honestly can't see this being an option for Hugh." Richard shakes his head ever so slightly; his disapproval is hard to disguise.

"You know, Richard, sometimes you really irritate me!" says Hamish. "Hugh has been a problem. He has made me very angry at times, too. Maybe with good reason, but he has also been a really good worker and a friend to me. I owe him a lot and would find it very hard to turn against him."

"Hamish, I would have preferred Hugh to be here when we discuss this situation. I find this part of the discussion very difficult. It's not good to talk behind the backs of others, and I very rarely do it. I know you have been aware of what was happening, but perhaps not the full extent of it. I will not report any single incidents that happened between us, but it is safe to say that I truly believe it is better for you—and the corporation—that I am a thorn in Hugh's side and not merely his echo."

"I would be negligent in my duty if I did not warn you of the potential situation. We are not talking a discontented person here … well we are … but we have a discontented person with the authority and capability to sink an entire division."

Michael interrupts: "Time is moving on. We can discuss this issue later." Hamish agrees.

"Let's cover Next Automotive, now." Mike puts up a new slide as he speaks. "The stated problem was the cost of premium freight. Interestingly, this is the same basic issue as at Ronson & Ronson: production schedules not being met and delaying deliveries."

"In addition to the delays, Next Automotive has cost penalties, a risk of losing their supplier certification, and a high risk of losing individual customers, especially those who schedule their production on the absolute understanding that their goods will be available on time and at the right quality."

"Our commitment is not to make a product by a certain date, but to have it at the customer's factory by a certain date and time, ready for use. Delayed production means that the normal, low-cost delivery channels are no longer available to us. Priority delivery becomes crucial as the only means to make up lost time. We need air freight or special trucks at significant extra cost."

"It was reported that despite taking actions to improve the problem, it just seems that the problems 'move around' as opposed to disappearing. They also continually come back to haunt us. This suggested one of two issues: first, that we are fixing symptoms and not root causes; second, that we are eliminating a bottleneck only to expose the next one in line."

Hamish looks confused. "Can you explain a bit more, please?"

"The first one is easy. We can be fixing symptoms and not the real cause. The best example I have is a system that was not loading properly—exactly like the press in Ronson & Ronson that uses the metal rolls. In my example, the load side was continually failing and needed constant adjustment.

Two sensors could be positioned to compensate and drive the table forward or backward by a small amount. However, these sensors are intended to confirm the loading pad is in position, not to align it. But, by setting this up *very* precisely, it can correct a small misalignment."

"This issue was around for years. The manufacturer bought tables from two sources: the original manufacturer and a second-source supplier that made similar tables much cheaper. Note the word *similar* does not mean they were the same. The alignment marks that the sensors use were not exactly the same on the different tables and vary much more between tables from the second-source manufacturer."

"The first issue was to correct the setup method. The proper process was to set up the *output* position first—not the input. The software then drove the pad a fixed distance to stop at the correct loading position. As I mentioned before, the sensors then only confirm the correct position."

"When this was the process used by all technicians, we still had issues. Proper analysis of the tables proved once and for all that the two different manufacturers had used different dimensions, so changing tables between manufacturers guaranteed the need for a new calibration. Thus, setting up the input sensor was only fixing a symptom. What we needed to do was use the correct setup procedure for the software and then try to match the tables to minimize the need for repeated recalibration."

"The real root cause was the different tables. The ones from the original manufacturer had the same dimensions for every table and were designed for the machines, so no calibration was needed on exchange. However, the second tables, from a different manufacturer, were not identical but were *much* less expensive to buy. The issue was long-standing, but Next Automotive's purchasing department did not believe the original vendor's engineers, thinking they were only trying to persuade them to buy their tables. It took a proper, measured analysis with graphs to prove the point."

"This is similar to the Ronson & Ronson issue, where the corrective work was always at the load side and the real issue that had to be fixed was at the output side." Mike asks Hamish, "How are we doing so far?"

Hamish nods his approval.

"So are we ready for the bottlenecks?" Another nod of confirmation.

Mike now draws a profile of a lake on a new page of the flip chart. The base of the lake has peaks of different heights. Thus each peak is at a different depth below the water surface. "The most common explanation, and the one I like best, considers a boat crossing a lake. Imagine a boat is traveling across the lake. Initially, there is enough clearance for the boat to get across with no problems. If the water level drops, however, eventually the highest peak will become an obstruction and will have to be removed. This will solve the problem for a while—or until the water drops to the level where the second-highest peak becomes an issue. When we fix this, if the water level keeps falling, the tallest remaining peak will become the next issue."

"The same situation happens with production bottlenecks. When we remove the first bottleneck, the next biggest (if there is one) will come into play. When that is removed, we get the next biggest, and so on."

"So, in Next Automotive, we have two possibilities: not solving to the root causes or exposing new constraints or, of course, a combination of both. We can map the product flow and highlight the capacities for each process. This will help us identify and predict the likely sequence of issues. Alternatively, we can work on the issues as they appear, confirming and fixing to the root causes. Besides, it is likely that the bottlenecks will already be recognized issues." Mike turns to the COO. "How is that, Hamish, any questions?"

Hamish smiles. "No, that sounds pretty good. I had heard the lake story before but never thought about it in this context. But what is the difference between a bottleneck and a constraint?"

"I was hoping you wouldn't ask that," replies Mike. "I have been in numerous heated debates about this one." Mike thinks for a moment. "As you know, I like to keep things simple. I have always thought of them as pretty much the same thing, like trying to decide if you are being eaten by an alligator or a crocodile."

"The bottleneck terminology is probably developed from the metaphor of the wide bottle with the narrow neck that slows down its pouring speed. To the scientist, the flow rate is proportional to the radius. To us, it fits nicely into production flows. Some regard bottlenecks as temporary issues, even though the neck of the bottle is permanent. This might be because, I believe, the bottleneck could be process dependent."

Hamish looks puzzled.

"I used to work with a machine that ran different raw materials. Each 'gas' required a specific setup to maximize the machine output. Boron was the most difficult to optimize. It could only run at a rate of 50% or less than, say, arsenic. So, if I run a process that needs product 'implanted' by boron, I can only produce half the amount of product that I can produce in an identical process that uses arsenic. The machine might become a bottleneck in the boron process but not the arsenic process. The *use* of the tool can create the bottleneck, not the tool itself."

Mike pauses for a moment. "Maybe there lies the meaning of constraint … The raw material we are using creates a constraint—something that limits the rate of production. So, a *constraint* is defined as something that restricts. The bottleneck can be a constraint, but perhaps it can also constrain other equipment."

"In a production line with five tools that can run 100 units per hour, if tool number 6 can only run 50 units an hour, there is nothing to prevent the first five tools from running to their maximum rates, but all we will do is create a pile of inventory at the bottleneck: tool 6."

"What about the equipment that follows the bottleneck? Even if rated at 100 items per hour, they can only produce 50 units. Their production rate is limited (constrained) by the bottleneck. To increase their productivity, they would need to be fed with more product, so a fix might be a parallel machine in position 6, effectively doubling the throughput capability to 100."

Hamish is still not yawning, so Mike goes on. "We can also have the same lineup but only sell 30 units an hour, so the machine is not *currently* a bottleneck, but it could be one in the future if sales took us to a need greater than 50 units per hour. In practice, for me, it as all academic: Whether we call it a constraint or a bottleneck, we still need to root cause the situation and implement an appropriate solution. But, if I was taking an exam, I have probably just lost a few points in my answer, even though the results will be the same. Happy?"

Hamish is satisfied, so Mike goes on. "OK, so I will continue, if we are ready?" Everyone nods.

"For a couple of years now, delayed production and other issues have been resulting in premium freight costs of $300,000 per year. At 3% EBIT, that means we need to sell $10 million more product to cover the loss. We have no budget for waste and—make no mistake about it—we all recognize it is pure waste."

"The company has $70 million per year in sales, with an historic profit of 3% EBIT or $2.1 million. At first glance, the casual eye would consider that eliminating premium freight would only increase the profit to $2.4 million per year, but this is a typical example of math not understanding science. The $300K is not the problem. It is only a symptom of all the production problems that cause the delays. By concentrating on the issues that cause late deliveries, we will automatically reduce the freight cost. But, we will also benefit from the savings to be made by the elimination of each of the problems."

"The premium freight can be seen as a burning platform to drive the improvements. Personally, I don't believe we need to create a cause to drive an improvement process but, if we have one and it is known about by the employees, it can help to boost the initial buy-in of the employees. But, please remember, a burning platform will eventually burn out and we will need a culture of improvement to take over."

"It is actually quite common to find that the burning platform is seen as the issue that hurts most. If we had no delivery penalties, we would still have problems. We would just be worried about our poor production and deliveries—the real problems."

"A machine breaking down can cause a delay, and yet the cost of the delays can go unseen. But if we have to pay $1,000 for emergency air freight because of this delay, it kind of slaps you in the face. We often forget about the costs of employee downtime during production delays, the cost of rework and extra materials, the wages of the folks waiting at the next process step, the wages of the shipping guys, or even the cost of any lost product that could have been made in that time. These are all *in addition* to the premium freight cost."

"Here, the premium freight is only a symptom of a number of other problems. It can be visualized like the center of a spider's web: a focal point with everything else connected to it. Given a normal intervention, we would conduct an in-depth analysis and look for all of these deeper issues. But here we have an issue that is screaming at us—and a time limit—so we will tackle the situation in two work streams and do the usual stuff in parallel, as the resources allow. So, the primary tool we have applied at Next Automotive is *short-interval reporting* or short-interval control. Every day, the cause of any new freight costs will be established, and the problem will be recorded and prioritized for resolution."

"If we had the resources, we would fix them all as they arose, but that may not be an option, as finding root cause solutions and implementing them sometimes takes time. Each issue is allocated to a specific person to be responsible for the repair. It also becomes an issue of focus until it is resolved. Support is made available as required."

"So, if we focus on the key delaying issues with determination that they will be eliminated, every time a cause is eliminated, we reduce the number of premium freight shipments. The improvement teams know they are all held accountable by their leader, as indeed that leader is aware he is being held accountable by you."

"Eventually, all of the problems in every function of the business will surface for resolution and get resolved. The most important causes are dealt with first. I must make it clear, though, that sometimes we will use a temporary fix to get immediate benefits, but we will *never* live with the temporary fix in place for longer than absolutely necessary. We follow up on the progress of each issue every morning at 9 a.m., because they are like time bombs waiting to go off. It's back to the weakest link theory, I'm afraid!"

"The good news is that we are largely on top of premium freight already. The focus on it has been absolute, and premium freight at Next Automotive is now as antisocial as smoking in a kindergarten. The main causes so far are as follows:

- *Changeovers taking too long*—Fix: Quick die change (SMED)
- *Dies and tools not working when fitted and needing repair*—Fix: Improved tool and die reliability and ensuring that tools are not stored when faulty
- *Too much time lost deciding what to run and jumping between production runs*—Fix: Improved production scheduling
- *No prestaging of shipments*—Fix: Prestage shipments to eliminate wasted time looking for parts and slowing down loading
- *No advance material preparation*—Fix: Kanban

"Basically, these are all the usual things that need to be in place in today's competitive business arena. Many should be used in all of the divisions, with all being driven by a developing culture of product excellence, empowerment, focus awareness, responsibility, and accountability, and a formal follow-up. The changes in Next Automotive will move the profit needle by a minimum of 3% or $4 million total and open up a further possibility of underused capacity for additional sales."

"From a people perspective, the management team was initially horrified at the directness of the 9 a.m. meetings. It was the same for me the first time I experienced them as an employee. It was a shock—after all these years of acceptance—to suddenly be expected to know the reasons for any premium shipments, let alone have already put a fix in place or be working on the fix now. The new culture explains the need to appreciate that, in business, there is a need for timely action, and three days can be seen as a lifetime."

"It took a bit of time for some of the managers to accept the need to turn up with all the problems already identified, the actions needed to resolve them, and to be able to report on the progress of actions currently underway—because they will be followed up the next day with someone's name against them. Although everyone was aware of the potential issues and had discussed them with the personnel in advance, there were still a few transitional phases before acceptance: Horror moved to fear and then to surprise when they saw how quickly their concerted actions bore fruit, to acceptance, and finally to support for the process and for each other."

"Don't you just love it when a plan comes together?" Richard quips, as if he did it all by himself. No false modesty here.

Michael mentions the key supporters and some of the team leaders who ran exceptional projects. Hamish looks at Richard sardonically but all he says is "Good job, boys."

The implacable Michael continues, displaying no concern about his embarrassing and overconfident partner. But, alas, like everyone else, they both have their own demons, and they make a person what they are. In Richard's case, that would be an absolute genius! "Ignoring Richard's inflated opinion of self, let's move on to Independent Pharmaceuticals, which is by far the jewel in the crown. This one will blow the doors off for you. Apart from production problems, there are no people problems here: no prima donnas." Michael can't help but glower at Richard over the top of his glasses. Richard, of course, completely ignores the look and graciously allows him to continue. "Lucie Bell and her team are brilliant, and I mean the whole team, not just the management. It's everyone—all the way to the operators. They really care. There is a genuine emphasis on responsibility and accountability that is so much a part of how they do business, which ensures that there is no need at all for people to boss each other around. Instead, they support each other and help each other solve problems. It is beautiful, like the gentle and flowing brushstrokes of an Italian Renaissance painter. The behavior we want to see at the bottom of an organization has to start at the top and flow down."

"The initial opportunity here was stated as spoilage in the powder-filling line, and so we focused the entire department on solving this—all levels and functions, everyone. This was a really interesting issue. Machine problems led to excessive variation in filling weights, due to the lower limit being the critical measure. It was easier just to increase the top limit, which pushed up the average fill. But remember, the weight difference between the bottom limit and the average is mirrored on the other side of the mean."

"It was discovered that we were running at nearly 30% to 40% excess fill—all to make sure that the minimum weight was met. To be honest,

I have seen this done before in a biscuit manufacturer, but in their case, the excess was deliberate at 10%, but maybe the cost of the extra weight was not appreciated."

"The first clue to our problem was in analyzing the leakers. Rather than just fixing the glue machines, which were not actually faulty, we weighed representative samples of the packages. The worst leakers were the heaviest packets."

"Carly Purdon led the analysis, which included a process map. But, we added the process limits for all the steps. This threw up some really interesting data, which we will come back to later, but the first point was that the failing packets were above 6.5 grams. We were simply putting too much into the bags. This caused two problems that reduced the sealing efficiency: One was physical and the other was contamination, where the analysis of the failed seals showed a high powder content mixing with the glue."

"Imagine a zip-fronted leather jacket being worn by a 140-lb man. It zips with no problem. But if his weight was to increase by 30% and went to 182 lb, the zipper simply would not close. We also had the problem of the powder puffing up into the glued seal during the knurling and closing process, which in turn stopped the glue working and caused even more leakers."

"The cause of the glue problem was identified, but not the reason for the overfilling. That was more interesting. The first step was to look at the specifications of the machine and the repair history. The team was comprised of process engineers, equipment folks, and operators. The first surprise was that the machine was capable of filling to an accuracy of tens of milligrams, so where we were averaging at 6 grams, we could have been running at levels of around 5.040 grams. Something was messing up the accuracy."

"The repair history showed that a number of pneumatic (air) valves were replaced due to sticking. After replacement, the values settled nicely at around 6 grams, the chosen average. But it would only run for a few days and fail again."

"The valves that controlled the powder dispensers were replaced frequently, so much so that every technician and engineer had spares in their own toolboxes. They never queried why they kept failing; they only replaced them. I checked the equipment log and found the vendor engineer did the same fix when he was called to the original fault. I suspect the techs saw that as the fix and just repeated it, not realizing it was only a symptom of the real fault."

"We approached the valve manufacturers, who sent an expert to analyze the system. He found that the valves were wet on the inside and a bit dirty, which was causing the valve operation to stick. We quickly found that other valves were also wet and some were very dirty, suggesting that the problem had been around for a long time. The root cause was tracked to a compressed-air line feed to the machine with missing water filters. This was causing a number of issues, but the weight was the biggest, most critical issue."

"Cleaning out the air lines, fitting new filters, installing a parallel filter system to enable a switchover for replacement, and setting up a preventive maintenance regime solved the issue. No blame was attributed to any department."

"The final task was to get some confidence with the new setting accuracy and to set a limit closer to the packet weight. The data sampling rattled out histograms in minutes using Minitab®." The major savings were estimated to be

- Increased machine availability of 40%
- Increased production capacity of 40% with no need for reworks, previously around 20%
- A steady reduction of QA checks as confidence grows and the SPC is relied on for spotting trends
- A saving of 30% in raw material use

"So, in summary, we used SPC (Statistical Process Control) to establish the equipment capability. This is how accurately the machine is able to fill the packets. It is indirectly related to the specification levels set for customers. Ideally, the customer limits and the process limits should be a close match, if not the actual limits set."

"Overfilling the pouches with powder to the upper end of their specifications was due to fear of underfills reaching the marketplace. This resulted in contamination of the sealing area with powder and, at the extreme end, the two faces not matching properly when sealing. These led to a chain reaction that caused production downtime, equipment adjustments, rework and spoilage, and then the need for overtime to avoid late shipments."

"This problem is now completely gone and the projected savings are $4 million. Better still, there is open capacity available for increased product throughput and sales into other regions. Lucie is keen to talk with the sales team at the earliest opportunity."

Hamish nods at Michael and smiles with satisfaction. "All good," he says.

Michael continues his report. "Not keeping the best for last, but not horrified with it, we move to the Phonethics call centers. We think it's very fair to say that this one could be looked upon as the best of times and the worst of times. It's an $80-million business that normally runs at 2% EBIT, which in itself is nothing to boast about, but to make matters worse, for the last three months it has been at break even!"

"The management is weak. The leader knows the industry and knows what has to be done, but has not been doing it. She believes that she asked for help and didn't get it, and so the problem was no longer hers."

"Then whose would it be?" asks Hamish.

"Well, she thinks it is yours, Jeff Lincoln's, the company's—anyone who either knows of the problem or should know of the problem—but certainly not hers, because she told you!"

Hamish leans forward and says, "Doesn't she realize that when you take the job, you take the responsibility, and with the responsibility comes the accountability, and that telling your boss does not mean that your accountability goes away?"

"Apparently not, Hamish," says Michael. "Anyway, the outsourced call-center business is highly specialized and generally depends on scale. Small companies tend to be eaten up by bigger ones through consolidation if they will not or cannot grow. The industry has largely moved offshore due to improvements in technology and labor arbitrage. This is largely because industry overall is constantly trying to cut its costs to stay competitive. What used to be considered as managing your most important asset, contact with your customers, is now considered as a cost to be reduced. However, the company doing the outsourcing never comes right out and says that they demand that the outsourcing provider deliver an even better service than they did themselves when it was in-house, so we go ever further down the rabbit hole."

"I'm afraid that the cost of getting the Phonethics business offshored at this stage would be prohibitive. It would cost you at least $4 million in infrastructure, and the inevitable delays and disruptions would likely doom your current overall plan. It looks like you have to sell it."

"I was afraid of that," says Hamish. "It all became very obvious at our meeting with Elizabeth Golden and her team."

Mike continues: "Yes, but there is still more good news and bad news—I won't ask you which one you would like first. The bad news is that if you sell it as is, you will get very little for it. A well-running business in this field might get you one times the cash flow, so $80 million. A poorly running business at, say, 2% EBIT, might get you seven times EBIT from someone who wants your clients, so seven times $1.6 million is $11.2 million—very unsatisfactory! A business that is at breakeven that relies on its existence to clients who are giving us less and less of their business would be hard to sell even at these multiples, so I'm sure you can see that this one requires special attention."

There is no disagreement from Hamish.

"So here's what we recommend," says Michael, moving to the flip charts.

- We get it ready for sale over the next nine months.
- We maximize the profit level of the business to ensure that it is a positive contributor to the improved fourth-quarter run rate for the entire company.
- We change the senior leadership.
- We identify any special needs our clients have and fulfill them at reasonable prices.
- Nine months from now, we market the call center business to larger outsourcers who already deal with clients that match our existing client profile, and we market it as a high-end, onshore contact center with a good profit level and client growth possibilities.

"Can we do it within the timelines?" asks Hamish.

"We can get the profit level up," Richard says. "We're working on it now. We have the four-point planning tool in place to drive results, which it is already doing. When we right-size the staffing—half the attrition rate to 5% per month or better—and get the average handle time to target levels, we will achieve at least a $4.2-million run rate in EBIT by the fourth quarter."

"On the face of it, that would be enough to satisfy our current mandate, but it isn't, remembering that the performance gains we achieve have to be sustained into the future. So we should consider and plan for consolidating the two locations into one; space will not be an issue."

"The top leadership needs to be restructured along with the span of control of the middle managers, and we need to ensure that our remaining call center becomes a model for the industry, probably around the same size at $80 million but with an EBIT of around 5% or $4 million. This should allow for a company sale of somewhere between 75% of sales or $60 million and 10 times EBIT or $40 million. In either case, we think it would be the intelligent thing to do."

Hamish is pensive. "Of course we will have to present this idea to the board," says Hamish. "It might not meet with their longer term strategy."

Richard responds, "You know we agree, Hamish, and we will of course be happy to work with you and the board in developing this ongoing strategy if they would like us to. Whether or not this is their desire, we will be happy to support you with ongoing periodic wellness checks and audits of the go-forward business, as we have discussed."

"Thanks, guys," says Hamish. "I'm very comfortable with that." He gives a wry grin to Richard, who matches it with a surprised smile.

Richard picks the presentation up, moving to the flip charts. "All right, so here's where we are."

- We believe we can achieve the desired productivity improvements to achieve EBIT run rates that are double those being achieved at the start of this project, and do this for the fourth quarter. This comes to a total of $18 million.
  - Phonethics call center company at $4 million
  - Independent Pharmaceuticals at $6 million
  - Ronson & Ronson Steel at $4 million
  - Next Automotive at $4 million
- We believe that corporate overhead should be reduced by 25% by the fourth quarter for a reduction of $6 million, which will fall directly to the bottom line as EBIT. We can do this through a combination of attrition for approximately 10%, voluntary severance for approximately 5%, and forced redundancy for approximately 10%.
- People who leave the business should be treated properly with dignity and generosity at the high end of expected redundancy payments. All of these costs can be taken as one-time restructuring charges.
- The last $12 million in EBIT becomes the task for increased sales; we will definitely have increased the throughput capability of our steel, automotive, and pharmaceutical businesses, so if we sell our excess capacity at 10% profit, we will require to make $120 million in additional sales. This will take clever cooperation between operations and sales and marketing.

"The only thing that is safe to say is that it will not work out exactly the way we plan. Anyone who has ever run a P&L knows that the targeted outcome never comes from exactly where you plan it to come from. That's OK; the goal is to hit the big target, and to do that we maximize on all of the small targets, knowing that there will be give and take. We can't guarantee that all of this can be achieved. We don't do miracles. Nevertheless, I don't think anyone would be in tears at tripling our fourth-quarter run rate from $9 million to $27 million, although our desired and targeted end-point is $36 million. So here we are, Hamish, what do you think?"

"I think it's fine, and here's what I'd like to do. First, I have to update Jeff Lincoln on all of this to get his buy-in and ask him in his role of chairman to inform the board. We need their buy-in on all of this, even the potential shortfall. I'll arrange the meeting with the four divisional presidents and the other members of the senior executive staff for two weeks from now. This will give them an opportunity to prepare. Both Jeff and I will lead that meeting. The agenda will be to go over the strategy we have developed together and get their buy-in for its execution. Jeff and I will have to think hard as to how and when to handle any announcement of the sale of our call-center business, that is, if the board of directors agrees."

"I'll ask you guys to get back to me as to what you think leadership in the consolidation of the four businesses could look like and I'll make that decision, again considering timing. We will also need a good follow-up technique in line with the other models that you have installed across the organization. We'll look at each of the financial targets and their actual performance achievements on a weekly basis with the viewpoint of what we will do to get back on target if we drift. We will do the same for productivity improvement, cost reduction, and sales. We'll also look at all the key operational and client measures."

"I'd like to do this weekly in a phone call with everyone present on the phone, and monthly with everyone here in the head office conference room. I want you guys to be at those meetings, sitting right beside me, but I have to run them! Don't correct me on camera if I'm wrong; just coach me between meetings, OK?"

Michael and Richard most certainly are OK—not bad for a morning's work!

27

Corporate Cost and Strategy

It's been ten days since Michael and Richard talked to Hamish about the need for cost reductions at corporate. A business that generates $300 million in sales simply cannot afford to carry a $24-million corporate overhead cost and also generate $36 million in profit!

Hamish, naturally, didn't take this well, but he knew it had to be seriously considered. The discussion was valid and led the consultants to suggest the next logical step. He took it to Jeff Lincoln, and if the CEO can't stomach a corporate cost reduction, it might be necessary to reduce the targeted profit increase. Today they find out.

"How are you Hamish?" says Michael. "How did it go with Jeff?"

"First I want to thank you two boys for the great work you have done in the business so far, and believe me, it hasn't gone unnoticed!"

"Uh-oh!" Richard thinks. "The project must be over for us. Maybe we've stepped on too many toes! At least we've done some good work and got Independent Pharmaceuticals working in the right direction."

"Thanks, Hamish, it's been a privilege," Richard says, stepping forward to shake his hand.

"What do you mean by that? Where the hell do you think you're going?" says Hamish.

"I thought we were done," Richard says. "It's a bit early in the project for thanks; it sounded like goodbye! I was just about to book a week's trip to Hawaii."

"It's too soon for you to be celebrating," says Hamish. "Most of the work still has to be done, and you know it! The CEO says it's full speed ahead. We know there will be disruption, though, and we want to keep it to a minimum. We have considered the proposed staff cuts for corporate and think it is too severe. We prefer to allow the attrition to work at its usual 10% rate and redistribute the work without rehiring. It also gives us time to reorganize, and it looks better for the company stability. If we let that happen for 24 months, it will leave only a 5% cut necessary. We think this is our safest route, as we have to think of year two as well as year one."

"So we are not being shut down?" Mike asks.

"If you can make the savings we have estimated, the business is now viable," Hamish says. "But we need to make the improvements first."

Richard thinks out loud about the new situation. "It looks like it's time we refreshed the strategy to help guide us over the coming year and the two years beyond. If everything goes to plan, we will need a further strategy that will be driven by the board and the CEO. The longer term strategy will likely need elements around new products and markets and potential acquisitions—a complex affair. But for now we need an operating strategy to take us through the next 12 months and beyond. It doesn't have to be complex; rather, it will encompass our overall direction and our basic beliefs. It will also help us look into the near future to determine some of the critical issues we will be faced with."

"I thought we had a plan. What about the one you did earlier?" says Hamish.

"That project plan needs to be amended now to give us a clear, desired outcome over the coming year," says Richard. "It was designed to achieve the desired increase in profit through improving existing processes. Now it will be required to encompass the sequence of the necessary activities so that we run smoothly into the following year to help us achieve the longer term outcome."

"An operating strategy is a very different thing than a project plan. It is meant as a view into the future that, among other things, will help us make decisions based on our values. Even then, a strategy is a living document. Situations will come up during the next 12 months and beyond that will require us to reexamine those values and the longer term direction of the company. We just experienced that with our acceptance of the need to cut corporate overhead."

"A strategy is a look into the future to show us what we truly want to look like as a company. It should define our goals, the types of beliefs we have, and any capabilities we might want to develop. We consider the position we want to have in our market, even geographical locations. The products and services we offer should be reviewed to see whether or not they should change in the future. Only when we know where we want to be can we identify any capabilities we need that are key to achieving our new vision and then, of course, the activities that all of this must trigger."

"So strategy, then, is more of a vision than a plan. It's a window to what we want to be in the future and enables a comparison between that vision and where we are now. This will create a gap that has to be closed over the strategic time frame—if we truly want to achieve the new vision."

"Well," says Hamish, "that might be slightly above my pay grade!"

"Your input will be essential, but we also need to get Jeff involved," says Michael. "Although we can suggest items, strategy is the domain of the CEO, with input from you and his other direct reports."

"It seems that great minds think alike," says Hamish. "Jeff told me he expected the next steps to be a bit touchy and that he'd make himself available for the whole day, today."

"Good, let's have him in," says Michael. They decide to have a coffee while Hamish contacts Jeff.

Jeff walks in and they bring him up to speed. "So you see, Jeff, with your agreement, it may be time to develop an operating strategy for the next 12 months and beyond. Would you like to involve the other members of your executive staff in the process?"

Jeff considers his options. "Not right now. Let's play with it a little between ourselves first, just in case it gets too touchy. I think it would be best for us to develop a blueprint, assess any implications, and then, when we have some concrete proposals, we can get the others involved and decide on any possible changes. So, how do we begin?"

"A bit of brainstorming or a SWOT (Strengths, Weaknesses, Opportunities, and Threats) analysis is as good a way as any," says Michael. "If we go for brainstorming, we can ask questions with the SWOT sections in mind and blend the two a bit."

"We'll ask open questions and you and Hamish should answer them as candidly as possible. Throw out all the ideas, even if you think they are a bit strange. We'll go through that for a couple of hours, or until the ideas run out, and then Richard and I will gather the issues under the headings of a strategic framework. After lunch we will go over it again, reconsider each point and determine any changes you would like to make. When happy, we can plan the next steps. Does that sound OK?"

Both nod, and Michael and Richard get underway, capturing the main points on the flip charts.

- The first 12 months is of crucial importance. We have to achieve the result before we can maintain it.
- Our low profit is a weakness that has to be overcome.
- We have to not only be ethical, but be *seen* to be ethical at all times. This will be a strength.

- Any gains we get have to be embedded in how we do business around here.
- This is an opportunity to define new ways of working.
- We should avoid layoffs where possible.
- Layoffs might seem as if we are in trouble and create a threat. We will also lose skilled personnel.
- If we conduct any layoffs, we should make any cuts once, across the business, and then tell the rest of the folks that it's done. People will not work to lose their own jobs.
- Turn the situation into an opportunity.
- Where possible, we should aggressively grow sales—opportunity.
- We should expand the geographies we sell into—opportunity.
- We should consider product diversification—strength and opportunity.
- The strategy of the business should be back to basics for the first 12 months at a minimum.
- Eliminate our weaknesses in production capability.
- Any mergers or acquisitions must complement existing business while bringing either new products or geographies—opportunity.
- Our new strategy and all success in our strategic objectives should be shared with our employees—strength and opportunity.
- We are still committed to $36 million in Earnings Before Interest and Taxes (EBIT) as a run rate by the fourth quarter of this coming year and to continue making improvements—weakness but already showing the strength to achieve it.
- Corporate staff must contribute to the success.
- Reduction in silos and building a new culture—opportunity.

All in all, they see many opportunities. The four have exhausted this approach before noon, and Hamish and Jeff leave for a while, giving Michael and Richard the opportunity to convert the points into the strategic framework.

When Jeff and Hamish return from lunch, they all go over the strategic framework to ensure that it accurately reflects their thinking, and with a few small changes it does.

"Because of the work we have done together so far, many of the immediate issues critical to our success in Year 1 have already been identified," says Michael. "Nevertheless, we will capture them again here at a high level. When we look at each element of the overall strategy for the coming three years,

Mission Statement and Strategic Time Frame

The Bow Corporation will be the leader in quality and productivity in its chosen lines of business. Over the coming 36 months, we will establish ourselves in the top quartile of privately held companies from a perspective of profit/return to shareholders. We will gradually expand our products and markets to serve a broader client base and geography.

Revenue and Profit Guidelines
Year 1
- Sales of $380 million as a run rate during the fourth quarter
- EBIT of $36 million as a run rate during the fourth quarter

Year 2
- Sales of at least $380 million for entire year
- EBIT of at least 10% for entire year—or $38 million
- Sell the call-center business

Year 3
- Consolidate business as per Year 2 performance

Basic Beliefs
We will display consideration and fairness to our three major constituents at all times: our employees, our customers, and our shareholders. This will not be a lip-service belief but rather a working mandate that will ensure the ongoing success of our company's mission.

Products and Markets
- During Year 1, our primary focus will be to service our current customer base and geographic markets with our current product offerings.
  - We will improve our quality and services and become the supplier of choice.
  - We will tactically expand our geographic area and client base to increase sales.
  - We will decrease our reliance on our existing customer base.
- In Years 2 and 3, we will continue to aggressively expand our geographical reach and our client base.

- We will develop added value to existing products and add new products where they fall within our key capabilities and core competencies.
- In Year 3, we will consider acquisitions that complement our existing business.

Candidates for Acquisition Must:

- Be accretive during the first year of the acquisition, delivering positive profit and cash flow
- Add new products, new customers, or new geographic reach to our core business
- Either add management strength or be within our current management's capabilities to operate
- Have the characteristics to ensure synergy savings and prompt an effective integration to the core business

Key Capabilities Required

- A strong, flexible, and cohesive management team
- An employee profit-sharing plan that benefits all levels of employees
- A pay-for-performance plan
- Superior human resources capabilities
- Superior sales and marketing capabilities
- A business integration team capable of temporarily being reassigned from their existing roles
- Superior human relations and communications at all levels of the company
- Superior client relations and flexible and speedy response
- Cohesive engineering, quality, and operations

it will likely trigger other critical issues that must be actioned and resolved to close the gap by the end of Year 3. Let's work on these together now."

They have a coffee and start to run through all the issues they can think of. They seem to drink a lot of coffee, but Richard feels a hot drink makes folks work better.

Michael steps back from the row of flip charts and looks at the lists. "How do you feel about the summary? Do you think it will serve as the foundation of a high-level plan?"

"I think so," says Jeff. "I'm certainly prepared to commit to it and take it to the board. I'll need you at that meeting, Hamish."

Critical Issues to Be Resolved

- Ensure all necessary change processes are in place and operating to plan
- Ensure communications with all employee groups are open and continuous
- Ensure all leadership and management are supportive of the change process
- Be prepared to change out any leadership and management who cannot commit to operating in the new environment
- Ensure effective plans are in place for any necessary layoffs, voluntary where possible
- Ensure effective and proactive planning for work distribution in a leaner workforce
- Have a plan to hire any essential new skills needed
- Integrate sales and marketing and operations to ensure commitment to new products and markets
- Obtain board approval of the strategy
- Obtain input from and acceptance by all leadership and management of the new strategy
- Ensure effective and appropriate communication of the strategy to all employees

"I'll be happy to be there, Jeff," Hamish adds, pleased to be recognized for his input. "In looking at the critical issues, it is apparent that this is where the rubber will hit the road. We will have to be prepared to trigger activities and projects over the coming three years to ensure that none of them become roadblocks."

"Yes," says Jeff, "this list has to be pretty much complete and revisited, along with the overall strategy, at least every six months. We have to ensure that it's still relevant and that there are no unpleasant surprises. After the board has seen and approved it, we will present it to all divisional and corporate leadership to get their input and their commitment."

Jeff turns to the consultants. "What do you guys think?" he asks.

Michael and Richard consider it to be a good day, and another brick in the wall!

28

Hugh Greenlees 2

"I have to give the devil his due, the figures show that business performance is improving…"

"It would have happened anyway, though, my team was on top of everything! Improvement always takes time, yet it seems it is now expected to happen in a heartbeat. It simply doesn't!"

I look across the table at my examiners. Here I am again, getting approval for all the excellent work I have done this month. I just have to get this wrap up speech over and then I can get back to my real work. Look at Jeff and Hamish and sitting there like proctors at an exam. I don't like it! There's far too much credit going to consultants and their disciples—to folks who used to work for me. I should be getting the credit for all these improvements, even if not directly, it should be at least officially recognized.

I wound up the meeting and become the attentive host again. "Hamish, I'll walk you back to your car."

I would say the meeting went smoothly, but I did feel a certain coldness as we walked, particularly a distancing in the relationship between us. This seemed more intense as we shook hands and said goodbye. I was relieved as I watched the car disappeared from sight.

"Ah well, back to the office." I felt the pressure dropping and even the heat of the sun on my back made me feel better.

Truth be told, I was feeling sorry for myself and the last thing I wanted to do was go back to the office. So I headed for the sitting area outside the canteen and sat, facing the sun, with my eyes closed: just thinking—trying to forget.

Looking back over the last nine months, I could see that my control over the business has diminished, while others' had clearly increased. "Isn't it supposed to be the opposite?"

People don't need me as much anymore, they just go off and do things on their own without seeking my approval. They are working in little teams and pretty much do as they please. I wonder how things would have been different if I had supported the changes? At the very least I would have been successful by association.

I am kept up to date with the progress but it's not quite the same as being involved. Superficially, I still have the power of veto but it's getting harder and harder to say no to most of the ideas and initiatives that are coming up—especially when they are good ideas and are usually successful. I must be seen now as only an obstruction to improvement.

Slipping my phone out of my pocket, I look for Ken's name and tap on the icon a few more times. Still no reply. What's he up to these days? I just can't reach him as often as before, so I try his cell phone number.

"Ken Hughes: how can I help?" Ken almost sings his reply.

"Hi Ken, are you off for the day already, you old scallywag?"

"No Hugh, I have a meeting with a major customer and it looks as though he has some more business for us—maybe a lot of business! The only time he could see me was 4 p.m. today."

"My Fridays have definitely changed. People are pretty busy, eh?" Ken's words echo a bit due to the "hands-free" in his car.

I was hoping for a few beers and a chat but that's not going to happen. I smiled, hoping it would make my voice sound happier. "It's good news, I guess. How much business?"

Ken answers, "Well, with all the changes, we've been able to reduce many of our costs by 10%. We wanted to find a way to pass some of this on to our customers, so we came up with the idea of offering a volume discount. To qualify for it, the client has to pass their current annual threshold by 20%. Working with Jose in production, we estimated we would only need 4 hours per week extra capacity to handle the offer. Availability on the tools that we use for their products has been increased by more than this, so we can easily increase utilization to cope. It's brilliant really."

"You reckon we take all that extra work from them and still guarantee our on-time delivery?" I should already know the answer...

"Yes," says Ken. "The new changeovers, production planning savings and improved uptimes all come together nicely. It should be no trouble at all. As I said, it is the productivity improvements we've made in the factory that easily allow us to offer the volume discount."

"Even better than that..." Ken sounds proud of himself, "...the beauty of the deal is that the additional orders are based on material cost only, all of our fixed and semi-fixed costs are taken care of and we still have open capacity in the plant."

"We just need to make sure we don't fall back into our old ways. It's different days, my friend!"

"Good luck with the sale, Ken." I am finding it hard to hide my disappointment at his success.

"Thanks, Hugh, see you Saturday morning at the kids' hockey."

I end the call and the time appears on the phone—a giant clock. It's a quarter to three and looks like a smiley face. Even the phone is laughing at me! I still have ages to kill, when I should be at the pub.

I meander back to the office, tidy up my desk and read a few e-mails. At five o'clock I am out the door. I drive straight home—much to the surprise of my wife, who never expects to see me so early.

"What happened, Hugh?" asks Mary. "I thought you would have been having a beer with Ken."

"No, he's meeting with a customer." Quickly changing the subject I add, "Something smells really good. What's for dinner?"

"Roast beef," answers Mary, "I'll get you a beer from the fridge, if you'd like. I'm so glad your home."

"Me, too, Mary, me, too..."

I flop into my chair, grab the remote and switch on the television but my mind is on a dozen other things. My thoughts are conflicted: I'm glad to be home and yet I miss the pub. I have been going straight to the pub after work for years. It was where I could unload all the stuff that bugged me. It was group therapy.

I used to worry about problems with the performance in the plant and with the customers, but now that concern no longer exists. Nature hates a vacuum, though, and there is a nagging concern at the back of my mind, pounding away like a toothache. I have to make a real change in my attitude at work before it is too late—if it is not too late already!

29

Hamish 2

Parking behind my wife's car, I lift my phone out of the hands-free cradle. Outlook pops up a reminder "9 months since the improvement process kicked off." I stare at the screen and think about all the ups and downs I have been through since then. On reflection, I guess it has been more ups than downs though. I decide to walk round to the back of the house as I am home from work early today and want to surprise Helen.

It worked. Helen is startled when she hears the back door open. "Hamish, its only lunch time, why are you home at this hour?" she asks.

"I'm ahead of the game: I thought I'd pop home to see you."

"Why?" says Helen again, unused to me just appearing home for lunch.

"I wanted to give you these." With a flourish, I make a large bouquet of flowers appear from behind my back.

Helen's bottom jaw drops in surprise, not a sound escapes her. She wonders if her husband is having an affair, but quickly dismissed the idea as ludicrous—not Hamish, not ever. She takes the flowers and almost buries her face as she breathes in the fragrance.

"And this…" Like a magician, I present Helen with a beautifully wrapped package about two inches square. She carefully places the flowers on the table and takes the gift.

I was grinning like a 5-year-old. Helen scrabbles with the wrapping and unearths a royal blue, hinged box. She pauses before opening it. Still looking at the box, she lifts her eyes toward me. I am still beaming like a lighthouse. Helen looks back to the box. Wide-eyed in anticipation she opens the box and gasps. Inside, there is a diamond ring. She can't hold back the tears and hugs me around the neck. "What's the occasion?"

"…Just that I love you and want to say thanks for all your support." I take her hand and lead her upstairs.

"Hamish!"

"Don't worry… I'll buy you lunch too."

30

Commitment

Looking around the boardroom table creates an interesting moment. It seems like a lifetime since Michael and Richard started this initiative with the Bow Corporation, and yet they are well on the way to hitting their targeted financial performance. The word is that everyone is happy with the progress.

"Did I say everyone?" thinks Michael. "What I really mean to say is that the key money guys and management leaders are happy. The four private-equity guys on the board think it's Christmas: They felt that their money was trapped in a sinkhole. They had no idea how they could salvage the situation without losing even more money. Indeed, they just expected to close the book on Bow, but being good businessmen, they knew that the better the results, the better the selling price. And so off we went on the task of going from $9 million to $36 million profit in 9 months."

In the back of their minds, Michael and Richard knew that 10% turnover is not unusual for a first-time improvement. Indeed, it can often be much more. But this time they had four companies and what everyone feared: a time limit.

Improvements should never be started with a financial target in mind. It is much better to work with the company and grow the savings, allowing the new culture to develop. In this case, however, Richard knew his "command-and-control" techniques would help fill the gap. While Michael prefers to work through empowerment, together, they both were able to reach a working compromise. Besides, they really did have a true burning platform: Do it or the corporation shuts you down.

It was certainly a roller-coaster ride in the beginning, with lots of people brushing up their résumés. But the recession worked to the advantage of the consultants, as there were not too many jobs out there. It took a lot of persuasion and reassurance to ask the guys to help make the improvements.

Michael and Richard had to make some compromises on philosophy and the desired approaches, as time was a luxury. It can take years to change a culture, and they had only months to prove viability or recommend pulling the plug. Even then, they had to prove that their plan was valid, which effectively required almost immediate buy-in—not a realistic expectation. There aren't too many people who see the excitement in a level of change that threatens to turn their world upside down. "I might have polished up my résumé, too!" thinks Michael.

Michael remembers how he felt when the stock market collapsed. The housing market implosion and ensuing financial crisis of 2008 affected pretty much everyone. The folks who lived paycheck to paycheck were hit worst. They had nothing saved except the equity in their houses—and even that fell. Everyone had been living life on credit, buying what they believed were life's necessities and paying banks huge interest on their loans. Then it all melted away.

For those who had saved diligently for a better life or for retirement, they saw their savings disappear over time. Contrary to beliefs, you don't get government support if you have savings in the bank. Since then, the volatility of world events and their resulting impact on the day-to-day lives of ordinary people has been dramatic.

The old adage "Once bitten, twice shy" has taken the lead—but not in a good way. The new approach seems to be based on "never again," a view that engenders excessive caution. Growth has taken a backseat for everyone but the money lenders. Companies stockpiled cash instead of investing it. Banks wanted to restore their balances—maybe even buy back their freedom from the governments (OK, the taxpayers) that bailed them out. Despite government requests for increased lending to support the rebuilding of the economy, the main drive as Michael saw it seemed more toward earning back that which had been lost and getting back on the gravy train—not spending. He admits to being annoyed with banks that failed who still pay huge bonuses to their senior employees when ordinary people, unemployed folks, low-paid workers, retirees, and women with baby strollers and young children were queuing at charity food banks because they couldn't afford to buy groceries.

Against this political and economic backdrop, it is no wonder that "rejected" buttons are being pushed everywhere in a drive to get back firmly on the road to success. The investors at the Bow Corporation made the same decision. But now that they have the taste of initial success, there is no going back, nor should there be. The world doesn't stand still, although maybe it should. Economics believes that if we are not advancing as a society, we are moving backward. Yet the well-being of every employee and their families at Bow was in the balance, and that's a pretty serious thing.

Richard and Michael are not about to let any one person's ego get in the way of this and, thank God, neither is Hamish or Jeff. These consultants have seen the result of inaction or too-little-too-late efforts: Businesses close, with thousands of jobs lost. But no more—not on their watch.

Michael looks at Jeff Lincoln, who stops writing and puts down his pen. He looks around slowly and clears his throat. The chatter around the table stops. "Thanks for being here today, folks. I see we have our four division presidents and all of our corporate department heads present. If you don't mind, I want to do a little level setting before Hamish takes the chair."

"First, it needs saying that, although I've poured my heart and soul into this company for 15 years, I am massively disappointed with both my performance and the performance of the company. At least that was true until recently. For reasons out of my control, I guess I got old and stodgy. No … that's not true … To blame my situation on age is a lie. I am older now than I was last year, and my drive has returned stronger than ever."

"I guess I fell victim to personal circumstances that caused me to lose my motivation. The fact that I stopped asking for the very best of myself was bad, even if it was a bit understandable, but that I stopped asking for your best, too, is inexcusable. It's true that the tone of an organization is set at the top, and mediocre leadership will produce a mediocre company. I had become mediocre. By default, I faltered and I dragged the standards of the company down with me."

"Time, itself, has been the cure, as have the world events of the past five years. They have roared a message that has woken me up. With age comes wisdom and experience, but it does not make you immune to the impact of living … or dying."

"Anyway, enough of this morbidity. We don't have the time to be complacent anymore. We needed a shake to wake us up to reality. So everyone in this room—and by extension everyone in this company—please consider yourselves shaken."

There has been dead silence in the room since Jeff cleared his throat, and there is no sign of him letting up. "The most common debate in driving change is how to motivate the people involved. For many, they feel there has to be a burning platform. For some, it can just be an explanation of the need to improve. For others, it is just a normal part of their culture. But for some folks to change their behavior, they need to experience some kind of significant emotional event. We need to understand the fears of our employees. Just as it can take developing cancer to stop someone from smoking or perhaps a serious car crash to finally see the true value of being alive, perhaps we need to experience being unemployed to appreciate the fear it invokes in others."

"I love this company and the people in it, and yet one significant emotional event stopped me from functioning. It took a second event to bring me back—one that smacked me right between the eyes. That was when our board of directors and shareholders told me we had to quadruple our bottom-line profits in a year or be broken up and sold off. I had a choice: Run for the trees or get in gear. I chose the latter."

"You all know Hamish, my right-hand man. Although he had only been with us for 12 months when this bomb went off, he has acted like a grand statesman to allow a path for the changes that have been necessary to create success." Jeff nods toward Hamish and adds, "I'm so very grateful you're here, Hamish." Hamish is noticeably moved by the compliment.

Jeff moves his attention to the other side of the table. "You all know our two guests: Michael and Richard. They are the consultants we asked to help us with this change process. One key benefit of their support was that they had no ax to grind—no agenda other than helping us perform better. Many of us gave them a hard time, but they never wavered in their task, not even when they had to tell us bad news as well as the good. They have won my respect."

"Mine, too," adds Hamish.

Jeff smiles once more. "Now I'm going to hand the floor over to Hamish and thank you all for your commitment to our ongoing change process. You have to belly up to the bar, ladies and gentlemen, just like I did, or we cannot possibly succeed! The floor is yours, Hamish."

"Thanks, Jeff," Hamish nods. "Now, this will be pretty clean-cut. I, too, am committed to this company and to Jeff, and to every other living soul who works here. I need all of you to be the same. I believe that all of us are needed to achieve success, but I also believe that anyone who cannot make this same commitment should leave now. If you are unsure, you can let me have your resignations after the meeting. I don't want to embarrass anyone."

No one moves. Hamish directs his attention to the four divisional presidents. "Each of you knows the performance expectations from your companies, and you are well on the way to achieving them. I ask that you stay the course on this, with no slacking or performance shortfalls. We will continue to monitor this performance on weekly conference calls."

"Attendance is mandatory. During these calls we will track your high-level revenue and profit performance against the plan. We will also check your key business performance indicators against plan, both from a quality and quantity perspective. I'll also want to be informed of any major issues that you are experiencing or that you can foresee arising in the future, both positive and negative. I also want to know how you are resolving them, or any help you might need. Remember that these are action and support meetings, and you are expected to be accountable." There is visible discomfort from some quarters, but overall there are nods of agreement and assent.

Next, Hamish focuses his attention on the leaders of the corporate support functions. "Everyone, with the exception of operations and sales, is working in a support function. It is worthwhile to remind everyone that these support functions exist only to ensure that sales can sell enough product to meet our company's objectives and that operations can produce and ship product. Sales and operations are the only two moneymaking functions in the business, and any other viewpoint than this can have us winding up with the tail wagging the dog. So, make sure you take care of your most important internal customers, folks. Give them the same respect and deference you would to our external customers."

"We were originally charged with an overall cost-reduction target at corporate of 25%, but through great teamwork we found a way to reduce that. Even so, not replacing staff and retraining those who remain on staff—on top of financial cutbacks—has been and will continue to be difficult. I know how much stress this is causing, but this target has to be met, and human resources will work with you to ensure that no critical work is dropped or lost during the transition. All current commitments must continue and be properly redistributed among the corporate staff."

"Regarding the sales department, you have a huge mandate: increasing sales by $125 million in a very short time. You might well have expected me to tell you how to do it, but in truth it's been your job all along, and the lack of new business has kept our top line performance flat for years. I remember all the reasons and excuses as to why we couldn't bring in any new business. I've heard how we have been uncompetitive in terms of price, but now we can sing another song. I need you to continue to work as cross-functional teams with the divisional presidents, the financial controllers, chief financial officer, and production managers to develop more and better pricing options. Our quality and delivery reliability has improved, and this will help. I expect these to improve further. This is not a one-time change effort but the start of a program of process excellence. Perhaps we should be redefining our manufacturing processes. The thing is, the choice is yours. Tell me what you need, and together we will decide what is possible and what is not."

Directing himself to the CFO, Hamish continues, "I want you to consider two-level pricing. See what we can do for new customers that we can keep segregated from our existing customers. Determine what costing could look like when all of our fixed costs are controlled and when inventory levels have dropped due to application of Lean practices. Please also consider the possibility of selling our goods on consignment, where we are only paid when the goods actually sell. This approach should work well with Lucie Bell in Pharmaceuticals Limited. Be open-minded and creative."

Hamish stops for a moment and asks for questions. There are none; everyone is taking notes and paying full attention. It seems that Hamish hasn't even drawn a breath; he is truly a man with a mission.

"I want to move on to strategy. Everyone here has received a copy of the plan we worked on recently. It focuses on Years 1 through 3, but with the primary focus being on Year 1. It is a far cry from previous strategies that had more pages than a phone directory. I'm sure some of you are shocked that it is such a short and concise document. I must admit I was too. But in truth, an operating strategy does not have to be a three-ring binder that sits on a shelf. It should be a living document that states our overall direction and values in such a way that all of our people can understand them. We intend to create a further-abbreviated version on a folding card that can be handed out to all our employees."

"Strategy is more of a vision—a direction rather than a plan. It is a yardstick that will help us balance our decisions going forward. If a major initiative or investment is deemed not to be in line with our strategy, then the decision for 'go' or 'no go' should be simple."

"I know you have all had ample time to review the document, so I won't go over it in full. Rather, I will stress the points that I'm concerned about and where I need your unswerving commitment, too."

- We will be the leader in our chosen industries for quality and productivity.
- We will gradually expand our products, markets, and geography.
- We will achieve our revenue and profit guidelines.
- We will have a strong, cohesive, and flexible management team.
- We will have superior sales and marketing capabilities.

- Sales must be fully integrated with operations and finance.
- All management must be supportive of the change process.
- We must be prepared to change out any management that is not committed to working in the new environment.

"The success of the entire strategy is crucial, and I know that you have reviewed and discussed all of it prior to this meeting. These elements are simply a few that are on the top of my mind, and I look at all your faces and see you are on board! We will review this strategy monthly on the fourth business update meeting of the month, which we will conduct here at corporate instead of the weekly conference call."

There is a still silence in the room as the folks digest the message.

"I'm going to hand the meeting back to Jeff now."

"Well, you've heard it," says Jeff. "It's all about us, me and you. Don't bite anyone's hand who's trying to help you!" he says, nodding to Michael and Richard with a grin. "If you can commit to this journey, all I can guarantee is that it will be a rocky one, but it will improve and change you. I have to ask once more: I want you all to be involved. You should also be fully trained in the Lean methodology—just ask Richard or Mike to help. But, if you feel you cannot get on this bus, then please move aside to make room for others who are willing."

Everyone in the room looks around the table at the same time. Some seem more worried than others, but there are no comments.

"Thank you all for being here today." And with that, Jeff stands up. Then everyone in the room stands up, and they give Jeff and Hamish a standing ovation.

31

Jeff Lincoln 2

Since the wakeup call I received from the board of directors, I feel like a different man. My viewpoint on life has changed and I have taken an in-depth interest in the business again. It was really like a light switch being flicked on. Today, I am visiting one of the divisions with Hamish. We now do this on a weekly basis. At each company, we do the round-robin and walk the floor, talking with the employees at all levels. The main focus is to be visible, interested, and supportive, and show folks we support all they are doing.

I answer every question honestly and, if I can't answer it, I will say why. If I just don't know the answer, I will find out and get back to them. Where help is requested, I will give it my full attention and support. There are lots of positives to be discussed.

It's 8:00 p.m. on a Tuesday and Hamish calls me at home for a chat on how he feels about the progress so far. "I think it's great Hamish, everyone's working together and they seem genuinely pleased to see us when we visit. I used to do exactly these types of visits all the time and I now wonder why I stopped…"

"But, what do you think, Hamish?"

"Yes, I'm with you on that Jeff. It seems that we can always find things to do around the head office or with the clients that take up all our time, but being on the floor with our people is totally necessary if we want to be a part of the team. I mean really be a part of it."

I sip my coffee, "You know Hamish, I'm particularly glad that we have the senior executive from each division and their teams do a formal presentation to us on every visit. It keeps them on their toes and us up to date on progress and any potential problems that may be looming. I know you have your weekly calls and they are invaluable and so these visits and updates are another link in the chain. What is it that Richard says? Focus, focus, focus."

"I'm glad you're happy with the progress Jeff. I'll let you relax and we'll chat again tomorrow. Sleep well."

I allow myself a brandy. I take it because I like it: the fact that it helps me sleep is irrelevant. Thinking back to the meeting with Patrick Edwards and Elijah Tobias—the one that kick-started this whole issue—my mind replays the progress made from then to now, like a video. I am absolutely certain that the 12-month improvement target will be met. It's clear to me that no single event caused the change, it's more like a jigsaw puzzle with every part coming together to create a bigger picture. I shrug my shoulders and wonder why it often takes a significant emotional event to shake us out of our comfort zones. One thing I know for sure though, it all begins with leadership, not just mine but at every level. It all has to link together and it won't happen by accident.

I allow myself to think about next year, just a little—golf, travel, the grandkids, reading for fun!

And then I think, "Maybe I could delegate a bit more and just work a bit less."

32

Phonethics Call Center Company 3

Elizabeth and her team had a meeting prior to the arrival of Hamish, Michael, and Richard, so they are ready and waiting for them bright and early Tuesday morning. The atmosphere is fine, albeit a little tense, but the smell of coffee and hot muffins always makes for a relaxed start. Hamish helps himself to a muffin and a cup of coffee as Elizabeth introduces the consultants. He picks up a tub marked "Authentic English Strawberry Jam" and stares at it for a moment. The word *authentic* puts him off, so he puts it back onto the dish. A few others top off their drinks, and some have another muffin as they wait for Hamish to kick the meeting off.

Hamish opens his notebook and flicks to the page with the agenda. Still holding his coffee, he begins. "Good morning, and thank you for taking the time to meet with us this morning. I know you have been having a hard time lately, and sometimes things feel out of your control and, to be fair, some things have been. However, we all know we can't sustain a business without profit, and that's where we have found ourselves over the past three months. My hope is that this morning we can decide together what we can do about it."

"Richard," Hamish nods in his direction, "who you probably all know by now, has spent a lot of time analyzing and running call centers. I am hoping he might be able to offer some positive input to our discussion that will help us move forward. It goes without saying that we need to be as open and honest as possible and that no idea is a bad one. The answers we need are probably in this room; we just need to find them. I ask for your full cooperation with this."

Elizabeth speaks up "Thanks for being here, Hamish. We all know how busy you are." There is a chorus of subdued agreement. "The fact that you have taken the time to be here with us this morning highlights how important you feel our situation is. I want to make it clear, though, that we have not simply been sitting on our hands and waiting for things to improve. We've tried everything that we can think of to get back to profitability and feel there are valid reasons as to why things are the way that they are."

"I believe we can fix things ourselves given time. The issues that Richard and Michael have pointed out to us are not new or surprising. They simply echo what we already knew, and so we are grateful for the opportunity this morning to explain why things are the way that they are." And with this Elizabeth sits down.

"Excellent," says Hamish. "Let's start our analysis from the list these gentlemen have prepared, but remember that a bad situation left alone invariably gets worse, and quite frankly we have no option other than to fix this one!"

Elizabeth bristles in her seat, but she smiles and asks her ops manager to address the first issue, which is the high average for call-handling time. The operations manager opens a stapled document and flicks to the correct page. She reads the data and the bullet points before speaking. "The average handle time has risen from 240 to 270 seconds. This has happened gradually over the last few months. The external reasons behind it seem to be that we have more and more angry customers, and defusing their anger prior to getting down to actual problem solving takes a fair portion of the additional 30 seconds."

"Why do you think there is an increase in angry customers?" asks Michael.

"There have been lots of problems on the client side of late. They changed their billing system—among other things—and so we have been inundated with complaints on incorrect bills. The calls come here even though we don't control the actual billing department, and so there are often delays, extra waiting times, and repeat calls while we transfer them to the correct location. Customers hate that, as they expect one-stop shopping."

"Anything else?" Richard asks.

"Yes, our telco client uses a subcontractor for the installation of new phone lines, and recently they bought the subcontracting company. Now that the subcontractor and the telco employees are both divisions of the same conglomerate, the subcontractor's employees expect the same pay scales—and they went out on strike for four weeks to get it. This created a backlog of work orders for the installation of new phone lines, all of which had passed the promise date for their connection."

"Customers were ignored and not informed about any of the issues. Indeed, some customers received confirmation that their installations would go ahead, even when it was known that this was very unlikely. This often resulted in customers actually sitting at home waiting for installation technicians who never arrived. Many customers had to take a day off to be home. I would have been angry, too."

"Thanks for this insight," says Michael. "Is there anything else you can think of?"

"Oh, lots of things," the ops manager continues. "We are one call center among a group of six that handles calls for our telco client. Three months ago, they moved a huge volume of their calls to an offshore supplier—driven, as always, by their desire to reduce costs."

"Just as with any start-up, the offshore supplier was unable to resolve all the issues that the customers called about. Although their agents may have the training, they simply don't have the experience. There are reports of agents simply hanging up on customers in the middle of a call, and when the customers call back, they default to the end of the queue—again. What makes it worse is that it can take half an hour or more to get back to an agent."

"When things get really desperate, the client redirects the calls to us, and the customers are very angry when they finally get through. They don't differentiate. They see us as the same folks—and I suppose, technically, we are—but they blame our agents for their bad experience, when in truth none of this is our issue, and we are the ones who solve their problems!"

"Is there any of the increase in average handling time that *we* are causing?" Richard asks.

"Yes, I suppose there is."

The manager's frustration is clearly visible in her body language. Michael tries to put her more at ease. "I'm sorry, we're not trying to find fault: We're just trying to get to the root of what we have to fix together."

The ops manager gives a false smile and continues, "Because most of the calls are now rerouted to the new offshore supplier, our agents are often sitting idle. When a call is routed to us, the agents handle it as if they have all the time in the world, which in fact they currently do. Also, the job is becoming so boring and demotivating that lots of our experienced agents are leaving to find other work. The new agents we hire, who have just come out of training, take longer with the calls while gaining experience. It's a vicious circle."

"How do you manage all of this?" probes Richard.

"Are you kidding?" Elizabeth intervenes, unable to contain herself. "These situations are out of our control. How can we possibly manage them?"

"Elizabeth," Hamish says softly, "fortunately or unfortunately, we managers have to manage every eventuality in business—everything that comes up. We don't have the luxury to pick and choose only the ones we like."

Elizabeth turns bright red and apologizes.

Richard picks up the conversation, "OK, so we understand why our calls are taking longer than we are paid for, and we also understand the impact the slowdown in the business is having on attrition. Can we talk a little bit more about this slowdown?"

Elizabeth is still recovering from her outburst and the embarrassment it caused her. She takes a deep breath as she settles down again into her role as business leader. "It's a few things, I think." She takes another deep breath, "The most obvious and glaring cause is simply globalization and the effect it has had on business overall. The cost of labor in itself has become a commodity. The telco sector is one of the most cost competitive sectors in the world economy. Gone are the days since Alexander Graham Bell had a franchise through invention. In those days and until quite recently, the individual telcos had a captive market for their customer bases due to their geographical areas. They could charge pretty much anything they liked."

Elizabeth is now up to speed. "Technology has put an end to that. Indeed, technology has had a huge impact on everything and, quite frankly, everyone in the world. Gone are the days when analog messages were sent over twisted pairs of copper wires running across telegraph poles or buried underground. The wires themselves were a physical barrier to entry for competitors simply because they were expensive to install and maintain."

"Today, digital messages, both voice and data, are sent at high speed over fiber optics using multiplex technologies to maximize capacity—all of which simply means oodles more calls per wire. If you tie all of this together with Voice Over Internet Protocol (VOIP) and the explosion in the use of cell phones and satellites, it becomes obvious that the days of having any kind of franchise with a local customer base is gone. Geographic boundaries for competition no longer exist. It has become a truly global marketplace and every telco is fighting to protect its market share."

"Mergers and acquisitions among the big telcos are now common. Where a local presence in the past could mean a country, in this day and age a local presence is a continent. It's either grow or be acquired, so large telcos have become a global presence."

"The mode of communication is also changing. More and more users would rather text than call, and e-mails are becoming predominant over the two other methods combined. Telcos are ever vigilant to any kind of change and carefully track all fluctuations in modes of communication. They are quick to exploit this new customer preference. Besides, it is much cheaper to answer an e-mail than a call."

"Of course the Internet has changed everything: Customers are being actively encouraged to go on-line with their inquiries and problems. The plan is to resolve them through the use of the telco's self-help options on their web page. Everything from billing inquiries to technical support is covered. Call *avoidance* has become a big imperative for the telcos. All of this is to maintain their profit levels in a new and aggressive price environment."

Michael questions, "But don't folks just end up coming back to a call? Personally, I find frequently asked question (FAQ) pages to be very irritating, and the inability to speak to a person, even by e-mail, is a real irritation."

"Perhaps that is another reason for the increased angry calls. I hadn't thought of that." Elizabeth notices her operations manager writing a note. "So, despite the continuing need for higher levels of quality and customer satisfaction, the telcos are driven in the opposite direction and reduce the amount of money they spend on essential call-center support. It is now relatively easy to cut costs in offshore, low-cost environments like India, the Philippines, and Africa, where wages are much lower than here in North America, and technology enables this approach. It is much more difficult here."

Everyone is listening intently to Elizabeth. Clearly she is well versed in what is going on in the industry and indeed in the world. Neither Michael nor Richard are surprised by these revelations, but Hamish's mouth is hanging open and the rest of her team look surprised, too, as if they are hearing all of this for the first time.

"So do you see any solution, Elizabeth?" Hamish asks softly.

"I don't," Elizabeth states with a defeated look on her face. Her managers sigh in unity, like air hissing from a tire. She continues in a depressed tone, almost quiet, "We've known for a long time that these changes were coming. They were gradual, but they didn't drop through a hole in the sky. In the old days we had a franchise with all of our clients, including the telcos. We built that franchise on quality and service, developing long-term personal relationships at all levels of their organization, from their middle management all the way up to their procurement and executives. For a long time our reputation carried us and we seemed—no, we were—untouchable."

"We never really believed the Internet could replace live calls, so VOIP was just a dream and not a reality. Soon, though, the clients began to ask for it, and all of the call-center suppliers were saying they had the capability, but in truth it was a long time in coming as, originally, the voice quality was so poor. This is the case no longer. We can now stream high-definition video with Dolby 5.1 surround sound. Virtually every long-distance call uses VOIP switching these days. It's the primary reason why long-distance costs to the consumer have come down so much."

"Managers, executives, and procurement professionals come and go within the industry. They are changed out by a new breed. Embedded in this new breed are contact-center professionals, every bit as savvy but considerably more demanding than anything the outsourced contact-center managers have ever seen before. As you can see, we don't even call ourselves *call centers* anymore: It's either *contact centers* or *back office processors* or *business-process outsourcing* (BPO). So here we are," Elizabeth finishes up with a long, sustained sigh.

"Well, that pretty much covers average handle time, attrition, and dropping call volumes. It touches on pretty much everything else, too," says Richard. "I have one last question regarding scheduling. Why do we run so overstaffed in relation to the call volumes we are offered?"

The operations manager speaks up. "The client expects us to staff to half-hour intervals. They give us their requirement and they manage the staffing level through their central workforce management team. They constantly monitor how many people we have signed on—whether they are talking, on after-call work, or available and waiting for a call. The telco does this with all six call centers they have in their network. It allows them to reroute the flow of calls from one location to another without having to pay for the people who are not actively engaged on a call."

"Thank you." Hamish smiles, "Any questions Richard? Michael? Elizabeth? Team?" There are no questions.

"What are the next steps?" asks Elizabeth.

Hamish defers the response to Richard. "Well, if we are going to be any help to you at all, we are going to have to come back and work with each of the individual department heads. This time we need to find the root causes of the problems. So, we will use a version of process mapping to develop a map. We will use the *four-point planning* tool—kind of like a current state Big Picture map but with a particular focus on intercompany communication. We will develop it across four elements, how we Forecast, Plan, Execute, and Report. It's a tried-and-true method, but it will only become obvious to all involved as we create it. The objective is to ensure that all of the steps and elements are highly visible and to highlight any *disconnects* in our work flow that are contributing to the problems."

"Next we will create a future state map using the same four elements and highlight any gaps between where we are now (the current state) and where we want to be (the future, desired state). There may be some things we can do little to nothing about in the short term, but working together we might find enough improvements to remain viable."

Hamish takes over. "Thanks Richard. Thank you all very much for your time and for your patience with us today."

And with that, the meeting is closed.

33

Phonethics 4: The Diagnosis

As they walk toward the door in reception, Michael notices the frown on Hamish's face is increasing. He is clearly not a happy man.

"Richard, I might as well wait here for my taxi." Michael places his bag next to a chair that has a view of the drop off area outside. "I can make a couple of calls while I sit."

He wants to say "I'll stay and help with Hamish," but they are too close together.

"Shall I postpone my meeting with Lucie, so we can discuss that meeting?" Michael suggests.

Richard shakes his head very slightly.

Michael tries again, "I can easily stay tonight and arrive a bit later tomorrow afternoon. I am sure Lucie will not mind."

Richard smiles at Hamish and back to Michael, "No, it's probably best if we stick to our original schedule. Why not call me tonight?"

Michael holds out his hand to Hamish. "Hamish, I will see you again in a couple of days and I can update you on the progress at Lucie's site."

Hamish's frown has found its way to his handshake, too, but he forces a smile, "No problem, Michael, see you soon."

Richard pats Michael on the back. "Later..."

As they leave the building, Hamish is still frowning. Consultants usually want to talk, to critique, to discuss and plan—probably because they have seen similar situations before, but the company's managers are often shocked. But, if Richard is honest, neither he nor Michael is particularly happy either.

When you look at waves on water, you see them as moving forward, but they're not. The water travels in more of a circular motion, oscillating back and forth. The waves are only carriers: a medium for an invisible energy to move through, just as sound travels through air. Well, it seems that meetings also have a way of creating their own invisible energy, but that energy has attitude. Here, people are the medium. They spread the energy from person to person—like an avalanche, always growing.

So it was with the meeting at Phonethics—the epicenter of a burst of negative energy, distinctly palpable. Everyone in the room was visibly affected, including Hamish and the consultants. Now they await the damage as the ripples race outward through all the employees.

"So what does this mean?" Hamish is almost whispering. "Surely, we're not dead in the water?"

"There are many ways to be dead in the water…" Richard responds philosophically.

Richard's outward display of confidence is too much for Hamish. "Don't philosophize, Richard. That meeting was pretty much self-explanatory. It was worse than bleak. So cutting through the crap, the obvious question is where can we go from here?"

Richard answers immediately and positively, "We do exactly what we said we would do." He reads the need for more detail in Hamish's expression. "We should continue to build a plan for the business that will meet the profit requirements set by the board. Exactly the same as we would have done yesterday."

"Is that even possible?" asks Hamish.

"Anything is possible, Grasshopper," says Richard, trying to lighten the mood.

Hamish explodes. Clearly he doesn't think it was funny. "Do we have a business here or not?"

Richard thinks for a moment, "To be honest, it looks like we will probably have to sell it." Richard responds to the not-so-subtle cue to be more serious, shakes his head, and gives a tight-lipped smile. "But even if that is the route we choose, before we can sell it, we still need to make it as successful as possible to attract a buyer."

"Attract a buyer!" Hamish seethes. "Why would anyone want to buy a business this bad?" Still having a massive problem with the idea, he points a fob at the car. The lights flash and beep and they enter the vehicle.

Richard buckles his seat belt. "You are right, Hamish. No one would buy it the way it is today—and definitely not if Elizabeth were doing the selling! But it will be much more attractive after a bit of work."

Hamish needs more convincing, so Richard explains, "We need to remember that outsourced call-center companies are a very specialized business.

I know everyone thinks their own businesses are unique, but they might actually be right in this case. Maybe call centers are the very ones that are."

"Call centers are a labor-intensive industry, so manpower costs were the original target for reduction. Most of their competitors moved offshore 20 years ago. They dipped their toes into the water in India or the Philippines. They made huge investments way back then and have been refining and fine-tuning their offshore businesses ever since."

"Somehow Bow either missed the boat or chose not to take that route. They were not alone, though: Many other smaller outsourcers stayed in the US, probably because of the fear of the initial cost which, even then, was in the millions."

"Over time, those who had not gone offshore with at least some of their call centers continued consolidating and preserving their own market shares. It was hard work, and *any* successes they had with this approach further convinced them they had made the right decision. After all, much public opinion agreed with them. There was—and still is—a growing dissatisfaction with foreign call centers. Indeed, only recently I was in the UK talking to a customer-support representative from a major cable group—and he was based in the Philippines."

Hamish looks thoughtful and asks, "Are you saying that we just believe what we want to believe and that we seek proof to support our own case and deny anything that doesn't agree?"

Richard gives the question a bit of thought. "More than a few companies have survived without offshoring, but many others were gobbled up by their bigger competition. Not all of them were losers, though. Just like selling a house, some held out for the premium price they thought their business was worth."

Richard looks Hamish straight in the eye. "These are just my opinions, Hamish. And, I know I'm not the decision maker, but we needed to consider the wider situation, warts and all."

"On the positive side, yesterday we knew we had some problems. Elizabeth had painted a picture of a company with troubles but nothing insurmountable. Today, we know the true extent of the issues. We should certainly talk to Jeff about it and get his insight…" Another pause for thought. Richard continues, "Trying to stay objective, I think our plans for the next 12 months should remain the same: We make the business as profitable as we can. Even if the final decision is to sell, it'll take at least a year to prepare."

"OK," says Hamish. "We inherited this situation, so let's get at it."

THE CONSULTANT'S THOUGHTS

That evening, Richard cannot switch off. He is uncomfortable that the picture was incomplete. He orders a beer in the hotel bar and tries to watch the football game on TV, but his mind keeps returning to Phonethics.

How can a company lose so much control? All they need is a system that allows the employee numbers—the fuel of a call center—to be modified at short notice. They *must* be able to adapt to any special circumstances or planned events that require a step change in the number of agents. Such events could include new product launches, recalls, billing system changes—indeed anything foreseeable that is big enough to impact the normal call volumes or patterns.

He wonders how they can be so wrong when technology makes data handling so much simpler. He remembers the early days, when everything was done manually and laboriously. They worked in half-hour periods to enable them to handle the predicted call rates. The *Erlang calculator* needs only three pieces of information to estimate the number of agents required to cover a period.

- The first is the *expected service level*—chosen by the client to ensure the agreed-upon level of customer service. This has a major impact on costs, as it has a huge impact on the number of agents required. This is obvious, as the more agents there are, the fewer the calls that are missed and the shorter the waiting time. High service levels require high numbers of agents. The actual number of agents employed is agreed on between the client and the company. This was one reason for the move to offshoring to countries where labor was cheap—more folks for less cost. An example of a service level input could be 80% of the incoming calls offered being handled within 20 seconds.
- The second input to the calculator is the *forecasted number of calls* for the half-hour interval being reviewed.
- The third is the *average handle time per call*.

The output from the calculator is the estimated number of agents required to handle the forecasted call volume for the specific half-hour interval under analysis.

Imagine the amount of manpower it used to take to run the workforce management department of a call center, as every single half hour had to be calculated manually over a year just to establish the required staffing levels. (For a 10-hour day, 5 days a week for 50 weeks a year, 5,000 calculations needed to be made.) The magnitude of this task effectively created a static forecast that was reworked only once per quarter to ensure its ongoing validity.

But that was 20 years ago. Thankfully, during the intervening years, technology has massively simplified the process. New software, that still works on the Erlang principles, now allows automatic downloading of call information and easy data analysis.

The irony is that the Phonethics management had the opportunity to experience the old way and yet still ended up with only a superficial understanding of the implications behind workforce management. This has caused them to miss the fundamental importance of staying in control of manpower and the need to respond to important inconsistencies, differences, and changes. As it turns out, even with all of today's technology, Phonethics has developed a 20-year-old static forecast, or, to put it another way, a wildly inadequate control plan.

Just talking to a few people raised Richard's suspicions about this problem. A few more questions confirmed the forecast had rarely been modified to consider changes—particularly following the reductions in call volumes due to the telco client's recent offshoring policy. Surely someone suspected this would redirect a large proportion of the calls away from Phonethics?

If a telco has three sites and they are treated like production lines, where priority is given to the line with the lowest production costs, there would be a controlling department that monitors the current status of each "line." If one site is very busy, calls can be directed away from it to reduce waiting problems.

However, that same feature can be used to control costs. If one site is more expensive than another site, calls can be directed away from the first site until the cheaper site reaches capacity, when they can choose to switch excess calls back the original site. Naturally this reduces income as well as costs.

Richard is certain if he checked the call data he would find there are significant changes in the call arrival patterns. With the telco having centers in different time zones, Phonethic's calls will be impacted by the availability of the offshore suppliers. So, where all calls once came directly to Phonethics, they could now be easily rerouted to the offshore suppliers during their office hours. This means the number of calls Phonethics sees is no longer dependent just on the number of calls offered, but also on the proportion of calls diverted to or away from them. They need to ensure they have a system that will detect and minimize the impact of all of this on their current and projected profitability.

System disconnects are not an unusual situation in contact centers (or businesses in general), but technology helps. Software monitors the agents and directs incoming calls to those who have been available for the longest time. Also, the current status of all agents can be viewed on their supervisors' screens. It is easy to tell at a glance how many agents are on a call, how many are available to take a call, how many are engaged in after-call work, how many are in the catch-all state of *other*, and how many are signed off. However, as with everything else, having information is not enough: It is how this information is used that is important! It requires focus, timely communication, *and* action.

Richard also has noticed that the supervisors are spending most of their time doing administrative work and that they often neglect their "day job" duties of coaching their agents. Some coaching sessions should be performed by the quality department personnel, but very few have been seen, and the feedback to the agents is often too late to do any good, as it is too far from the actual call event. With calls running 30 seconds longer than they should, Ruchard would have hoped to see action being taken to help those agents most affected to help them take control of their calls.

The overall picture tends to suggest an organization of silos with disconnects between the various departments that should be working together in the call center. The management seems to be 100% reactive. The workforce management team is not updating the supervisors of their agents' work patterns to highlight where agents are needed, and the recruitment function doesn't seem to talk to anyone.

Despite having more information than anyone could ever ask for, the team leaders and managers protest that they simply don't have the time to work through the reams of data available to understand what is going on. They are not wrong. The data is poorly presented.

Particularly obvious is the omission of short-interval reporting. There should be triggers that scream out any deviation between what is planned and what is actually done. And there is no link to the financial information on performance available at the level of team leader or manager.

All of these problems have been discovered by just talking to folks in the company and asking a few questions. Now it is time to turn the suspicions to facts. Now the problems begin to involve the employees. To get their buy-in to the issues, the consultants need to get them to see the problems and find their own solutions—with a bit of help.

THE COMPANY ANALYSIS

Two days have passed since the initial shock and realization of the situation at Phonethics. The gloom has settled a bit and turned to a desire to see what can be done to save the situation. Michael and Richard are digging in with the various department managers, keen to understand and quantify the issues. They know that there are systems in place, but these systems have failed and they need to find out why.

The core of the operational process covers four crucial, linked processes:

1. *Forecast*: The forecast defines what they need to do to meet the client's needs. It is the estimate of the cost to carry out the contract. However, the client's need is not the only consideration; it must also include Phonethic's profit requirements. It goes without saying that any financial loss must be avoided, something that is occasionally forgetten once a project is running.

   The forecast is where the determination is made whether taking on a new piece of business should be accepted or rejected. Assumptions like future productivity savings can be built in *if* it is certain they will be in operation when the contract begins. The bottom line is companies are in business to make money.

   The starting point is the method used to forecast the annual call volumes for each client. Not just *x* calls per year, but in detail—how the volumes will change over the contract period. Remember, since the number of incoming calls offered defines the staffing levels, it seems simple! So accurate data is needed to plan numbers, hiring, and training—again staying at this high level.

   The contract values for *any* client will include the cost to provide the service they want, graphed on a scale that will show all trends in costs due to any seasonality issues: variation in staffing levels, overtime, profit levels, expected usage (the staff numbers on which the contract is based), and how any deviations from the forecast will impact profitability.

2. *Plan*: Once the forecast has been completed, the consultants look at how to plan to do this work in detail. The objective is to predict the staff needed to cover every minute the phone lines are open. Half-hour intervals are a useful measure. Consideration is again given to the impact of seasonality, sales promotions by the customer, and any other changes that might comprise the individual pieces of

the puzzle: call volumes, staffing (agents and support staff), hiring, revenue, profit, and cash flow.

This approach also forces the customer to consider any promotions they have planned over the year to estimate a demand. The sole purpose is to *know* what support is needed from the call center. The team's focus at this stage is to refine the actual impact of every eventuality they can think of on how the business will have to run. The map helps the team to "see" more succinctly how they currently do all of these things.

3. *Execution*: In the execution stage, the goal is to understand how the business will run day to day. Here the team will examine how they currently conduct each of the company's main functions: call center operations, quality, IT, human resources, training, management, *and* supervision. Again, everything is considered, remembering to record what is actually done—*not* what the policies and procedures say should be done.

4. *Reporting*: Finally, consideration is given to how progress is reported in all aspects of the business. Once more, daily, weekly, monthly, quarterly, and annual meetings are implemented—both formal and informal, among the internal team, with corporate, and with clients.

Areas are identified where controls are needed: the triggers and warnings received from the system of anything that is changing and risks drifting out of control. The team must also track anything that is going wrong—or right—and define the key performance indicators (KPIs) to track and what kind of feedback the team needs—and gives—to the clients.

The Four-Point map looks for disconnects in the system—points where the checks and balances fail. For example, Michael and Richard know how many folks the corporation agreed to hire, so why do they have more (or fewer) than needed? How did the company decide the new number of agents? The calls are longer than they should be, but why? The supervisors don't supervise adequately—they just file reports, but why? For this situation, the consultants decide to develop a high-level analysis of the four key management processes: forecast, plan, execute and report. The map will take up at least one whole wall in the conference room (Table 33.1).

Michael and Richard take down a couple of pictures and hang three horizontal strips of white wallpaper; this will become the base of the map. They lightly draw a two-column, two-row table dividing the paper (Figure 33.1), creating four separate workspaces. On the top left side of

TABLE 33.1

Summary of Key Considerations with the Four-Point Plan

Area	Forecast	Plan	Execution	Report
Contract content	✓	✓		
Staffing levels	✓	✓		
Events that will impact staffing numbers	✓	✓		
Staff utilization	✓			
Processes		✓	✓	✓
Human resources			✓	
Hiring		✓		
Training			✓	
Overtime	✓			
Impact of deviations from forecast on profit	✓			
Call volumes		✓		
Management and supervision			✓	
Operations			✓	
Quality			✓	
IT			✓	
Reporting systems				✓
Purpose of internal and external meetings				✓
Key measures (KPIs)				✓
Corrective actions, triggers, and responsibilities				✓
Profit	✓		✓	✓
Revenue			✓	✓
Cash flow			✓	✓

Forecast	Plan
Report	Execute

FIGURE 33.1
Blank table for the four-point map.

each of the four cells, they stick a sticky note. Written on each sticky note is a one-word header: Forecast, Plan, Execute, or Report.

The process of mapping has more benefits than the simple production of a map. It brings folks together, minimizes ego issues, builds involvement, helps to visualize where things go wrong, highlights where procedures aren't followed, and shows where resources are needed to fix problems. It also helps increase the pool of communal knowledge and creates the motivation essential for change in the culture of a company.

Starting with a blank canvas looks foreboding. Working with a team of employees involved with all the tasks, the consultants begin by gathering the actual documents used for each of the elements that make up the process. Some members like to shrink the documents to half size. It helps save space when they attach them to the wall below the relevant step.

The consultants' initial intention is simply to identify how the company *currently* carries out the four processes—not how the company thinks they should be done. The map will show them what they don't do as well as what they do! In creating the map, Michael and Richard identify the sequence of the tasks, recording the major steps on individual sticky notes. By using sticky notes, they can easily rearrange tasks and add any steps they miss. They can also use sticky notes to temporarily represent feedback loops. If they find that they need more detail on any point, they can either create an additional map or reposition the notes and add them to the main map.

Remember that the goal is not a perfect map; the goal is getting the right information. Many will disagree and argue that maps have to be exactly the same for every user. Mostly, they will be. But the consultants remind the team that it is important to remember that the map is only a tool to help them find out what they need to know. It is their map, and they can change the format to suit the experience of the team to help them achieve what they want to get from it.

A simple color code makes maps easier to read, even from a distance. The consultants record only one task, problem, or idea per sticky note. They also have a trick they have learned from experience: Don't place the first sticky note at the edge of the wall. Leave a bit of space to add steps that may have been missed. As the map develops, they often find steps that originate prior to where the team expected the start point to be.

When the team has completed the map sequence—all tasks shown in yellow sticky notes—they then add any information/data they have on problems and how they impact

- The revenue
- The profit
- The volume of work
- The method of executing the work
- In-house communications
- Staffing levels
- Client relations and communications

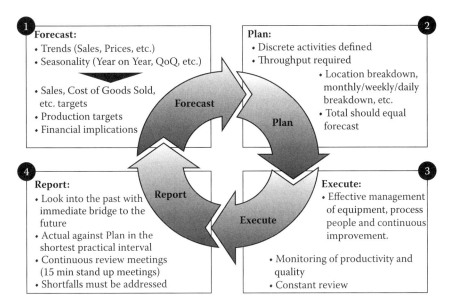

FIGURE 33.2
Main requirements of each section of the four-point map.

Richard reminds the team, "This map is looking at costs and profitability as well as how the business operates" (Figure 33.2).

"Financial losses are usually represented in red, so it seems appropriate that red sticky notes be used for problems. The problem note is located above or below the task to which it relates. This keeps them process related. Finally, should there be any ideas for solutions, write them on blue Post-its—again, located next to the task and problem to which it relates. One note is used for one problem only, so counting the red notes is the same as counting the problems."

Michael and Richard do this for each of Phonethics' clients and for the four sections of the map: forecast, plan, execute, and report. The complete analysis consists of two stages: the initial map, which is called the current state map, and the corrected system, the future state map. The current state map shows what is happening now. The future state map shows what the team is aiming for: what the processes should look like after correction. But the future state map is more than just a correction: It also includes a link to the company strategy, showing where they want to be. Any new operations that will help them achieve the strategy and eliminate any steps that would take them down the wrong path must be included.

Understanding the Current State Map

Once the current state map is complete, the consultants must go over every step to identify whether any issues have been missed. Michael tells the team, "If you find that there are too many employees in the *execution* stage, then look back to the *forecast* and see how you made your initial calculations. Did you estimate the numbers correctly? Did you use the right information? Did you put in any steps to consider changes in the contract? Next, look at the *plan* and see if it has procedures to convert your forecast into actions. Then look in detail at the *execute* stage to see if you have followed the steps in the plan. Finally, look at the *reporting* system to see if you noticed the issue before and, if recorded, what actions were taken to correct the numbers."

"The steps in the forecast relating to the numbers are linked by a line to the numbers section in the plan, which in turn link to the relevant section of the execution stage, which finally links to the report. If the system is working, all the lines are drawn as solid, but where there is a disconnection—a step that is missing or not followed—the line is presented as a broken line of dashes."

"Look for any other issues you can think of. We'll leave a sticky note pad of a different color so that you can add comments to the map. The new color makes additional points easy to see."

"It will take a week to complete the map, iteration after iteration, as each department discovers something new and everyone works *together* to understand exactly how the departments and the clients interface and work with each other. Confirm again, again, and yet again what is actually going on as opposed to what should to be going on."

"When the current state map is complete, you will pretty much have what you would expect it to be: a big mass of colored sticky notes, specifications, and documents, with processes running in straight lines that branch off with decisions and feedback loops. It might not be very pretty to look at, and it will have disconnections in places. It might even have the data under the wrong headings. Nevertheless, it will be *your* map with your processes. It will show what you are doing now and how you do it, and it will show you what you need to fix to make it work properly. It will not be a perfect map, but then we are not looking for perfect maps. The solutions are more important."

Richard adds, "Every person who has helped in building the map must agree and accept that it is accurate. Now you will need a couple of days to go over it, to see where you can quantify any issues, pinpoint any questions that need answering, and work with the relevant folks to determine how to eliminate the disconnects and fix the problems. The map can even help you prioritize how you will implement the solutions."

The Future State Map

The consultants work with the team to create a second map on the wall adjacent to the first using the same process. Michael explains, "This map will represent a *possible* future state for the processes. It will show how the processes will look when you have fixed the problems, eliminated or corrected any faulty processes, and introduced any new procedures."

"The future state is where you need to be."

MAKING FOUR-POINT PLANNING WORK: THE CURRENT STATE PLAN

Hamish and Elizabeth, being the most senior managers, have an open invitation to participate, but they choose to attend on only a few occasions, and never for the full session. Their goal is to show support for the process. They limit their attendance because they are worried their presence might stifle involvement, which can happen. When everyone has given their best efforts and the map is complete, Michael and Richard will then present their work formally to them and then to the entire management team for final approval and fine-tuning.

Even if this all goes as smoothly and as easily as it sounds, they are only at the beginning. Next they have to implement the changes!

One point to remember: all maps are intended to be a *living* process—to be used for reference and future improvements and be regularly updated. Michael and Richard soon get into the swing of building the current state map, working hand in glove with the management, support departments, and agents of Phonethics.

Most companies have a process map of some sort. The four-point plan is more of a consultancy tool, designed to find problems. Phonethics does have a rough plan, but it is not very comprehensive. Michael and Richard use it for reference. Fortunately, call centers tend to have the expertise and the equipment (IT) necessary to produce effective forecasts and plans.

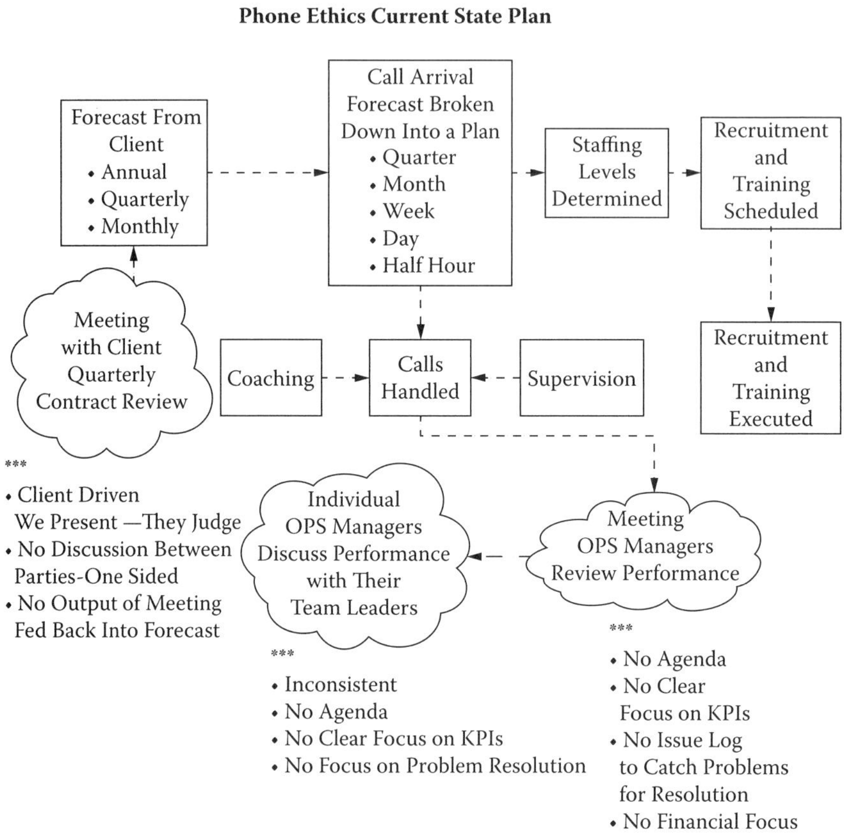

Phone Ethics Current State Plan

FIGURE 33.3

Part of the one-point plan: a hand-drawn current state map.

They have the technology and knowledge as to how to run effective operations and *execute* the work of their business. And they most certainly have the technology and information required to spit out reams of reports on virtually everything.

So what could possibly be wrong with this picture? (See the current-state plan in Figure 33.3.)

There are broken links (disconnects) in almost every area. Some problems are chronic, mostly related to meetings. The call-handling meetings, run by the ops managers, had no formal agendas; KPIs were not discussed in any detail; there was no "issues log" to catch problems for resolution, so no one was allocated the responsibility to fix anything. All of this, plus there was no alignment made between the problems and the financial issues they caused.

The meetings between ops managers and team leaders to discuss performance also had no agenda, and the KPIs were not discussed here, either. Add to this inconsistent content and no focus on improvement, and Phonethics had the perfect recipe for recurring problems and a culture of firefighting.

Even the quarterly meetings with the client were one-sided: The client led the meetings. Phonethics presented the situation, and the client judged the company's performance. Any issues arising from their disregard for the contract would not be discussed, and there was no feedback from the meeting to the forecast, so even a basic "Plan, Do, Check, Act" loop would never be closed, allowing the numbers problems to fluctuate freely—always at the company's expense.

As seen in Figure 33.2, the consultants worked in a clockwise circle as they analyzed the current state map, and so it is perfectly normal that the first big problems appear under the heading of *Forecast*. It's not that it's been done wrong; it's more likely that it is incomplete. In truth, the method of forecasting work in a call center is easier today than in most businesses. The complexity of the task means that much of the guesswork has been engineered out using technology and computers.

Michael and Richard needed to know how the calls varied over the day and over different days, weeks, months, and years. They used histograms to show the data spread and simple statistics to predict how many calls could be expected between 12:30 and 1:00 p.m. or 8:00 to 8:30 a.m.—in fact, for any time interval on any day of the week. They needed this data to determine the staffing levels of the call-center agents—the folks who actually answer the calls. Since the number of calls varies hour to hour, the compromises are tricky.

Although the map showed that all elements were in place, they were disconnected from each other in one way or another. The forecasts were seldom updated to consider changing call arrivals or average handle time, and so the company often found itself to be overstaffed due to working with outmoded schedules. Add to this the fact that the budget was not connected to the forecast or the plan, and they began to see how the overall impact, from a financial perspective, was not seen in real time.

Data showed that the call volumes had been trending down, while graphs from the training department showed that the recruitment and training functions were continuing at the original planned level. Comparisons showed a complete disconnect between needs, training, and staff numbers. Add to this a client that continually would leverage its power by insisting on ever-higher levels of staff, even though the call volumes did not support it, and there was a recipe for disaster. It seemed that the company's main goal was to keep the contract, even if that meant running it at a loss.

It is surprising that no one took any high-level action regarding the overstaffing on the floor. Anyone who bothered to look could see the idle agents becoming bored and taking as long as they liked on calls. After all, there was no reason to manage the call time to the contracted level—right? The easy life for the agents led to boredom, which then led to discontent, which in turn led to high levels of attrition. The high number of staff leaving the company supports the false sense of urgency seen by the recruitment and training functions. There is a clear disconnect between call volume and the number of employees.

To top this off, the management at all levels in the organization seemed to be loaded down with admin tasks that could be better handled by associates. All this paperwork prevented the team leaders and ops managers from actively managing their people—allowing lethargy to creep in.

Regarding the quality coaching of the agents, to avoid customer complaints the company followed the letter of the contract and coached evenly across all agents. Could the company not consider prioritizing training on the people who really needed the help and less on the star performers who clearly did not need it? There was no focus on coaching to "need" or having a basic requalification program, and the training department was never seen on the floor. They were too busy conducting full-blown classes and growing the number of employees to make up for the attrition due to job dissatisfaction.

There was very little formal interaction with the client other than a quarterly contract review meeting, where the company presented the previous three months' performance stats to the client, which then beat the company up—asking for lower prices and more value adds! Phonethics went into these meetings already on the defensive and was actually happy when they gave up less than expected, even knowing it was detrimental to their profit margins.

Michael and Richard found that all of the major elements of how to run the business were present—they were just completely dysfunctional! They needed to improve on this, and so they started to build a future state plan with the help of the employees. When everyone agreed that the plan was right, they would present it to Hamish and Elizabeth for their approval prior to implementing the changes.

THE OBJECTIVES OF THE FUTURE STATE FOUR-POINT PLAN

The objectives the consultants wished to achieve are, on the face of it, quite obvious:

- Return to profitability
- Review key performance indicators (KPIs) and agree what needs to be measured
- Ensure the achievement of all KPIs
- Develop a long-term partnership with the clients

To achieve the goals, the consultants had to create an environment where there was an equal focus on meeting *all* objectives—those of the clients and those of Phonethics. Somehow, Phonethics had drifted away from this and concentrated on the clients' wants only. There can be no losers in any business transaction.

So, they went back to basics. Working with the team, they brainstormed to find options for achieving their objectives. Then they took the thoughts and ideas and developed them into actionable activities with checks and balances built in. When complete, they built them into the future state plan and determined its feasibility.

The main changes are as follows:

- Initiate a biweekly meeting between Phonethics' client services depart-ment and the client, the purpose being to ensure the ongoing under-standing of *both* parties regarding the need to achieve the four main objectives stated above, and to improve overall client relationships.
- Connect the budget to the forecast. We must ensure a clear, real-time understanding of the financial impact caused by shifts in call volumes and any related decisions.
- Monitor actual average handle time and act on the data. We must understand how it affects overall staffing requirements.
- Ensure all planning meetings focus on optimizing the efficiency of our staffing and the handling of the incoming workload.
- Relieve the managers and supervisors of as many admin tasks as reasonable and return their focus to actively managing their people.

- Coach to need. Have the training department personnel spend time on the floor conducting remedial training as guided by the supervisors.
- Create a performance index board that measures each individual team's performance on the KPIs, always showing actual performance against plan.
- Develop and utilize a report on the KPIs per team, again tracking actual against planned performance.
- Promote the most effective operations manager to site director. This person will manage the remaining operations managers and report directly to the president.
- Initiate daily morning meetings with the site director and the operations managers to review the previous day's performance. The goal is short-interval control and issue resolution. Actions will be allocated to specific managers with a time frame for completion.
- Operations managers to conduct daily 15-minute stand-up meetings with their team leaders. Focus is to be on the performance of the previous day and the coming day based on KPIs. As always, the goal is actual performance versus plan and issue resolution. An action log will record any shortfalls and corrective actions.
- Ensure that the quarterly contract review meeting is two way and honest, highlighting both the performance regarding the client's goals and the impact of the incoming call volumes to our company.
- Ensure that there is a financial focus included at all levels of management reporting, including the support functions.

In addition to all of these items, Phonethics will strive to ensure that all of its call-handling activities fall within the contracted average handle time. They plan to right-staff their organization through attrition and, where necessary and appropriate, through performance management of underperforming employees. They will also consider the consolidation of the two locations into one building.

The company would like to attract nonphone work into its business (business process outsourcing [BPO]), including answering e-mails and web queries. This will allow them to optimize the efficiency of their agents, as e-mails do not require handling in real time, but can be used to fill up the spaces between call arrivals. The company will earn the right to this work by performing up to and beyond their clients' reasonable expectations.

Michael and Richard are ready. They will present to Hamish and Elizabeth tomorrow!

34

Elizabeth Golden 2

Elizabeth wakes up in a fog; her head and her heart hurt, and she doesn't want to drag herself out of bed. She calls the office and tells them she has a bad cold and she will work from home today. However, she can be reached in all the usual ways. Ah, the blessings of technology.

For the first hour she doesn't even move—just stares at the ceiling drifting in and out of sleep. Her mind is fully active and reliving the previous day's issues. Perhaps if she listens to the news on the radio, the sound will distract her from her own problems. Nope. Not even the world's problems are enough to distract her. She feels like crying, and before she knows it there are tears streaming across her cheeks.

She is pleased the call center is running better now and even with the role she played in getting it there. Finally, the right people are in the right places, at the right time, and doing all the right things. But her managers still call endlessly for directions. Maybe she didn't delegate enough; maybe it was a control thing or a trust thing. More often than not, all they ask for is permission to take action. For whatever reason, they need confirmation that they are doing the right thing, and they seem to need that reassurance.

Then there are the calls from the clients. Every time they want to maximize the power of their complaints, the calls come straight to Elizabeth. Even though performance is much better, they still apply pressure for reduced costs and push for ever-higher customer satisfaction, never considering for a moment that the two objectives might be in direct conflict with each other. Except, they know well enough: They just want more and more and for less and less. What's new?

On the brighter side, some tough negotiations have led to the clients giving Phonethics some *back-office processing* work as well as new phone marketing. This is a definite plus, as it can be organized and carried out in blocks without the concern of random arrivals. When a call comes in, it has to be answered in real time, but e-mails can be answered within 24 hours. Indeed, some rivals take 48 hours to respond. The main benefit of the back-office work is the increased flexibility in the labor force, which is a major relief, as cross training allows the agents to be moved around to help cover any surges of incoming call volumes. It creates a nice buffer that avoids the panic and pressure of understaffing.

It takes her a couple of seconds to realize her phone is crawling about on the bedside cabinet. She reaches out to catch it before it jumps over the edge. She presses the green phone icon. It will ring a lot today! "Hi Elizabeth, we might need an extra training class for February's call volumes. Should we start recruiting?"

Elizabeth is in no mood for it today. She clears her throat and answers abruptly, "You know what to do. Make the decision yourself!"

She has barely hung up when the phone starts buzzing again. "Hi Elizabeth, you know we are a good client and that we are giving you lots of additional work. But you said there would be volume discounts. When can we expect to see them? We have other alternatives, you know. Lots of other suppliers would like the work!"

"Suppliers, hmm, whatever happened to partners?" thinks Elizabeth. She forces a smile, hoping it will hide her mood, "Hello, nice to hear from you. I'm waiting for word back from corporate," she lies, wiping her nose with a Kleenex. She knows she has lots of leeway and direct communications with the CFO. "Thanks for calling. I will chase that up immediately and get back to you tomorrow." She hangs up the phone, thinking "God they've got their nerve!"

Then her boyfriend calls. "Hi Elizabeth, I tried you at the office and they said you were working from home today. Can I come over and see you?"

"Why? What would be the point? You know we ended it yesterday. I don't want to see you ever again!" Elizabeth slams down the phone and stares at it angrily. She thinks, "How could I have tolerated this relationship for so long?"

The decision is made. All of the decisions are made. She was informed yesterday that Phonethics would be put up for sale and that she could go forward with the new company as part of the sale, or accept a buyout payment. Elizabeth knows she should feel something inside herself about this, but she feels nothing, except maybe a little relief.

She has a healthy balance in her savings account, her condo is fully paid for, and a buyout payment to top it all off would add up to a tidy sum. She will put her condo on the market and play along at work until the end of the year, take the buyout, and head off to the south of France!

35

Lucie Bell 2

It seems unfair that really happy folk get happier, while unhappy folk seem to become only less happy—unless you are the happy one, of course.

Lucie finds herself to be happier by the day, not because life is easy, but because it is incredibly interesting. Her positive personality has been an asset all her life. It seems that any two people can be faced with the same situation, and one of them will be terrified by it, while the other is thrilled. She wonders what makes the difference. Why should she bother? "Well, it might be a useful character trait for a play," she thinks.

For some unknown reason, Lucie has always felt that it's good to be alive. Certainly she has had her fair share of disappointments and even failures—as viewed by other people. Lucie most certainly has been daunted by roadblocks and production failures, but she kept going through them, simply licking her wounds and keeping her head up. The old maxim of "what doesn't kill you makes you stronger" is an ingrown belief for her.

This particular year in Lucie's life, difficult as it has been, has proven to be one of her most productive. When it came to learning, people close to her considered her to be a sponge. She was always taking notes and memorizing new techniques, which she lost no time in applying for the good of the business, turning theory into applied knowledge. Where better to learn than inside a pressure cooker, where there was actual help from knowledgeable colleagues and consultants who actually wanted to share their skills with her?

"Lucie, you've no idea how nice it is to see you at home more. How can you do that in the middle of such an upheaval at work?" asks her husband. She can see her husband's reflection in the mirror as he shaves.

"It just seems to be getting easier, dear," she replies. There are now three jackets lying on the bed, plus the two she is alternately holding against her body. She glances at the bed and continues, "I have always believed in empowerment for my employees, but with training and their new skills, I can trust them to ask for help if they need it. They can even call me here at home, but they don't. Each new step we take seems to follow logically from the last, and when we talk about them and plan their introduction as a team, things just seem to flow. We don't just do stuff; we consider what to do if something goes wrong, too. Who knew it could be this exciting? And then, when we install successive procedures on top of each other and monitor the results, it's like a landslide of progression."

"Is that why you have more and more time to spend with us?"

"It is," responds Lucie with a cheeky grin, picking another jacket from the wardrobe. "I will still pop in to work on weekends, but I'll only do it at random for an hour or so each day to give my support. I might even have coffee and a chat with a few folks, depending on how busy they are. The fact that I appear at random gives the impression that I am always there, and I multiply that effect by ensuring that I don't waste the opportunity by sitting in my office."

"That's why I'm able to be with you and the kids: to go riding, to attend drama class, all in all to be the best mother and wife that I can be. I'm keeping fit, too! Going to the gym and working out increases my energy. If I want a full life, it will be easier to enjoy if I'm fit and healthy, and God knows I feel so much better for my new lifestyle, so much more excited by what every day brings."

"Does your COO recognize your value and commitment?"

"Absolutely! Both Hamish and Jeff are full of praise for me and my team. I never curry favor, though; you know I'm not into politics. I'm simply doing the job as best as I possibly can, and we are always willing to make adjustments to our approach by adding something new and monitoring the outcome. It keeps us all fresh."

Four of the jackets are now back in the wardrobe. "Did I tell you Hamish has hinted that I should be prepared for a promotion to group president? I'm not exactly sure what that means, but it sounds like an exciting opportunity—and I'm certainly prepared for that. Everything is just unfolding around me. I love my job. It's an important part of my overall life. And, if this is success, it can follow me anytime."

She stares into the mirror, with her head tilted slightly, "How do you like this white jacket on me?"

"It's fine … Come on then, Lucie; stop blabbing at me. It's time for us all to get off to drama class!"

36

Strategy Meeting with the Board

It's been 10 months since the beginning of the Bow Corporation project. Both Mike and Richard have found it to be an exciting time. There have been highs when it felt like the world could not stop them, and then there were the lows when they felt totally blocked. Their initial project is all but complete, and here they are, once more, meeting with the board of directors.

Jeff and Hamish have been asked to present an update on the overall project results, and both of them felt it would be good to have Michael and Richard attend. The board is a diverse group: two men and two women. Two are very young, and two are middle-aged or a bit older.

Mary seems to be in her mid- to late-forties and represents a pension fund. She is very aware of the need to maintain steady returns for the fund members. Her company expects 8% or better. To feed this, the fund has the majority of their investments in bonds and cash-related investments. This is currently not generating a good return. The best rate comes from the equity, mainly blue chip, but with a few higher risk forays into the ownership of small companies and individual growth stocks to perk up the average return and get them to the 8% target.

Elijah is in his sixties. He works for one of the larger New York investment houses, where he heads up their Small-to-Medium Business Division. He has been in the game of picking small and medium-sized enterprises (SMEs) with higher-than-average potential for so long he is considered a kind of prophet—one who is mainly interested in profit.

Patrick is a bit of a crackerjack. He represents an aggressive growth fund with international holdings. Their portfolio includes some developing nations that have become drivers of fast and high returns over the past few years. Their ownership in the Bow Corporation is a leftover from the old days, when they were considered more as value investors. This is how they saw the old Bow Corporation: a leftover. Patrick is 28 and new to the private equity business; his nature seems to tilt to the impatient side, and yes, he also sees the Bow Corporation for what it was, an old conglomerate that has been unable to meet the expected returns of its investors.

Sheila is in her mid-thirties and full of life. She has an infectious laugh and interacts well with her three fellow board members. Sheila represents the investment arm of an old and well-respected English bank. Mostly, she is interested in value investing and, during her tenure on the board, has always believed that Bow had lots of potential just waiting to be unlocked.

Finally, there is Jeff Lincoln. Jeff has guided the continuity of the business for 15 years of self-ownership and through the four years since it was sold to the private-equity firms, who now each own 25%.

Jeff opens up the meeting and introduces Michael and Richard. He tells the other board members how happy he is about the turnaround the business has made during the past 10 months. He is generous in his praise of Hamish, Michael, and Richard for their part in this. Then he drops the bomb: "I've been in the Bow Corporation for the past 25 years of my life, 15 of these as CEO. I love the company … it's like my child …" He takes a deep breath, "But it's time for me to move on, maybe even to retire."

There is shocked silence in the room, and Jeff continues. "You all know that I lost my wife, Martha, three years ago and that I considered retirement at that time. It's very hard to lose a loved one, especially one who has been your lifetime partner. I know that for quite a while her loss impacted my focus on the business. That's one of the many reasons I was so glad to have Hamish come on board as COO two years ago."

Sheila can't contain herself any longer. "Jeff, we don't want you to go, not now … This company still needs you!"

Elijah speaks up, "I know I speak for the others in the room." He looks around, and Mary nods her agreement. "You most definitely had a hard time dealing with the heavy blow of Martha's passing, but you kept going, and now more than ever the company needs the benefit of your years of experience."

Jeff is visibly moved. He expected no argument. "You are all very kind, but I made this decision some time ago and have been waiting for a time to arrive that I could hand the company over to my successor in better shape than it has been in the past few years. This time has come thanks to the work done by Hamish and his team—and I include these two men who worked as part of the team to help steer us with their experience and facilitation during this past year's initiative. I know that there will likely be a formal search for a new group CEO, and yet my preferred choice and support goes to Hamish, who I hope the board sees fit to consider."

Once again there is silence in the room. Changing CEOs in a company is not like changing the baton in a relay race. There will be some serious private deliberations by the members of the board as they determine how to proceed.

"How long will you stay, Jeff?" asks Mary.

"I think six months should be enough," says Jeff. "The company has good day-to-day leadership, and you have seen the operating strategy that is in place to guide our decisions. I will stay until the new CEO is in place and has had a chance to familiarize himself or herself with the business."

The board nods their agreement.

"This brings me to one of the other reasons that I asked you to meet with us today: There are two. I would like Hamish to say a few words about the change process we have just completed, its current status, and the future implications. Then I would like Richard and Michael to talk a little about corporate strategy and how it can help guide us into the future. I know you all fully understand the need for strategy and are well experienced in its development, so it's with humility that I ask your time to listen to the thoughts of these three gentlemen on the topic."

Patrick talks first. "We are full of respect and even delight at the changes that have occurred in the company over the past 10 months, and we would be pleased to hear Hamish's thoughts on it. We also know that Michael and Richard have had their part to play, and this also commands our respect. Regardless of what any of us know about strategy, I think it is always prudent to listen to new ideas." He looks around the table for agreement. "We are, after all, four different people representing four different organizations, and so it is likely we will have four different approaches to strategy. Nevertheless, I, for one, am all ears."

The others nod their agreement. "Hear, hear!" says the prophet of profit.

Hamish begins, "I'd like to thank you for the opportunity of being here today to talk about the change initiative we are going through. I'd also like to thank Jeff for his kind words regarding me being a candidate for the role of CEO. I admit I never saw that coming, but I would be pleased to be considered." Hamish gives a respectful glance to Jeff. "I guess there will be many good candidates out there for the role, and I promise here and now to support the board's choice, whoever they choose."

"To talk briefly about the past 10 months is not the easiest thing in the world to do. So much has happened. So much has changed. When Jeff told us that we had to quadruple the bottom-line profit in only nine months, I thought it was impossible. When Michael and Richard showed their willingness to go after this result with us, I was astounded and, quite frankly, had high levels of disbelief. My opinion of consultants was not very favorable at the time. Most executives I've worked with would rather solve their own problems, and that's how I've grown up in industry."

"From that starting point, you can imagine how I felt about two strangers agreeing to what seemed like an impossible task. I viewed it in terms of the old story about consultants being like a dog chasing a taxicab: They don't know or care where they are going until they catch it. But I have to admit, these two knew where they were going and how they planned to get there." There is a small round of good-natured laughter in the room that actually breaks into mild applause.

Hamish continues, "I'm pleased to report we are on target for a run rate of $36 million EBIT for the fourth quarter of this fiscal year. It's not a flash in the pan, either; the gains are across all four operating companies."

Hamish is clearly proud, "Remarkably, it has not been achieved by bullying or by excessive cost cutting; rather, the business improvement has been done with high levels of employee involvement. Any job losses have been handled, where possible, through natural attrition and voluntary buyouts. All of the functions across the Bow Corporation are working in harmony with each other. At the pointy-end operations, sales and finance have done such a good job of collaboration that our business is now running at $425 million in sales. This could not have been done without the efficiency improvements that opened up untapped capacity that was previously invisible to us. All we could see were the problems."

"You are aware that most of these gains were achieved without any capital expenditures. Any capital expenditures incurred were small, and you know this because you OK'd them."

"Throughput has been the watchword in all our divisions. While we still watch all meaningful productivity measures, our ability to sell product at more competitive prices in the marketplace is largely due to improved equipment performance, increased throughput, and lower inventory levels, as product is shipped virtually as it is produced. Recognizing and acting on this opportunity has brought great cohesion between sales, operations, and finance. We now (mostly) operate as one team."

"The tools that we have applied together to achieve these results range from Statistical Process Control (SPC) to strategy. In between those two bookends are Lean, the Theory of Constraints, managing the performance system, project management, organizational mapping/four-point planning, and short-interval reporting. Employees have been trained in all these tools throughout the organization and systematized to ensure the continuity of their use."

"Both Michael and Richard have committed to being available ongoing as required, and they will also conduct wellness audits quarterly to help us with any necessary adjustments." Hamish turns toward Michael and Richard with a broad grin. "I want to thank you two personally. You have taught me a lot, especially what I don't want to be when I grow up!"

It's quiet in the room again, embarrassingly so. Hamish catches it and feels that a small explanation might be appropriate. "It's our sense of humor," he explains. "There have been times when these two boys have been so direct with me I almost cried, but I love them … I really do … please believe me."

Finally, there is a chuckle from the room. "We'll do the funnies, thank you very much, Hamish!"

"I'd like to hand it over to Michael and Richard to talk a little bit about ongoing strategy." And with this, Hamish sits down.

Michael nods to Richard, who gets up from his chair. He's not the most outgoing guy in the world, but compared with Michael, he is the one who prefers the heat of the spotlights and the smell of the greasepaint melting on his face. "Hi everyone," he says, giving the room a big wave. Staid business people as they are, they smile and wave right back. Works every time!

"The reason for talking about strategy at this point was pretty much summed up by Patrick a little earlier. As shareholders, each of you represent ownership of approximately 25% of the company, and each of your businesses might want to take a different position in going forward in the future. The decision and guidance given by the board as to how the Bow Corporation should proceed at the beginning of this fiscal year has largely created what might be considered a very different company. The top-line sales have grown by over 41% with an EBIT of 8.5% on the new enlarged business. The new question is, 'What would you like to do with it now?' It could be that you might just want to put it on the block and sell it. In this case you will have a healthier company to sell than you did a year ago and will make a better overall return on your original investment. On the other hand, some of you may see this improvement as the tip of the iceberg and feel that it just might be a good business to stay invested in. So, if your current thoughts are to sell, I really shouldn't waste your time with any thoughts on strategy and we should simply thank you and move on."

Michael whispers out of the side of his mouth, "Aren't you ever the direct one!"

"Please continue, Richard," says Mary. "We really should hear this."

"Well, there are a couple of loose ends in the business that either you or a future ownership will have to address. The obvious issues are in leadership. If you want this company to continue to shine and grow, its leadership at the division level has to be reviewed and improved."

Mary asks, "Do you have any specific ideas?"

"I think two division presidents would probably make more sense than four. Besides, currently only one of the four really shines. One other has potential, but will take a bit of time to become a true leader."

"Next would be the overall fit of the conglomerate's business portfolio. We have done a lot to improve the competitive stance of Phonethics, the call-center company. We have improved the efficiency of the call processes, and the capture of back-of-house work from our existing clients has improved flexibility in manpower and helped stabilize the attrition rate. It has now become a business-process outsourcing (BPO) company as opposed to an outsourced call-center company."

"By strengthening ties with the existing client base and improving pricing models, the clients are prepared to provide back-of-house work like billing, arranging service appointments, etc. But that's just for now. In the BPO space, the outsourcing companies tend to be specialized as opposed to conglomerates. They also tend to be large. Years ago, the industry began to capitalize on labor arbitrage in offshore locations such as India and the Philippines due to the ongoing requirement from their client base to reduce costs. It's still a reality in the industry today, and it takes significant investment to get a foothold offshore."

Richard builds up to the bombshell: "You have two options, really. You either choose to follow the route of increased investment or you choose to sell this division while it is profitable and marketable with its client base. Whatever you choose, you can see this is definitely a strategic decision."

The room clearly wants Richard to continue.

"We are not going to try to facilitate a strategy session here and now, but I feel a few points on strategic awareness might be useful." It would be an exaggeration to say that the crowd roared its approval, but they clearly want Richard to continue—even though they are looking at their watches.

"I'll be brief. When you develop your strategy, it would be appropriate to decide on your major goal first. It will likely cover the coming three to five years. I'll lose you if I try to go through it all with examples now, so it's best that I get Michael's help, and together we will list a few of the major objectives that should be considered in the formulation of a proposed corporate strategy. This will largely be off the top of our heads, so please forgive us if we end up out of sequence or with the occasional omission."

"You can take notes as we go, but we will summarize the discussion and send you all copies later and, if at the close of the fourth quarter, you are still interested, we will be happy to facilitate you through your corporate strategy. At that time, together, we will make sure we miss nothing. OK?"

Hamish can't resist. "Ever the salesman," he mutters.

"I beg your pardon!" Richard laughs indignantly.

"Nothing, nothing," Hamish says, clearing his throat.

The room has a slight, ever so restrained chuckle at the Mutt and Jeff show.

"On your feet Michael," Richard urges as he moves to the flip chart. Together, they brainstorm the major elements to be considered in the formulation of corporate strategy, inviting discussion from the room.

1. The major goal should encompass three to five years.

    It should reflect what the business will look like at the end of the chosen strategic time frame. It would likely encompass:
    - The size of the business
    - Its expected profitability
    - Any future growth potential
    - The geographic reach from an operating and customer perspective
    - The type of products and markets the business will be in

2. Major objectives: achievement of these should meet the overall goal. Consider short term, medium term, and long term.

    The vision of the end desired result should be broken up into its major parts, and these should then be sequenced and prioritized against each other and set against a timeline within the strategic time frame.

3. Agree on the strategic timeline, but review validity and progress annually.

    Following on from Point 2, even during the planning stage as we set our milestones for the major objectives and sequence them on a timeline, we will see the potential enormity of the task.

    Knowing that resources are always limited to some degree and will vary over time, we may choose to change parts of the original schedule and expand the time frame to allow the achievement of all of our major objectives.

4. Consider geography.

When considering geography, it is often an emotional choice to decide on the whole world. However, we must consider what products and services we choose to be in and where the greatest opportunity is for the expansion of their sales.

We would then consider whether or not we would manufacture in the newly chosen location or ship to it from our current base of operations.

5. Consider acquisitions.

Acquisitions tend to be a consideration in future strategy when growth is a primary goal. It allows for the possibility of capturing new products, enhancing management capability, and inheriting an expanded client base. It can also provide an established foothold in our targeted geography and open up a new opportunity to sell existing products from the parent company.

6. Which industries?

The industries we are currently in might prove to influence our choice of new industries. We should be looking for synergies between them.

We also should be considering the point in the life cycle any new targeted industries are in. We don't want to get into manufacturing buggy whips regardless of how well the operation runs!

7. Consider investment amount. Decisions must be made within the framework of limited total resources.

If we invest too much of our growth funds in any one acquisition, it could adversely affect our ability to support existing operations.

8. Consider divestments.

It may be that businesses in our existing portfolio will no longer fit our new strategic objectives. It might be prudent to sell them off and use the funds from the sale for the expansion of the business into our chosen future business.

9. Consider know-how requirements regarding acquisitions.

We must ensure that we know enough about the business we plan to get into.

– Will we use existing senior management?
– Hire new expertise?
– Plan to ensure the new business brings the required expertise?

10. Consider current administrative and operations capability.

    Determine whether or not our current administrative and operational capability will allow for cost reductions in any acquired organization or in any new industry we intend to enter.

11. Competitive advantage.

    Determine what we will offer the marketplace that will make us the vendor of choice.

12. Profit/return expectations.

    Determine what financial returns we expect over the strategic time frame, and test future investments or divestitures against this.

13. Centralized policy/decentralized operations?

    How will we operate and manage any new business locations?

14. Balance of attention between operating existing business and strategy implementation.

    Business growth or the integration of a new business will require resources, both financial and physical. They also require executive time and attention. We must ensure that the appropriate resources are directed at the existing business while we expand.

15. Set up search criteria for possible acquisitions.

    Prior to considering specific acquisitions, we should narrow the field by considering criteria such as geography, industry, current sales and profit levels, products offered, market share, expected synergies, etc.

16. Constant surveillance of the market: We don't know what's out there.

    A reputable broker will be required to work with us in unearthing opportunities. New opportunities that match our criteria can pop up at any time.

17. Possible acquisitions are tested against the goal as well as long-term and short-term objectives.

    Set up a decision tree specific to our needs.

18. What competition exists or may exist in the market?

    Consider whether we can be in the top three in our industry and geography with the products we offer. Determine what market share we need and how we will get it.

    Is there room for us now, or must we capture market share from existing competitors? Consider that suppliers can become new competitors.

19. Should we acquire or grow internally?

    What would be a suitable timeline and cost considerations?

 Consider time to market, current capabilities, geography, and customers.

20. Due diligence of potentials acquisition: What can be gained through synergies?

 Set up a blueprint for conducting due diligence; ensure that the team is capable and has enough experience. Test any financial gain expectations through synergy for realism. Most synergy targets are not met.

21. Analyze the potential acquisition's strategy.

 When acquiring a new business, their value will be enhanced if they have an existing strategy that propels them forward.

22. Assess risk in any acquisition, cost of exit, etc.

 Consider the probability of failure when acquiring a new business. It may be necessary to exit, and the costs of doing so could be prohibitive.

23. Be prepared for organizational resistance in the acquired company.

 Determine how you will integrate the new business with the existing business. Determine how to ensure that the new employees do not feel like poor stepchildren.

Richard turns to the board of directors. "We now have a list of 23 items to show for two hours of brainstorming and discussion. The only thing we know for sure is that it's incomplete, but it's a start—a skeleton."

Looking around, Michael and Richard see that the people in the room are closing their notebooks. Hamish is starting to inch toward the door. They might have outstayed their welcome! They thank everyone and head out the door, closing it as they leave. Only the board remains.

Hamish, Michael, and Richard are headed for the pub!

Index